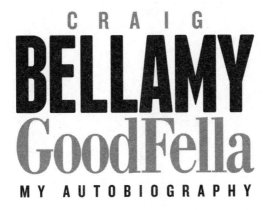

CRAIG
BELLAMY
GoodFella
MY AUTOBIOGRAPHY

CRAIG BELLAMY

GoodFella

MY AUTOBIOGRAPHY

Sport Media

For Nana Mary.
Not a day goes by when
I don't think of you.

Sport Media

By Craig Bellamy with Oliver Holt

Copyright: Craig Bellamy

Published by Trinity Mirror Sport Media
Executive Editor: Ken Rogers
Senior Editor: Steve Hanrahan
Editor: Paul Dove
Senior Art Editor: Rick Cooke
Production: Chris McLoughlin, Roy Gilfoyle, James Cleary
Design: Colin Harrison

First Edition
Published in Great Britain in 2013.
Published and produced by: Trinity Mirror Sport Media,
PO Box 48, Old Hall Street, Liverpool L69 3EB.

ISBN: 978-1-908695-30-7

Photographic acknowledgements:
Craig Bellamy personal collection,
Trinity Mirror (Daily Mirror, Western Mail, Liverpool Echo),
PA Photos, Football Association of Wales,
David Rawcliffe.

Front and back page images: Tony Woolliscroft.

Printed by CPI Group (UK) Ltd, Croydon, CR0 4YY

Contents

I

Acknowledgements

First of all, I want to thank my kids, Ellis, Cameron and Lexi, the three most important people in my life. I hope I've made you all proud.

My mum and dad have always loved and supported me and I'm so grateful for the fact that we are as close again now as we ever were.

My brothers Paul and Matthew are two good men who I'm proud to call my family.

Sometimes divorce obliterates the good memories but my ex-wife Claire and I shared some happy times in our years together before we grew apart and went our separate ways.

I'd like to thank every manager that has had to put up with me. They have all left a mark on me. I didn't really want to mention any of them individually but after this season with Cardiff, I have to state my gratitude to Malky Mackay. He's been tremendous.

I could not have asked for a better agent than Steve Horner. His advice has been fantastic. I might not have listened to him all the time but I should have. I wouldn't have got into as much trouble.

Phil Baker, my business adviser, has been a good source of advice, too, as well as a mate. And my PA, Suzanne Twamley, has been a true friend who has been watching me play football since I was eight.

Dr Steve Peters has had a huge impact on me and still does now. He has shown me what happiness is.

I am not the easiest person to work with when I'm recovering from injury so I'd like to thank all the physios down the years who have allowed me to keep playing. I would like to single out Andy Williams, the knee surgeon, as well. A huge thank you to him.

Not many people know Kieron Dyer properly but I am grateful for the fact that I do. He's an intelligent man and my best friend in football.

I owe a lot to Dato Chan Tien Ghee, better known as TG, the former Cardiff City chairman. His determination to get me to come to Cardiff never waned and his passion was amazing. He had many kind words for me in tough times.

In the moments after we won promotion, I was lucky to be able to share some of the joy with the Cardiff City doctor, Professor Len Nokes. I can't think of anyone I would rather have been with right then.

I want to mention James Reardon, better known as Jimmy Ray, a great friend of mine who died too soon.

ACKNOWLEDGEMENTS

I want to mention all the clubs I have played for, all the people who work for those clubs, all the fans who support those clubs.

And, of course, I want to mention Gary Speed. The impact he had on my career while he was here was incredibly important. In a strange way, his influence on me since his death has probably been even greater.

Craig Bellamy, 2013

II
—

Forewords
By Steven Gerrard and Mark Hughes

When I first heard that Craig Bellamy was joining Liverpool in the summer of 2006, I thought that, as captain of the club, I might have a challenge on my hands.

I had played against him, had a few spats and arguments and words. I was expecting a bit of a hothead. I was expecting someone who was more interested in being a footballer rather than actually living like one.

I was totally wrong. It was my fault. I was guilty of judging someone before I had met him. And when he arrived, he was the opposite of what I thought he would be.

Nothing surprised me on the pitch because I had seen him with my own eyes. I knew he was a good player and I knew he would offer us a lot.

But his character surprised me. It surprised me how professional he was. It surprised me how much he loved the game.

He is a bit similar to me in a way. He has got certain small insecurities. If he doesn't train well or play well, it hurts him. And if he loses, it hurts him. But I think they're great insecurities to have as a player because they help you to find consistency and they help drive you to the top. But you wouldn't think that of Craig if you hadn't met him. You'd think he'd be a person who doesn't care. Well, he isn't.

On the pitch, he is one of those players that you would rather have with you than against you. Everyone knows what he can do. On his day, he can destroy any defender out there because of his pace. When you are playing against a side he is in, every manager is wary of Craig Bellamy. It's his character, too, the way he never gives up, the way he never stops harrying you and hassling you.

He played for Liverpool in two different spells, of course. The first time he came, when Rafa Benitez was the manager, I was disappointed he did not stay longer than a single season. I thought that, if he had stayed, he would have offered us more and more. I felt we would have been a better team with him in it and when he left, we didn't really find anyone of his quality to replace him.

I wanted him to stay. He was a player with real quality and that is one of the reasons the club brought him back. After his second spell at Anfield in 2011-12, I understood why he wanted to go and play for Cardiff City and to be closer to his children. I know that he is a Liverpool fan but he loves his hometown club, too. I think he has got the same love for Cardiff that I have for this club.

I think what people will admire about this book is that there will be an honesty about it because there is an honesty about him. A lot of footballers say the politically correct thing. They want to be liked too much. Sometimes, you have to say what you really think and be honest and I respect Craig's honesty.

When you are a footballer, people say you have to respect the media but he hasn't done that really. Rather than saying the nice thing over and over again, he has said what he thinks and sometimes that upsets people.

At Liverpool, he worked incredibly hard in the gym and set a good example of how a senior pro should behave. If he saw anything around the place that suggested people weren't pushing in the right direction, he would help you as a captain and back you up. He wanted the right thing for this club.

He ended up being a terrific ally for me at Liverpool, as well as becoming a good friend.

Steven Gerrard, 2013

If I had to pick out one reason why I always loved having Craig Bellamy in my football teams, it is the intensity he brings. It's his desire to affect the game every single time he plays. He has a strong will and I like that about him.

Some people thought he was trouble without ever really getting to know him. Some of the things he does can be misinterpreted and maybe there were some who did not like his intensity. Maybe some of them were unsettled by it or worried about the reputation he earned in his younger days

Sure, there were numerous occasions when he played for me

for Wales, Blackburn Rovers and Manchester City when he looked like he was going to combust on the pitch. I didn't have any dramatic remedy for that. There was no particular secret. I just gave him a smile and a knowing look and he tended to calm down fairly quickly.

He was always a great asset to me. He is the type of player the fans love because they know he is giving it everything he has. He inspires players around him, too.

It has never really occurred to me that he is difficult to manage. I actually always found him very rewarding to manage. If you understand him and support him, he will play his heart out for you.

I played with him for Wales when he was younger and, yes, he could be quite volatile but a lot of people have also been surprised by how professional he is.

Like most of us, he has changed as he has grown older. He had some injuries and the fear of losing a career that was precious to him turned him into someone who is utterly dedicated to the game.

He doesn't take any prisoners. He says it as he sees it. He is honest and up front and he expects people to be the same with him.

He has got a lot of strengths. Diplomacy isn't one of them.

Mark Hughes, 2013

III

The Human Snarl

I don't know what you see when you look at me. A human snarl, maybe. That's pretty much been my image for the last 15 years. A snarling, snapping, hungry, feral player who loathed himself and everyone around him. Someone who was unhappy. Someone who had a lot of things eating at him. Someone always moving on. Always falling out with people. Always running.

I have always been restless. That's true. Restless in my personal life and in football. In my own world, maybe I feel I deserve more respect than I get as a player so I am always chasing it as aggressively as I can. And if I don't get it in one place, from a manager or from a crowd, I search for it in another place.

Steven Gerrard says I am driven by my insecurities. He's right. I'm always looking for a chance to show people how good I am.

I went through much of my career without winning anything. So I started to chase trophies. I went to clubs where I thought I would win medals. When I failed, I moved on. I wanted something to show for my career. If I didn't win medals and trophies, my career was just a big waste. I was convinced of that. The fear of failure was one of the reasons I kept on moving.

That changed in November 2011 when my friend Gary Speed died. I was playing for Liverpool then and the club doctor, Zaf Iqbal, said he was worried about my mental state. He said he thought I needed help. He recommended that I went to see Steve Peters, the psychiatrist who is probably most famous for working with Britain's gold medal cyclists Sir Chris Hoy and Victoria Pendleton.

I had always refused to see a psychiatrist before. You may not be surprised to know it had been suggested to me several times. And there were excellent practitioners available at several of the clubs I played for. But I thought it was weak to seek that kind of help. I thought I was doing okay. I was a good footballer. I didn't want to talk to anyone in case it opened up a mess of issues that would affect my game. If it ain't broke, don't fix it. That was what I thought. But it clearly was broken. I was broken. I was just in denial about it.

As a young kid, I was happy. I grew up on an estate on the outskirts of Cardiff. I had loving parents and a group of close mates, many of whom spiralled off into delinquency and drugs. I loved football and played every minute I could. I was a daydreamer, yeah, and I didn't achieve much at school. But I was happy. And then I had to move away when I was 15.

I moved to the other side of Britain, to Norwich, to play football, to pursue my dream. It sounds melodramatic but it killed a part of me. It taught me to isolate myself, to be single-minded, to be selfish, to exclude others, to keep everything inside. I learned to be emotionally detached. I grew distant from my mum and a lot of people who were close to me.

The more I rung home back then, the more I missed home. Nothing makes it better. In fact, everything seems to make it worse. You ring home, you get upset, your parents get upset because they can tell how unhappy you are and they can't do anything about it. And then you start feeling guilty because you're upsetting them. And before you know it, you're in a phone booth outside a fish and chip shop in Norwich crying your eyes out.

That's what it was like for me. That's what it was like for a year. A year of homesickness that hurt like hell. A year of trying to conceal my feelings. A year of trying to cope with everything that was being thrown at me as a young footballer trying to make it with hard taskmasters for coaches and senior professionals that enjoyed treating you like shit. Sounds like self-pity, doesn't it? Well, I was the master of self-pity.

I spent most weekends on my own. I played a match on Saturday morning, watched the Norwich first team play in the afternoon. Then I'd stick around, clean up all the kit, watch the players and study their happiness in victory or the raw pain of defeat. Then it was the long walk home to my digs at The Limes, half an hour in the dark. Sit in my room for a while on my own. Then go to the chip shop. And the phone box.

I had a girlfriend by then. Claire and I got together before I left Cardiff. In time, we had three beautiful children together. We got married in the end. And we stayed married until 2012 when she decided she'd had enough. Enough of the moving and the following me round. Enough of the absentee husband. Enough of the selfishness and the black moods and the times when I wouldn't talk to her because I was worried about a knee injury.

So we got divorced and it nearly tore me apart. I have had months of guilt about not being the husband I should have been. And not being the father I should have been, either. For a while, I didn't think about the lifestyle I had been able to give Claire and my three children, the life I have been able to give my kids who mean more to me than anything in the world. The pride in what I have been able to provide, the pride in some of the sacrifices I made, has come back now.

I caused the breakdown of my marriage. Not football. It's about more than football. I suppose this is controversial because people will say that no two people are the same but I feel that high-profile sportsmen and sportswomen are different. We're wired differently. We're not the same as other people. The same goes for a lot of other people who are very successful at what they do.

Why? Because we have to sacrifice so much. And some people can cope with that and maintain a happy family life. And some people can't. I had no experience of being around people who were doing something similar. There were no people in my area who were following that path. I had to learn for myself. I never asked for advice and saw how they behaved.

The way I saw it, my life would begin when I was 35. When I finish football, my life starts. That's how I looked at it. Until then, nothing matters. It's the game and that's it. I want to be as successful as I can. I want to earn as much money as I can for my children. And then I can sit back and relax.

The thing is, you have to enjoy what you are doing at the time as well. Otherwise you're just punishing yourself. The sacrifice is too great. I didn't understand that. Not until it was too late. Too late for my marriage anyway. I missed out on years and years of fun. I didn't enjoy it. Not even close. I didn't enjoy my career. If a team-mate made a mistake, I might not speak to him for a week. It was bullshit.

If I did something good in a game, I'd just tell you about all the bad things I did instead. That's what kept me up at night. And I thought keeping myself up at night was improving me. If I woke up at 3am, thinking about something I didn't do, that's what made me a better player. If I wasn't doing that, I thought I was taking my eye off the game. If there was a game on television on Friday night and I didn't watch it, I thought I was showing football a lack of respect and I would pay for it on Saturday. That's how crazy I was.

I wouldn't leave the house two or three days before a game because I wanted to save my legs. If I didn't save my legs, I thought I would pay for it on Saturday. If I won on a Saturday, I would wake up at the same time the next Saturday, leave the house at the same time, drive the same route to the game, wear the same suit. If I was forced to do something differently, I was convinced I was going to lose. It was borderline insane.

So, yes, I was difficult to live with. I worked away a lot. I was apart from my wife and family for long periods. Several years ago, they moved back to Cardiff to give my children a stable base for school and I commuted from London or Liverpool or Manchester or wherever I was playing to see them. It's hard to have a successful relationship when you're living like that.

Being away from my kids on a daily basis made me very

unhappy so why the hell was I doing it? Why did I put myself in that situation? I felt that when I came home, it wasn't my home. I felt guilty for not being around the children so I tried to make up as much time as I could with them in the short while I had. But I also had a young wife who wanted my time and affection and I couldn't do it all at once and the next thing I am back up the road.

That was part of the reason I became the human snarl. I was unhappy and if I was going to be unhappy, I wanted to make damn sure everyone knew I was unhappy and that they were unhappy, too.

It took the death of Gary Speed for me to step back and find happiness within myself. It wasn't my wife's fault that I had been unhappy. It wasn't a club's fault or a manager's fault. It wasn't because I had had an argument with Graeme Souness or Roberto Mancini. I was stopping myself from being happy. I'd been doing it since I left Cardiff at the age of 15.

If I had not got help, if I had not begun talking to Steve Peters, I was facing a dark, empty future. Gary Speed's death, the fact that he apparently took his own life, shook me to the core. It scared me. There are a lot of similarities between me and Speedo.

I understand myself a lot better now, I think. I have been able to cope with the separation and divorce from my wife. I still find it very hard not being able to see my children when I want to but I am coping. I am not sure how I would have dealt with it if it had happened a few years ago.

It's not always been pretty but I am a better man for having been involved in football. It's taken me to different countries. It's put me in a position where I have been able to found a football academy in Sierra Leone and try to help people make a better life for themselves through the game. Maybe one day, people will be able to see beyond the snarl.

There was a time when I thought that when I retired from playing, I would have a period away from the game but I know now that I can't be without football. I would miss it too much. If anyone else comes into my life, they have to be prepared to share me with football. It doesn't drive me mad any more but it still consumes me. Any job can make you unhappy if you let it. Finally, just in time, I've come to understand that if I love football this much, why not just enjoy it.

And I am enjoying it. I'm enjoying it more than I've enjoyed it at any time since I was a little kid dashing around on ABC Park in Trowbridge with my mates. I'm enjoying it more than I've ever enjoyed it. It's the greatest game in the world but it's nothing more than that. Apart from my children, it's been the best thing in my life. I wake up every morning and I can't wait to go to training. I feel grateful for that.

Craig Bellamy, 2013

1

Where I Belong

My home is Cardiff. More specifically, my home is Trowbridge, on the eastern edge of the city, on a 1960s estate near the Eastern Avenue, the dual carriageway that cuts a swathe through the suburbs on its way out to the M4. I live in Penarth at the moment, on the south side of the city, in an apartment that looks out over the sea. I'm recently divorced. I'm exiled from the house I once lived in with my wife and children in the countryside to the west.

But I'll always think of Trowbridge as home, the 1960s estate, with its streets named after Welsh towns and areas. Abergele Road, Caernarvon Way, Prestatyn Road, Aberdaron Road, Menai Way.

They're the names of my childhood, the names of the streets

and crescents I used to dash along to get to ABC Park, where I'd play football with my mates.

Along those streets I'd sprint, through the little alleyways where knots of youths used to gather to smoke dope or sniff glue or try to get high from air fresheners. I'd join them in time, watching and shuffling around uneasily, trying to be part of the group.

I suppose some people would think of it as a rough area, a place of unemployment and delinquency. It never seemed that way to me. I had a happy childhood. I grew up a happy kid. Happier there than I ever have been since, happier than when I was a footballer living behind gates and walls and fancy inter- com systems with built-in cameras.

When I was a small kid, we lived in Swinton Street, by Splott, close to the docks, closer to the city than Trowbridge was. The railway tracks were at one end of our road and trains trundled past there, heading out of Cardiff Central east towards Eng- land and London. At the other end was Splott Park and behind that was the giant spread of Allied Steel and Wire where my old man worked. They closed it down in 2002. It was sold on to a Spanish company. Its great blue bulk still dominates that part of the area, but most of the jobs went.

There was a time in Splott when you could see the flames and the sparks dancing in the night air from the famous old Dowlais ironworks and women worried about putting their washing out on the line because it would get covered in a film of fine red dust. Cardiff used to be an ironworks and steel town but the industry was dying when I was a kid. In 1978, the year before I was born, thousands of jobs were lost when the East Moors Steelworks closed down.

But there was a great sense of community. Originally, people had been transported there from the Valleys to work in the factories and it was still a traditional working class area where it felt like every door was open. If my mum ever shut herself out by mistake, she'd knock next door and the neighbour would send her kid round through our back garden, through our back door and he'd open up for us at the front.

I always felt like we had a decent living from what my mum and dad did. We were happy enough. My mum was a cleaner and my world was all about playing in the warren of streets round our house, Baden Powell School, Splott Park and Splott Baths. My dad, Douglas, worked at Allied Steel and Wire for as long as I can remember even though we moved away from Splott, a few miles further east to Trowbridge, when I was five.

My dad knew his place in the family. My mum was the number one and she ran the house. They were great parents and even though I was a bit of a daydreamer, I was a happy kid. I knew my mum loved me and we were a happy family. A lot of the men in the area would spend all evening, every evening, down the pub but my dad knew that if he went up there, there was a certain time he had to be back and he was back at that time. He abided by that.

My mum and dad still live in Trowbridge. They live in the same house they lived in when I was growing up. In times of trouble or uncertainty, that's where I've always returned. I see now that it was called one of the most deprived areas in south Wales when I was growing up but I never thought of it like that.

We had a bigger house in Trowbridge than we'd had in Splott, the roads weren't as busy and I began to play an awful lot of football. My dad loved football.

CRAIG BELLAMY

He used to go and watch Cardiff City as much as he could. He had three kids – me and my brothers, Paul and Matthew – so I'm not sure my mum allowed him to go that much but he would come home talking about players like Jimmy Gilligan and Paul Wimbleton, the mainstays of that team that played in the old Fourth Division.

My first game was Cardiff City against Newport County in the 1987-88 season. It was 4-0 to Cardiff. Gilligan got two and Alan Curtis got two. Cardiff got promoted that year and they were great days even though there were rumours practically every week that we were close to going out of business.

I hear people now talk about fans 'deserving' something at clubs for the bad times they might have endured. In that era, Cardiff supporters turned up and watched a poor standard of football week in, week out in dilapidated, decaying stadiums.

You could stand where you wanted and I flitted around so much at one game that I realised afterwards I'd watched from all four stands. When it got to five minutes from the end, I'd go and meet up with my dad at a pre-arranged spot so we could go home together.

I'm not sure whether my own love of football followed on from my dad's. Maybe. Or maybe I was just a naturally competitive kid. My brother, Paul, was two years older than me and I hung out with a lot of his friends. That made me into a better player very quickly. We used to play down the field at the bottom of my road. It was called the ABC Park and we played there constantly.

It was a bit of a higgledy-piggledy park, shoehorned between the rows of houses on the estate. It sloped quite heavily from north to south. I'm not even sure why it was called ABC Park.

I think it was because there were some climbing frames there and they had been labelled A, B and C to differentiate them from each other.

There were no goalposts and there were so many kids playing that, most of the time, you couldn't find a spare patch of grass. They've built a BMX track there now. I see articles about it in the Western Mail sometimes. The last one was about the fact that the council had had to put security guards there because gangs of kids were congregating and throwing stones at local houses. There's graffiti sprayed on the garden fences that back on to it.

I played my first match for my school, Trowbridge Juniors, when I was seven. My dad was surprised when he found out I'd been selected. Most of the kids in the team were a couple of years older than me and I was small for my age, too. I was skinny and under-developed but I was quick and clever and I was always desperate to win. My dad was still dubious about it but Paul told him how good I was, so he came to watch.

We played against Gladstone Primary School from Cathays and I won a penalty when a kid tripped me in the box. Whoever got brought down for the pen usually took the spot-kick. Those were the rules in park football, anyway, so I thought it was mine. But this was serious stuff. They told me there was a regular penalty taker and it was my mate Stuart Solomon. The Gladstone goalkeeper had glasses. I thought we couldn't miss but those specs were working wonders for him and he saved it. We drew the game and went away feeling very deflated.

I soon got other opportunities to play. When we had our kick-abouts down at ABC Park, a scout from Pentwyn Dynamos would turn up sometimes. We were miles away from Pentwyn, on the other side of the Eastern Avenue, so they must have been pretty desperate but they still wouldn't consider me because I was too small. So my dad told me that if I got enough players together, he would help me start a team.

I went around loads of kids' houses, knocking on doors. My dad found someone who ran a team called Caer Castell, near Rumney High School, and I had soon found enough kids for us to start an Under-10s side there. Our first game, inevitably, was against Pentwyn Dynamos. We played on Rumney Recreation Ground and won 4-0 and I scored all four. That was the start for me. I played on Saturdays for the school team and on Sundays for Caer Castell and when I was nine or ten, I was selected for the Cardiff and District boys side. I played for Cardiff Schools, too. One cup game over two legs, we played against Deeside Schools and Michael Owen was playing for the opposition.

I became a good player just by playing. By playing constantly and by playing with kids who were both older and better than me. I saw tricks other kids did and I had the ability to absorb what had just happened. I'd try to imitate it myself and then I'd practise what they had done. Then I'd try that trick on another kid.

I still do that now. I never stop learning. I could see a 19-year-old kid do something today and I'd try it tomorrow in training. I think that's given me an edge sometimes, that ability to innovate. My biggest concern with most young kids now is that they don't have that edge to want to be better than their mate. You don't see kids on the parks now, not the way it used to be anyway, and when they're attached to clubs, I think they're comfortable in their own zone. Football takes such good care of you now at every age group that some of the hunger's gone.

I wanted to be the best against everyone. Mainly, when we were kicking about, we used to play something we called FA Cup Doubles or Singles. I'd be distraught if I didn't win it. If we had an eight v eight game, I had to win that eight v eight. That was when I got the most pure enjoyment out of football, better than any time I've been playing as a professional.

There are a lot of kids I haven't spoken to since then whose names I still know off by heart. I hope they've gained some satisfaction from what I have been able to achieve because I certainly appreciated what they gave me. Even some kids who might not have thought they were any good, I learned something from them just by the fact they were enthusiastic enough to come out and play every day. Playing against them every day improved me as a player.

There was one kid I remember in particular. His name was Andrew Evans. He was four or five years older than me and when I was eight or nine years old, I thought he was a kind of football god. We used to play in informal matches on Tesco's Fields, which was an expanse of pitches a couple of miles from my house, and Evvo played in this brilliant blue Everton strip with white shorts. He had tricks. He could do body swerves, he had everything. Whenever I tried to tackle him, I couldn't get anywhere near him.

He could have been somebody. He really could. There are kids like him in a lot of communities, kids that have got a raw talent that makes them stand out when they are young. But, like a lot of those players, Evvo just didn't have the commitment you needed to make it. He was such a good player but he was totally relaxed about it. Too relaxed.

A lot of people tried their hardest with him. One of the

coaches used to go round to his house just to get him to matches and now and then Evvo would say he didn't fancy it. He'd say he was staying in bed. One day, when I was 11 and he was 15 or 16 and still in school, he told me he was going to be a dad. I asked him whether he wanted a boy or a girl but most of all I wondered how the kid was going to grow up and how Evvo was going to provide for it.

It hit me a bit, that. He was still a hero of mine and he was a hero round the area because he was such a good footballer. He went to play men's football when he was 15 or 16 and he was scoring five or six every game. But he was never going to go anywhere because he didn't want to. He was never going to push himself through it. Seeing the way he drifted out of the game helped me because I knew what I had to do.

It made me realise that it wasn't enough just to be supremely gifted. It made me realise, even as a kid growing up on an estate, surrounded by normal kids who just wanted to have a laugh, that I was going to have to live a different kind of life if I was going to have any chance of making it. I was going to have to be separate. There would be loneliness and I realised that, too, but I wanted to be a footballer so badly that it didn't deter me.

Evvo drifted into doing what most boys drift into. He had the ability to be special but only I know his name now. The only time he has ever been mentioned in the newspapers is when I have mentioned his name in an interview.

I find that sad, really, because people should have known his name, all around the world. He had the talent but he did not have the strength. Every area in every city in Britain has got people like that.

2
—

Choices

I began to live a kind of double life. I was football mad, devoted to it, determined to succeed. And then there was my life on the estate, trying to fit in, trying to be a normal kid, trying to be part of the gang. Suddenly I was at Rumney High School and there were kids from St Mellons, Rumney, Harris Avenue and Llanrumney and it was a melting pot. I wanted to look right. I wanted to make sure I had nice trainers. There were girls, loads of girls. I saw a lot of kids grow up quickly.

Around that time, a guy called Stan Montgomery, who had played for Cardiff and been first team coach at Norwich City, scouted me for Bristol Rovers. I was training with Cardiff at Trelais School by then but the facilities were beyond poor and so when Stan approached my dad and we realised I would be given kit at Rovers and the coaching would be better, we went for it. It was about an hour's drive but I didn't mind. It was just another place to go and play football.

I did well there and word got around. One night, the phone went at home and my dad answered it and I heard him talking for a while. He came back into the room and said that it had been someone from Norwich City. They wanted me to go and play in a game in Somerset. It was like a trial, I suppose. I went, I played well and then they asked me to go and play for them in a tournament in Denmark called the Dana Cup.

I'd never heard of it. My horizons were not exactly wide at that time. But it is one of the world's largest football tournaments and it takes place at the end of July every year in the town of Hjorring, way up in the north of Denmark, about 300 miles from Copenhagen. It felt like a massive jamboree when I got there. There were thousands of kids from all over the world. I had never experienced anything remotely like it.

I'd been on the odd holiday with my parents. We'd been to Benidorm and Corfu but this was way outside my comfort zone. It was challenging enough just travelling with a football club. All the other kids were from places like Colchester and Ipswich and there was me, fresh out of Cardiff, a long way away from home.

The people at Norwich could not have made me feel more welcome. Perhaps it was partly because I was a good player. That always helps when it comes to being accepted as a kid. I felt, even in that company, even at that age, that I stood out straight away. I played well in Denmark. I really enjoyed it and a month later, I started training with Norwich's young development team, which was called Canary Rangers. I trained with them for a week and had a great week. I did well again and from then on, all my football development was with them.

That was when my double life started in earnest. I would head off from Cardiff to Norwich or to a tournament somewhere abroad. We slept in dormitories or camper beds. Training was brilliant, the facilities were brilliant and I started to learn about what it meant to be a professional footballer.

I learned a bit more about life, too. Norwich started to educate me about pleases and thank yous. I'm not saying that my parents didn't but Norwich really did develop a professionalism in me that I managed to keep. We had a youth coach called Kit Carson, who was a big influence on me. He wanted us to keep the ball at all costs so I was brought up to pass the football, to play one-twos, not to hit it long but to be patient, to pass it across the back four. Kit Carson just stood there quietly, watching us play, never saying a word. Parents weren't allowed to come and watch training or come to the games. We were allowed to swear and, as long as we were responsible and respectful, we were treated with that kind of respect from Kit Carson as well.

That was one half of my life but at home, I was still hanging around with kids who were two or three years older than me. We used to meet at the Trowbridge shops: me, Anthony, Gareth, Stuart, another Anthony, my brother, Paul, and Omar and Mohammed. Omar and Mohammed were new. They were refugees from Iraq and from day one, they could look after themselves. Omar was a hard bastard. Fearless. They were good kids to grow up with. There was a gang of 13 or 14 of us and we used to meet up at the shops down the end of my street and then wander into school.

By the time I was 12, my mates who were 14 or 15 weren't really interested in playing football at the park any more. They were doing stuff that was a little bit out of my league. Girls were being chased and I was getting roped into that. I mean, I was an immature kid. I was small. I didn't mature like most boys. I was a late developer. I found that tough.

So I was playing for Norwich, then going back to Cardiff and hanging round with kids who were drinking and smoking. It seemed the coolest thing to do at the time and I felt pressure to be a part of it. I started having a few drinks when I was 12. The odd bottle of cider, a beer here and there. I stayed away from cigarettes because my old man told me it would make me slow and I would lose my pace. I didn't want that.

After being introduced to alcohol, I drank fairly regularly. Maybe it was another way of chasing girls. It gave me a bit of Dutch courage. I felt I had to do it, which was a weakness in me. All my friends were doing it and although I knew it wasn't right, I didn't want to be on my own.

So I would go off and drink with my mates. My parents caught me a few times and I can't imagine what was going through their heads. Then, I saw other kids smoking cannabis and on other drugs. Glue was frequent around the area. At first, I viewed those people as down and outs. But I started seeing people who were close to me smoking cannabis and doing air fresheners and it started to seem normal.

Glade, the air-freshener that was sold in those tall, thin canisters, was a big thing round our way. You put a sleeve over the nozzle at the top and pumped it and sucked through it. Apparently, you got a ridiculous head rush for five or ten seconds and then you did it again.

Being left on my own was too hard to contemplate at that age. Some of them were trying to lead me down a particular behavioural route because maybe they didn't want me to have success. They knew about my other life in football and the chance I had. Others could see that I was risking everything just by hanging around with them. Some of them would say 'Bellers, no chance, don't do it'. They wanted to protect me.

Perhaps inevitably, some of my mates started getting into trouble. If they were buying £15 worth of cannabis, well, they had to get £15. A lot of the people who sold it let them buy it on tick. They would give you a deadline and you had to have the £15 in four days or a week.

If you're a kid, you don't have the discipline to save up. So you have to find another way to get the money. They turned to crime. The main target was car stereos, the pull-out ones. It was like a dream if you found a car with one of them. People were looking for pull-outs like you wouldn't believe. It was an easy way out. It would be a window, an elbow through it and 'bang!' You could sell that pull-out for £25. If it was a Panasonic, brilliant. If it was anything else, a different make, you could still get a few quid.

I used to hang out with mates who did that. Generally, it was more about me going along and watching them do it. I would keep an eye out for them while they were stealing from the cars. I never physically stole anything myself but I know that's no excuse. Helping out is just as bad as stealing.

There was a period when I was 13 or so when I was skiving off school quite a lot. Once, I went missing for two weeks. How can you go missing for two weeks as a 13-year-old kid without anybody from school ringing up? But they didn't.

The only reason I got found out was because another lad got caught. His mum was dragging him up to school and she made him grass me up to the head teacher.

Because a lot of my friends were a couple of years older, a lot of them just stopped going to school. One or two of the boys in my class got expelled. A mate called Bingham was expelled for abusive behaviour. He wasn't that kind of kid but when he got up to read in class and the other kids started sniggering, he would feel so embarrassed that he would shout at the teacher. He went to another school and got expelled again. And his parents wouldn't allow him to go to a special school, so he was 13 and not going to school at all.

Bingham was one of my best friends. His dad left for work about 7am and his mum left at ten past nine. I'd wait for her to leave and then I'd go in and wake him up and spend the morning at his house until his mum came back at lunchtime. And then I only had a few hours to kill before I could go back to my house, pretending everything was normal.

There'd be a few of us round Bingham's house every morning. I kind of liked that excitement of being somewhere you shouldn't be. It would be wrong to say I wasn't concerned about my parents finding out but I also knew it wouldn't be the biggest thing in the world. I think my parents wanted me to learn but in the back of their minds they thought I was going to make it as a footballer with Norwich so they weren't quite as bothered.

They were right about Norwich, too. I began playing for the club's schoolboy team and when I was about to sign schoolboy forms, a couple of other clubs tried to tempt me and my family away. Leeds United offered my parents £10,000 for me to go to sign with them and Norwich fought them off by guaranteeing me a two-year YTS apprenticeship when I was old enough to take it up.

We took that like a shot but it was one of the worst things Norwich could have done for me. My life after school was sorted now, so what did I need to go to school for? That was my attitude. My friends weren't going, so why should I go? My parents would have come down hard on me for not being in school but as long as they weren't confronted with it, they turned a blind eye. They didn't chase it up and the school didn't ask them about it either.

When I started playing for the Norwich schoolboy teams, I would get the 4.25pm train from Cardiff Central to London Paddington on Saturday afternoon. I'd get the Tube from Paddington to Liverpool Street and another train from Liverpool Street to Norwich, which got me in at 9.10pm. I'd play for Norwich's schoolboy team on Sunday morning, then get a train back to Cardiff. My dad would come and pick me up.

Usually, I brought a bonus home with me. We used to get expenses and the older lads played the system. They'd claim £100 for their fare, whatever it actually was, and they would have killed me if I'd only put in for the £25 it cost me for the Cardiff-Norwich return. So I claimed the same as them and when I arrived home in Cardiff, I'd give my mum and dad the £25 and keep the rest for myself.

On a Monday, I'd often be walking into school with £75 in my pocket. That's if I went into school, which I usually didn't. I had begun to feel I could do whatever I wanted and pay for whoever wanted to come with me, too. So I'd spend the money on booze or have an entire day at an amusement arcade somewhere. Or if I liked a pair of trainers, I could get a pair of trainers. Or I could buy some cigarettes. I could do whatever I wanted and I usually did.

I learned absolutely nothing at school. That was my fault most of all but there was a lack of enthusiasm from the teachers, too. They seemed weary. They seemed to have given up. Before every class, the teacher would say 'if you don't want to learn, go and sit at the back of the class and don't interrupt the kids who do want to learn'. I was a kid who knew he was going to be a footballer and thought he knew it all. I would go and sit at the back, daydream and kill a couple of hours. I deeply regret that. I wish I had knuckled down and picked up as much as I could but I lived another life.

I was soon drinking and smoking cigarettes every day, ignoring my dad's warning. My football started to go downhill and because of the lifestyle I was leading, I wasn't maturing like other kids, who were getting bigger and stronger. By the time I was 14, I was drinking more and more. I'd started off on cider and moved on to cheap lager. There was no way I looked 18 but it was all easy enough to get hold of round our way. If there was a lad walking past the off-licence, we'd ask him to buy the drink for us. Usually, they'd do it if you gave them a box of matches or a packet of Rizlas. It couldn't have been simpler really.

Drinking was taking a bigger and bigger toll on my football. During the Christmas holidays at the end of 1993, there was a residential week in Norwich that was used to decide which of the kids in the schoolboy team would be signed up to apprenticeships. My place was already guaranteed but it was made clear to me that week that the Norwich coaches felt I was going backwards.

I was playing for Wales Schoolboys, too, and things weren't

going well there, either. We barely won a game. We were a poor, poor team. There was a lot of infighting and jealousy. Some of the parents of other kids had been ringing up the manager, apparently, and saying that I was too small to be in the team and wasn't worth my place. The manager even singled me out after one defeat and asked me in front of everybody whether I thought I deserved to be playing.

I told him that, yes, I did think I deserved to be playing but inside I was starting to have doubts about whether I wanted to be a footballer. We were losing and I did begin to feel that maybe I wasn't good enough. In a way, those kinds of thoughts are what made me a top player. I have always been haunted by self-doubt. I have always wondered whether the next game or the next move is the one that will find me out and expose me as the ordinary player that deep down I fear I am.

The way I was living my life was eating at me, really gnawing away at me. I hated myself for my lack of discipline and the weakness I was showing with my drinking and smoking. I knew it was affecting my football but I felt torn. I was 14. It's young to have to dedicate yourself to something. It's young to cut yourself off from your friends.

I wanted to fit in. I wanted to be one of the lads. I was going through puberty, too, of course, and I started to entertain the idea that maybe I would like to do what my mates were doing. There was a freedom about that.

I knew how hard I was going to have to work if I was to become a professional footballer and I didn't know whether I wanted to work that hard. No one from the area had ever done it. I had no one to look up to. There was no role model for that, no example to follow. I started to think 'what's wrong with what my mates do, would it be so bad to stick around in Cardiff and drift along with them?'

I don't know if I could say there was a low point, a point of maximum danger, a moment where I realised I was risking more than my football career. Perhaps it was the time I rode in a stolen car. I only did it once. I was skiving off school with a mate and a lad pulled up who was known around the area for stealing cars.

Me and my mate jumped in and this lad screamed up the road to my school and roared out on to the playing fields. All the other kids were in the classrooms staring out of the windows at us and this lad pulled a couple of doughnuts on the football pitches and then drove back out on to the streets. When we got a couple of hundred yards away, I asked him to let me out. I was scared stiff. I hated every second of it. I thought then 'I am never, ever going in a stolen car again'.

That episode still haunts me now. It was one of the stupidest things I have ever done. What if it had crashed? I could have lost everything. The other thing that haunts me is the mate that was with me carried on riding in stolen cars with the lad who was driving. He ended up stealing cars with him. He started taking heroin. He travelled along a different path.

Perhaps most people are like this but when I did the wrong thing, I always had a voice in the back of my head telling me to stop. I always had a limit.

When glue came into my little group of mates for a couple of weeks, I remember putting the bag to my mouth once and wondering what to do. In that split-second, I thought about this young kid who was well-known in our area for being a gluey. I had an image of him in my mind, thin and miserable, with cold sores all around his mouth and his face red and raw. I didn't want to look like that. I thought 'no'. I put the bag down and passed it on.

I was always aware of what went on and I knew what older kids were doing because you would see them smoking stuff and it wasn't just cannabis. I realised quickly that the ones who were doing hard stuff didn't look great. It was the people who were selling it who were clever. They would be around boys my age with wads of cash, exploiting the image that they were flash and super-successful. A lot of impressionable kids loved that.

You know what I thought? I looked at them and I thought 'great, but this is bullshit'. I saw the drug dealers hanging around and I saw the local kids heading up to the Trowbridge Inn, the pub that was the focal point of our community.

Some of my mates had to go up there if they wanted to see their fathers because they were in there all the time. They couldn't wait to grow up so they could go and start drinking in there, too. My dad wasn't like that but I knew I was close to choosing that way of life. The drink, the glue, the Glade, all of it. I knew that was how life could go for me. I could see how it might work out.

I knew some of the older boys were starting to make appearances in court. I could see the route their lives were taking, where it was leading. All the time, I looked at what was going on around me, at the kids trooping up to the Trowbridge Inn, at the little circles of kids sniffing glue and a thought kept going through my mind.

"There has got to be more to life than this," I kept saying to myself. "There has got to be more."

3
—

Life Changer

In those months, I came incredibly close to blowing it and never having a football career. One of the things that saved me was meeting Claire. Claire and I got divorced at the end of 2012 but we had been together from the day at the end of 1993 when my brother, Paul, came up to me and told me that she fancied me. I met her on the corner and we had our first kiss. We quickly became inseparable and I began to spend less time with my mates. Suddenly, it was Claire who was my focus, not sitting round with my pals, drinking.

The following summer, it was the 1994 World Cup and even though people don't remember it as one of the great tournaments, it helped me fall in love with the game again. I made up my mind I was going to watch every match. I loved studying

Roberto Baggio and Romario. I had a brilliant summer and I felt like football had become my priority again. I came back from the brink at a time when some of my mates were falling over the edge.

I was lucky in other ways, too. I had a great relationship with my nana Mary, my dad's mum. She looked after me and my brothers from an early age because both my mum and dad were often at work. So I would spend most of the school holidays in Adamsdown, quite close to where we used to live in Splott, with my nana, my brothers and my cousin Sarah.

I thought Nana Mary was unbelievable. She showed us pure love. We had to kiss her when we came in and kiss her before we left. She was a lovely woman who wasn't scared of showing emotion. She was also an important influence on me. My parents would never have a real go at me if I did something wrong but my nana would and I felt more guilty letting her down than anyone. I adored her. She was a brilliant, brilliant woman.

It was in that summer of 1994 that I began to realise that my time in Cardiff was almost at an end. I was dreading leaving. There might have been social problems in Trowbridge but I still loved it. It was what I knew. In my area around Trowbridge Green, every door in every house was open. There was music playing in the street. You could walk into anyone's house.

And inevitably, some of my happiest memories are simple ones linked to football. I remember the 1990 FA Cup semi-final when Liverpool played Crystal Palace; flitting from one mate's house to another. I went into one house and Ian Rush had scored, then popped into another house and someone else had scored and suddenly Alan Pardew was scoring the goal that won it in extra-time for Palace and it was 4-3. And then after the match, the ice cream van appeared in the street and it was carnage.

But those days were gone. Things had moved on. Some of my mates had already gone to jail for crimes they committed trying to feed their drug habits and it had got to the point where my dad actually wanted me to go to Norwich because he was so worried about what might happen to me if I stuck around at home in Cardiff.

Norwich wanted to move me over to the club early but they were restricted because of my school age. But I wasn't going to school anyway, so one way and another, I started spending more time in Norwich. I began playing for the youth team and the more football I was getting, the more they were coaching me and improving me.

I still found the final separation from home very hard when it came. I joined up on July 1 and the night before I left, it dawned on me that this was it. I knew life was changing. I knew life was never going to be like this again. I knew I had to do it or I was never going to be a footballer.

Leaving Claire was very difficult. She was still at school. There was no possibility of her coming to join me and I worried we would drift apart. And suddenly, simple parts of my routine that I had taken for granted, like hopping on the bus to go and see my nana, seemed unbelievably precious now that I knew I was never going to be able to do them again. These are the rites of passage that many kids go through when they leave home but I was 15 and I found it very tough.

It had an impact on those around me, too. My elder brother and I were two different people but I was close to my younger brother. He was my kid brother and we shared a bedroom when we were kids and I was very protective of him. When I look back on it now, I feel for him because I moved away at 15. One minute your big brother is looking out for you and the next he is gone.

He was at a difficult age and all of a sudden, he was alone. We have drifted apart since then and I think it's because I moved away at a young age. It wasn't just the geographical separation. It puts a psychological barrier between you, too. Me moving away as young as I did affected a lot of relationships in my close family. That determination to make it, it can set you apart.

My mum and dad drove me up to Norwich. My dad had been counting the days to me leaving because he knew the dangers I was facing at home. My mum was different. She would have been happy if I'd said I wanted to come back home. She would have driven me right back to Cardiff there and then. She was losing her 15-year-old son and it was tough for her. My father told me later how upset she was in the car on the way back but she couldn't show that in front of me. She thought she had lost me, which she had. I wasn't going to be there any more.

In many ways, I think the pain of that separation and what I endured in the following weeks and months shaped the person I became. That first year of my apprenticeship at Norwich was the hardest year of my life. For the first few months, I cried myself to sleep most nights. I learned to cope on my own. I didn't ever turn to others.

Everything about it was difficult. I was in digs and the house was owned by a family who hadn't put anyone up before so they weren't quite sure how to act. They imposed curfews at night. It was strict and formal, a bit of a culture shock after the life I had been living in Cardiff.

I shared a room with another apprentice who had grown up in a village a few miles away. So at weekends, he could go home. I couldn't. I was down. I moped around quite a lot and the family who were putting me up found that difficult, too. I probably wasn't the best introduction to lodgers for them. They wanted to try to make me feel better but they couldn't.

Pre-season was difficult in those days. It was hard work and it was unforgiving. It was all about long runs and supposed character-building. It was what I imagine it's like in your first few days in the army. The senior professionals treated you like dirt. So did some of the staff. All the apprentices had a senior pro we had to do jobs for and mine was John Polston, the defender, who was a club stalwart by the time I arrived.

I had to clean his boots, get his kit for him, make him a tea or a coffee if he wanted one and generally clean around after him. He was difficult. He made a point of it. Every so often, I would go away with Wales Under-17s or 18s and every time I came back, I'd have to introduce myself to him all over again. "Who are you?" he'd say. He knew who I was but he wanted to try to humiliate me.

If he wasn't happy with the tea, he'd throw it in the sink and tell me to get another one. He complained about his boots all the time, too. He wasn't unusual. I think the rest of the players saw it as character-building, too. Look, I agreed with certain aspects of it but it felt like bullying really. You were intimidated. It felt like they were trying to break you.

Every six weeks, I was allowed home for a long weekend. I played on a Saturday and the deal was I had to be back in training the following Wednesday. So I would get a few days off but then I found it difficult to go back. The first occasion I was okay but the second occasion, I was crying at my parents' house when the time came to leave. I didn't want to go back.

My father rang Norwich and they gave me an extra couple of days off. They didn't rush me. They had probably seen it before. In the end, my father got firm with me. He said I needed to go back. He said I'd get over it and it would get better and if I could cope with this, I could cope with anything. I wasn't so sure. I was missing my girlfriend, I was missing everything.

I had just turned 16. When I came back to Cardiff for a couple of days, I wasn't really one of my friends' group any more. There was a distance between us. It was kind of understood that I had left, that I had chosen a different route. I suppose at a basic level, my friends felt I had rejected them and, at a basic level, they were right. I had gone in another direction. I became alone when I was at home as well as when I was in Norwich.

That period of being ripped away from my old life was agony. I refused to go back to Norwich during another one of my home visits and one of the other apprentices, another Cardiff lad called Tom Ramusat, came round to the house to persuade me to return with him. He put me on a guilt trip about how he couldn't face the journey back by himself. I owe a lot to him. He went out of his way to make sure he looked after me. I've stayed friends with him and his family ever since.

Things were difficult for a long time because of how I felt. Once, I got involved in a fight outside the Norwich training ground with a triallist. It didn't go too well for that kid. He was a goalkeeper and I broke his arm. I felt embarrassed about it afterwards and Norwich warned me that if anything like that happened again, I was gone.

The thing was, part of me wanted to be sacked. I was looking for every excuse I could to get sacked. I thought if I got sacked then I could come home and I could say it was their fault. I could say it wasn't my fault that it didn't work out. It was theirs. And then I could do what I wanted to do and blame everyone else for the loss of my football career.

But Norwich knew what I was up to and they didn't half bend the rules for me. I was pushing certain things. I walked off the training pitch once. Then I refused to come back out for running. When I felt really unhappy, I was looking for ways to get myself out of it. But the people at Norwich were absolutely fantastic. I will always be grateful that they persevered with me.

Martin O'Neill had been appointed the first team manager that summer. He wasn't particularly sociable with apprentices like me. In fact, he didn't even look at you. The only contact I had with him was walking past him in the corridor at the training ground but even in those circumstances, I knew there was a kind of magnetism about him.

Because I didn't go home at weekends, I had to clean up the first team dressing room after matches at Carrow Road and the best part of it was hanging around just outside the door, listening to the way O'Neill talked to the players. He would praise some of them like you wouldn't believe and he made some ordinary footballers play very, very well. Some of them never played at the same level again after he left that Christmas.

But he wasn't shy about getting stuck into someone if he felt they weren't pulling their weight. I remember one occasion. He had signed a guy called Matthew Rush for more than £300,000 from West Ham. It was O'Neill's signing, a biggish signing for Norwich and Rush was a flash Londoner who had a healthy opinion of himself.

But in one of his first games, he came on as a substitute for about 20 minutes and didn't do particularly well. Martin absolutely destroyed him after the game. He called him a big-time Charlie and generally lambasted him for his lack of effort and quality. I was impressed. It showed he didn't care who he got stuck into. I admired that about him.

Martin didn't take any interest in the apprentices but the reserve team boss, Steve Walford, who has been part of Martin's coaching team wherever he has gone in football, went out of his way to get to know me. He was brilliant to me. Even when I was 16, he gave me a lift back to my digs a couple of times. He told me about his debut at Spurs and about how, when he first began playing for West Ham in the early '80s, the hardest team he played against was Liverpool. As a Liverpool fan, that was music to my ears.

Then there was John Robertson, who until recently was the other constant in Martin's managerial life. Someone told me that he had been a proper player once. I know that now. I know that people thought he was a genius, that he was Brian Clough's favourite player at Nottingham Forest, that he won European Cups. But back then, I'd look at him with bandages round his knees, puffing on a cigarette and think 'no chance'.

It didn't work out for O'Neill and his staff at Norwich, though, and they were out before Christmas, 1995. They were replaced by Gary Megson and although I didn't really think it would make much difference to me who was the first team boss, Megson soon made it plain he thought I had a future and the homesickness that had been crippling me began to fade a little.

I moved out of my digs after a few months. Tom Ramusat lived in some digs called The Limes with six or seven other apprentices from the club and I asked Norwich's youth development officer, Gordon Bennett, if I could move in with them. It was more like living in a B&B than being cooped up in someone else's home and Gordon fixed it up for me. I began to settle in a bit better. I was quite professional. For all the problems I had been having, I was trying to take my football as seriously as I could and do the right things. Most nights, I would go to bed on time. If we had a game the next day, I would go to bed on time because I wanted to play well.

Most of the other boys would stay up. There was no one to keep an eye on us like there would have been in more traditional digs. As I was the youngest of the kids in there, I became the victim of a lot of practical jokes and pranks. One night, we were playing Scrabble, which wasn't really my strong point. We had Arsenal the next day so I headed off to bed. The rest stayed up playing Scrabble and I fell fast asleep.

The next thing I know, they've all come rushing into the room, all dressed and ready to go. They were in a panic, shaking me awake and saying we had overslept and that we were going to miss the coach. They looked scared. We'd been late before and been disciplined for it so I was in a real state. I started saying I had to pack my bag because I was being allowed home after the game but they said I didn't have time.

I rushed outside and started trying to get into the car. Then I looked around and everyone was on the floor, laughing. It was only then I realised it was pitch black. It wasn't time to get the coach at all. It was about 2am and they'd just finished their Scrabble. I had a major strop. I went stomping off to my room and all through the game against Arsenal, I was in a foul mood. I played rubbish. I made sure I blamed them for that.

The youth team boss was a guy called Keith Webb. He was strict and I found his regime hard to deal with in the first year. A lot of the time I was a substitute because the second year apprentices were generally given every opportunity to try to prove themselves. But when you are homesick, not playing regularly doesn't help.

Keith was actually a brilliant coach and he was a great help to me in my second year but in those first 12 months, he intimidated me. The youth team played in the South East Counties League and because we had a number of centre forwards, I would often play on the right wing. My chances were limited and I was moved around quite a lot.

I was small, too, don't forget. In youth team football in that era, strength and size were prized as much as anything and I was a late developer. But I got my head down and learned a lot, even though at times I tried my best not to, and at the end of my first season, Megson's first team coach, Mike Phelan, came to watch one of our games and immediately promoted me to the reserves.

That hadn't happened to anyone else from the youth team so it gave me a huge boost. In another game soon after that, Megson pulled me to the side and said 'you are going to be some player you, lad'. That made me think I had actually got a chance. I played well in the reserve team games and one of them was watched by the Wales Under-21 manager, Tom Whalley, who called me up for a match against San Marino. I was still 16. I ended the most difficult year of my life on a real high.

I had the summer of '96 off and watched as much of Euro 96 as I could. I was only on £40 a week so Claire and I didn't have enough money to go on holiday but we were still inseparable and it was still very difficult when the summer ended and I had to go back to live on the other side of the country. But being a second year YTS was a bit easier. We were given a little bit more respect by everybody and when I arrived back in Norwich, it didn't feel nearly as bad as when I had got there a year earlier.

I looked around at the new kids and funnily enough, seeing lads who looked as though they might be feeling as uncertain and as homesick as I once had, reassured me. When you see other people miserable, it makes you feel a bit better. Perhaps it was my first inkling of a sense of responsibility. A couple of the first years were from Plymouth. One of them was a kid called Darren Way, who behaved like he wanted to fight the world, just like I had done. I understood when he was homesick. He was a long way from home. I knew what he was going through.

I had ended the previous season so well that I arrived back feeling renewed and excited. I set my target on getting a first team debut when I was 17 because that was what Ryan Giggs had done. But any hopes I had harboured that Megson would champion my cause had come to nothing during the summer when he became a victim of the first team's disappointing season in Division One and left the club.

He was replaced by Mike Walker, who took over at the club for the second time. I had been led to believe that Megson had been ready to give me a professional contract but now I knew I was back to square one. Pre-season training was hard, hard work. We didn't see a ball for what felt like weeks. We just ran and ran. I knew I was going to have to prove myself all over again.

Then I got the phone call that changed my life.

It was Claire. She was pregnant. She was 16. I was just turning 17. A lot of thoughts rushed through my mind.

'What am I going to do?' 'Are we going to keep it?' 'What do I have to offer a child?' 'How are we going to be able to look after a baby?'

Well, Claire was from a Catholic family for a start. There was no way we were not going to have the baby and that was fine by me. But I was daunted by the idea of becoming a father. What do I have? I have nothing. I am living in digs. I am on £45 a week. What am I going to do? So I went in to see Keith Webb and told him my situation.

He was brilliant. He told me I had to go out and play the best football I had ever played and get the best contract I could. He told me it wasn't just about me any more. "You better eat and sleep football," he said. "You better think about nothing apart from football." 'That's right,' I thought. 'I know I can do this.'

And after that, my attitude was perfect. There was no looking for ways out any more. I didn't cut any corners. If we were told to do 45 seconds on a bike, I did 45 seconds. If we had to run to a cone, I ran right to the cone. I thought constantly of providing for Claire and the baby. It influenced everything I did, every drill in training, every recovery session. Everything.

I knew what my options were. If it wasn't football, we would be living in a flat in Trowbridge. Claire would have been okay with that. It wasn't as if she liked me because she thought I was going to be a professional footballer. But I wanted her to have the best life possible. I wanted my kid to have everything. I had to do something about it. I wanted to be able to provide for the baby. It was all clear to me.

I couldn't afford to bring Claire over to Norwich. She had just left school and was working at the Forbuoys newsagents. Lads would just go in there to rob stuff, basically, and as soon as it was possible, I wanted us to be together. So I worked and worked and worked. When other boys went home, I stayed. I did extras. I trained and trained. The more I trained, the less homesick I felt. I went from looking like I might be a good player to people saying with something approaching certainty 'he's a player'.

I was moving ahead of the other lads in the youth team. I was taking care of details. I cut out fizzy drinks. I drank water. I started doing weights. I found a new level of discipline. I didn't know anyone in Norwich anyway so all I did was football, morning, noon and night.

I have had the career I have had because of that moment when Claire phoned me up to tell me she was pregnant. I watched as much football as I could. I played as much football as I could. I trained as much as I could. I rested as much as I could. And if it turned out that, after all that, I wasn't good enough, at least I could look at my child and say 'I gave it my best shot'.

4

Rebel With A Cause

At the end of my first year of YTS, all the second year boys I lived with at The Limes – including Tom Ramusat – had been called in for contract talks with Gary Megson and Keith Webb. One by one, they came out looking crestfallen. One by one, they said they had been released. Tom took it on the chin but I could see how down he was.

The image of their faces kept coming into my mind. It was my other motivation. I was desperate to do well for the child we were going to have and I was also determined not to hear the words of rejection that those other lads had heard when my time came to be judged.

I became very selfish and single-minded about that and the club loved it. I was supported fully in all the extra work I was doing. The reserve team coach, Steve Foley, was fantastic. He was strict but his football knowledge was brilliant and if I stayed late, he stayed late with me. I think it meant a lot to him that a kid like me was willing to do all this work, but I got so much out of him. I was educated so well at Norwich.

We had a good youth team in my second year. Robert Green was the goalkeeper and Darren Kenton, who went on to have a good career for the club, was also in the side. Green lived at The Limes, too, but he wasn't for me. He liked to come across as someone who wasn't your stereotypical footballer, but that wasn't the Robert Green that I knew.

My determination to get a contract drove me on but it also brought me into conflict with people. I had been selected for Wales Under-21s in my first year and made my debut when I came on as a substitute in an away match against San Marino. We'd travelled out to Italy with the first team squad – players like Mark Hughes, Ryan Giggs and Gary Speed – and they must have looked at me, this kid who was so small in all my over-sized national team gear, and wondered who the hell I was.

That performance in San Marino made me the youngest player ever to appear for Wales Under-21s but when I found out I was going to be a dad, the next time I was called up, in November 1996, I told Norwich I didn't want to go and asked them if they could tell Wales I was injured. It wasn't that I didn't love playing for Wales. I did. It was a real privilege to be around some of those senior players. But I felt it set me back at Norwich.

I'd go away with the Under-21s for 10 days and miss a couple of youth team games and when I got back, I'd find that some-body had played in my absence, done well and was suddenly ahead of me. I needed a pro contract. I was totally focused on that. It was my number one priority. And if going away with Wales was getting in the way of that goal, if it was harming my chances, I didn't want to do it.

Norwich were sympathetic. I think they could see why the situation was difficult for me. And two weeks after the conversation about the Under-21s, they offered me a professional contract. They told me they wanted to remove any of the doubts and worries from my mind and reassure me that I had a big future at the club. What a moment that was. It was just an incredible relief. And I can still remember calling my parents to tell them. That takes some beating as a moment, I promise you.

But, quickly, other thoughts started crowding in. First of all, I told myself I had done nothing yet and that the hard work was just beginning. I wanted to get into the first team and make myself a regular. And even though I was so grateful to Norwich for offering me the contract, I was also determined to get the best deal possible for me, Claire and the baby.

That wasn't the norm. The idea was that you were offered terms and you accepted them, no questions asked. In my case, the offer was £200 a week. If I played 10 games for the first team, it would be renegotiated and renewed. If it had just been me, £200 would have been great but it wasn't just me. I had my girlfriend and my kid, too. And the way I looked at it, I was probably better off on £40 a week with my accommodation paid for.

Norwich were a bit taken aback. They called my bluff but I said I would play on until the end of my second year and then take my chances and see what was available elsewhere in the summer. Two other lads had said they were going to do the same thing but they buckled under the pressure straight away and signed. I was painted as some sort of renegade. Some of the senior pros regarded me as an object of curiosity. Other people at the club started to shun me.

I didn't care. I'd made a lot of sacrifices. I knew I was going to have to make a lot more. I believed in myself and I thought that if Norwich did not improve their offer, I would secure a better contract somewhere else. It wasn't easy, though. Norwich decided they'd teach me a lesson. I found myself on the bench for the reserves. It lasted four or five weeks but I didn't buckle.

Then they called me back in. They offered me £250 a week and I agreed. That was funny. If I'd accepted the £200 a week straight away, I would already have had that and could have still negotiated a rise. I probably would have been better off. What an idiot I was. But at least I had got my way. And I felt satisfied that I had done my best. It wasn't much money, not enough to move Claire up to Norwich, but it got the ball rolling. Next, I wanted to get in the first team, get more appearances, get another contract.

I was playing well for the youth team. We were sailing in the league and progressing in the FA Youth Cup and I was scoring hat-tricks from the position they were playing me in, as a free man in the centre of midfield. I had a licence to go wherever I wanted and it suited me. I found it very comfortable and I felt that I was getting closer and closer to a spot in the first team.

Then one day in late February, I came in from training and Terry Postle, the kit man, called me into his little room and asked if he could have a word.

He told me my dad had just called to say that Claire had gone into labour. I was just a kid. I didn't know what to expect. I didn't know whether to be excited or afraid for her or what. They got me over to the station and I got the train to London and then on to Cardiff. I was on the train for five hours and I thought I'd probably miss the birth. But when I got up to Heath Hospital, the same hospital where I had been born 17 years earlier, I found the room where she was, with her mum and her auntie. She was still in labour.

I wasn't sure whether I wanted to be in the room. We were kids. I didn't know what to do. I felt like a spare part. Then my nan rang. So I went outside and chatted to her and during that call, Claire gave birth to our son, Ellis. I froze a little bit. I didn't know what to do. I was just praying she and the baby were both well.

It all seemed like a blur. It was amazing when I saw him for the first time, amazing when I knew everything was okay. I slept at my parents' that night and then went back up to the hospital the next morning. There were other new parents in the ward and I felt embarrassed because I was still a boy. But I wasn't going to have anyone looking down on us, thinking 'we'll have to pay for those kids'.

I knew I was going to provide for Claire and my baby. I was going to pay my own way. We were young and it was going to be difficult but I knew I'd do it. The first night Ellis came home, we were in Claire's bedroom and we slept on a mattress right next to him. Just listening to him breathe…I didn't sleep a wink. I was just listening to him, holding my own breath until he breathed again.

It was a magical couple of days but I knew I had to go. I had to get back up the road. Football doesn't stop. I knew I needed to get back quickly because I needed to get into that first team.

I knew that the task of providing for Ellis had started in earnest now and I had to move up to another level. It had to start with me going back to Norwich that day. Claire's mum promised me they would look after them both. And so I left.

Nobody mentioned it much to me back in Norwich. Football's football. Everyone's looking after themselves. You're here, you're back, that's it. No little gifts from older pros. Nothing like that. You just got on with it. That was how I approached it. I didn't expect anything different. I went back to The Limes with Robert Green and Darren Kenton. I made Tom Ramusat the godfather. I threw myself back into training.

I was hardly at the digs because I was training all the time. The other YTS boys knew what I was doing. Maybe in other circumstances, some of the other lads might have thought I was being busy, trying to make myself popular with the coaches, being a teacher's pet. But they had seen how I had behaved the year before and the change that had come over me since I had found out I was going to be a father and I think they understood. I think they were thinking 'look at Bellers now'. They understood my focus.

I made my first team debut against Crystal Palace at Selhurst Park on March 15, 1997, less than a month after Ellis was born. Norwich were in the First Division, the second tier of English football, and by the time I broke through, we were no longer contending for promotion. We had started well under Mike Walker but we went 10 games without a win before Christmas which put paid to our ambitions of going up to the Premier League. We lost 5-1 and 6-1 in consecutive matches away at West Brom and Port Vale in December.

There were a lot of decent players at the club, though. Bryan

Gunn was a good keeper, Ian Crook and Mike Milligan were fine midfielders, Darren Eadie had a lot of pace out wide and there was Robert Fleck up front. I got about two minutes at the end of that game against Palace. There was no question of a call to my parents so that they could get to the game to watch my debut. It all felt very last minute. I was wearing a kit that was about three sizes too big for me, I touched the ball twice, we lost 2-0 and it was over.

It wasn't the proudest time in Norwich's history. That had probably come a few years earlier when they led the Premier League for most of the season during its first year of existence. They finished third in the end but the following year, they beat Bayern Munich in the Olympic Stadium in the Uefa Cup before losing to Inter Milan.

Those were the years when I first started travelling over from Cardiff to play for the boys' team but by the time I joined as an apprentice in the summer of 1995, it was very different. The club had been relegated from the Premier League at the end of the previous season and there was some brutal cost-cutting going on as the club tried to adapt to its reduced circumstances.

I found out how ruthless football was that season. Martin O'Neill left after a few months in a row over money. I saw kit men who had worked at the club for years and years sacked. And the same with tea ladies. That was my introduction to the reality of football. It is ruthless. Clubs don't care. Money's tight and if things have to give way, they will give way. It does not matter how many years you have been somewhere. There is no loyalty in this game. I saw that early doors due to all that. What is more important: players or the club's existence? It's the club's existence. Not us. Players come and go.

I wasn't under any illusions about that. I knew how easy it would be to become a victim of football rather a beneficiary of everything it could offer. I was disappointed with my debut at Palace because I barely got a touch and it felt like an anti-climax. But it was one more goal achieved. I was 17 when I made my debut, just like Ryan Giggs had been, and now I wanted to kick on.

The week after my first team debut, I was sub for the youth team. It was their way of saying 'don't think you've made it'. That was fair enough. It was my motto anyway. It was perfect for me. I didn't think I was a professional yet, really. I wasn't expecting that everything would suddenly start coming easily. I knew I had to go away and work even harder.

At least I could see some rewards for the effort I was putting in. The youth team won the South East Counties League and soon after we had clinched the title, I played for the first team again in the last home game of the season against Manchester City on a Friday night. I got 10 or 15 minutes this time and I felt like I made a contribution.

City had been relegated from the Premier League the year before and they still had some good players but I did okay against them. Ian Crook fed me the ball all the time and I played a couple of quick one-twos with him. I played centre midfield and I was roaming everywhere. The crowd took to me straight away, this little kid playing in a kit that was still way too big for him.

The last game of the season was Oldham away. I came off the bench again. It was all part of my education and a place like Boundary Park was a hard school. I nearly gave a goal away with a loose backpass and it gave me a real shock. I felt uncomfortable in that game.

The Oldham players seemed like giants. They were strong, direct and physical. It didn't scare me but it did make me realise I was going to have to work hard that summer if I was going to impress in the first team. We lost 3-0.

I went home to Cardiff. I lived at Claire's mum's that summer, getting used to being a father and caring for Ellis. I was also coming to terms with the fact that I had an awful lot to lose and that I couldn't afford to take any risks any more. I knew by that stage that I wasn't too far away from getting a full cap for Wales, which would bring a new level of recognition, particularly in Cardiff.

It hit me with a jolt that I couldn't really go round to my mates' flats any more. What happens if I'm round there and they invite some other lads round and they start smoking cannabis or other stuff? I can't tell them what not to do in their own place. And what happens if the police come running into that place? I'd get arrested and my name would be all over the papers even though I hadn't done anything.

Not many people cared about Norwich City in Trowbridge. I knew that. In fact, interest in football generally in the area was at a bit of a low with Cardiff stuck in the Fourth Division. But people were aware that I was a footballer and I knew that, with my career looking as though it might be about to take off, I couldn't afford any suggestions of bad behaviour to get back to Norwich. That would set me right back.

So I totally shut myself off from my old friends. I stopped going to the Hippo Club in Cardiff, a dance music place behind the train station, which had been one of my haunts. I knew then my life had gone in a different direction and even though they were my friends, my friends knew it too.

CRAIG BELLAMY

My life was different. My focus was different. Providing for Ellis was what really mattered to me. I couldn't afford any mistakes. I felt that I had a genuine chance of making it to the big time as a footballer. I was close now, really close. It was hard but I knew I had to completely sacrifice my friends.

If I couldn't speak to them ever again, I wouldn't.

5
##

In At The Deep End

An agent called Johnny Mac had started sniffing around me.
I looked at his profile on the internet the other day. Next
to the slot where it asks for your education, he had written:
'Hard Knocks'. He was okay. I was 17. I was going to be in the
Norwich first team. I was doing interviews without having a
clue what to say. I needed some representation.

I hit my quota of 10 first team appearances fairly quickly at
the start of the 1997-98 season. That triggered a clause that
said the club had to renegotiate my contract. They called me
in and offered me £500 a week. I refused. I wanted to move
Claire and Ellis up to Norwich so we could be together but I
wanted to do it properly.

Johnny Mac said he would go in and sort it out. He had a

meeting with the club. He got the wages up to £750 a week with various add-ons and that was fine by me. I just wanted to get it done. I went to watch a reserve team match that night and bumped into the chief executive. I hadn't spoken to Johnny Mac but I told the chief executive I'd sign the next day and we shook hands.

The next day came. On my way into training, my phone rang. It was Johnny Mac. "Whatever you do, don't sign that contract," he said.

He told me that Crystal Palace, who had been promoted to the Premier League the previous summer, wanted to buy me. The Palace chairman, Ron Noades, had offered Norwich £2m to buy me and they were offering me £2,500 a week. I was a bit wide-eyed about that. It was a big jump in salary. And they were Premier League. It was my dream to play in the Premier League.

I had to go in to Mike Walker's office because I knew they were waiting in there with the contract for me to sign. They were all smiles when I walked in. It was awkward. I just told them I wasn't signing. Mike Walker and the chief executive looked at each other.

"Can I ask why?" the manager said.

I just said that I had been told not to sign it.

He and the chief executive looked at each other again.

"Get out of my office," Mike Walker said.

So I was public enemy number one again. I felt bad about it but it wasn't just about me. If it was just about me, I would have signed every time and just got on with my football. But I had made a conscious decision that everything was for Claire and Ellis. I had to stick it out for them. I wanted them to have more.

Norwich didn't banish me. I stayed in the first team. Crystal Palace's interest got even stronger and so Norwich called Johnny Mac in. They told him the club wanted ridiculous money for me and if I wanted to go, I would have to ask to leave. Johnny Mac asked me what I wanted to do but then said that staying at Norwich would be my best bet. He said there would be other moves in the future. He said I still had a lot to learn and I just had to keep progressing.

I didn't know what was going to happen if I went to Crystal Palace. My mind was in turmoil. I left it a couple of weeks and then I went back in and signed exactly the same £750-a-week contract Norwich had been offering me in the first place. So much for the great negotiator.

It was for the best. Things went well for me at Norwich that season. I'd spat my dummy when I wasn't included in the squad for the pre-season tour to Ireland and I pulled my thigh in training a few days later but, after that, everything was okay. Steve Foley told me to stop feeling sorry for myself. He reminded me it was a long season and that I had plenty of time. I knew he was right but when you're a kid you want everything now.

Everybody was hoping that 1997-98 would be the season that Mike Walker would recapture some of the magic of his first spell in charge at Norwich and there was a lot of optimism around the first game of the season against Wolves at Carrow Road. I came off the bench for the last 20 minutes but it turned out to be the Robbie Keane show. He scored twice on his Wolves debut and we lost 2-0.

We got battered in the next game at Nottingham Forest and then lost at home to Crewe, too. But I found I was playing all the time. If Mike Walker didn't pick me one week, I'd be back in the next week. I made 38 appearances that season, usually in centre midfield. I scored 13 goals and revelled in the role. I was probably responsible for plenty of the goals we conceded, too, many of which originated from the fact that I didn't track the opposition's runners well enough.

The optimism around the club had died but perhaps in a way that helped me. Maybe if the club had been pressing for promotion, first team opportunities for someone like me would have been limited but Norwich had been plunged into a financial crisis as it tried to adapt to no longer being in the Premier League and as a result, young lads like me were getting a chance.

I probably wouldn't have had such a good career if I hadn't got all that experience with Norwich. I probably wouldn't have developed into the player I became if I had been stuck in the reserves at a club where it was impossible for a kid to force his way into the first team. I felt for the fans that the club was at such a low ebb but it became more and more obvious its circumstances were providing me with a golden opportunity.

I got more games than my ability deserved. I found some games very difficult physically and I was fatigued by playing twice a week. That meant my performances were inconsistent. My body was still maturing and I was still growing but I wasn't rested because we had a lack of players. There wasn't really anyone else they could draft in. Some games I felt drained. Some I felt great.

Robert Fleck and Iwan Roberts played up front and Darren Eadie scored plenty of goals, too. Eadie was decent. He was quick and direct. He wasn't a clever player but he could do something. He scored plenty of goals. Iwan struggled with his weight a bit. I liked Fleck. He knew he was on his way out. He knew he was coming to the end of his career and his legs were gone but he was always generous to me with advice.

During that year, a guy called Peter Grant came in from Celtic and played alongside me in central midfield. He had been a cult figure at Celtic because of his love for the club and his combative style. His attitude was immense. He was in his early 30s by the time he arrived at Carrow Road but I was impressed by the way he looked after himself, the way he trained, the weights he did and the commitment he showed.

I kind of attached myself to him and he took me under his wing. A lot of the other players were a little bit intimidated by his work ethic because there was still a bit of a drinking culture in the game in those days. After every game there was a crate of beer on the bus, that kind of thing. Actually, a lot of the time, I'd be pouring the beers on the bus. As the youngest member of the team, it was one of my duties. I bit back occasionally but it was just the way it was.

Some of the other senior pros resented me. I seemed to rub them up the wrong way. They thought I was a bit of an upstart. So in training that season, one or two of them would try to clean me out with flying tackles. They wanted to bring me down a peg or two. They were suspicious of the fact that I wanted to work hard. Again, that was the way it was then.

There was a guy called Kevin Scott, a lad from the north east, who had been signed from Tottenham in February 1997 for £250,000. He was a big defender and there was one training game in particular where he took it upon himself to boot me up in the air the entire match. I was nearly in tears. I felt like walking off. Iwan Roberts looked out for me a bit and told me not to bite. The coaches didn't do anything, though. They were in on it. They didn't want to penalise Scott, so I just got on with it.

I had to learn the hard way but the thing that kept me going was that I knew I was going to be better than them. I looked at Scott and I thought 'I ain't going to be like you. You can say what you want and treat me how you want, but I am going to be a better player than you ever were or ever will be'. They probably knew I felt like that. I didn't care.

I loved Norwich and I will always be grateful to them for everything they did for me, everything they taught me and the patience they showed me. But I wanted to go on to bigger and better things. I knew I had to work hard and, as far as I was concerned, people like Scott were the example not to follow.

I felt the club had too many players with the wrong attitude. I respected many of them but even though I was a young player, I felt they needed to earn my respect. I was getting players in their 30s who thought they were the best footballer in the world because they once finished fourth in the league talking to me as if I was a piece of shit. But if I had a go at them, if I told them they should have passed the ball earlier or covered back more quickly, they found that impudent and disrespectful. When I play in a match, giving everything to try to win, if I feel you are not doing something right, I am going to tell you. It's just the way I am. I had Peter Grant on my side, too.

"Wee man," he used to say, "I wouldn't change you for the fucking world. You got something to say, you say it and I will back you up." It was great to have that kind of support from a pro like him.

He was 33 and I was a raw teenager but he would invite me round to his house and I'd have something to eat with him and his wife and his two kids. I thought that if I could train as well as him and look after myself as well as him, knowing that I had more ability than him, then I could have a good career. He said that, too. He said he had got the maximum out of what he had. He told me that if I could apply myself, I would be able to go wherever I wanted to and achieve whatever I wanted to.

I had Claire and Ellis with me by then. After I signed my new contract, I bought an apartment and moved them over. It was a fantastic feeling to be all together at last although it was daunting, too. We were still kids and we had a kid to look after. Everything I had went on that apartment and all my focus was on trying to provide a good life for us.

I was a lot happier once they arrived and I went from strength to strength, even though we were struggling as a side. Between January and April 1998, we went 14 games without a victory and slipped to within three points of the relegation zone. The atmosphere around the club was grim and even though we staged a minor recovery to finish 15th, Mike Walker was sacked just before the end of the season.

It had been hard for Walker. He had been forced to blood a lot of young players and at the same time, some of the older players, stalwarts of the club, were moving towards retirement. Being exiled from the Premier League was really taking its toll financially by then. It had felt like a cutting edge club when I was coming up through the ranks, full of new ideas and optimistic about the future. That had gone.

Players like me were thrown in at the deep end. I benefited from that but he probably didn't. I'll always be grateful to him for giving me my league debut but did I learn anything from him? Not really. Did I learn anything tactically? No. Did I learn anything about how to motivate players? No.

Maybe that was partly because I was still very close to Steve Foley. I was still learning in the game and I was always aware of that. When training with the first team finished, I would still go back with the reserves in the afternoon. I didn't need to but I wanted to improve. I didn't settle for just being a first team player. I wanted to play at the top and I knew there was a lot of work to be done.

Foley was my motivation. He watched every game. He was on my case if I did stuff wrong but he was encouraging, too. Walker was sacked at the end of April 1998 and Foley took charge of the last game of the season. It was Reading away and I scored the goal in a 1-0 victory. It was the last game at Elm Park, I think.

Bruce Rioch took over for the start of the 1998-99 season, with Bryan Hamilton as his assistant. It was clear immediately we got back for pre-season training that improvements had been made. That summer, the club had created a new sports science department. We had heart monitors, there were finger pricks to take the bloods for fatigue, there was a new emphasis on diet with a nutritionist. Instead of buying a player for three or four hundred grand, you might as well spend the money on that kind of stuff and get the club right. It felt like the cutting edge was back again. Everything was very professional.

I liked Rioch. He knew the game. He had an army background and was very strict. He struggled to warm to people and some players struggled to warm to him. But he was always willing to try and improve you as a player which was right up my street. He was a sharp observer of the game, too, so when we went on pre-season tour to Ireland and he saw me playing centre midfield, he knew immediately I wasn't a natural fit there. He had been a pretty good central midfielder himself, which helped.

After we got back from Ireland, he called me into his office the day before another pre-season game against Spurs. He said he could see I was a goalscorer but that he felt I left too many gaps and the team had to adjust to me. He said I sometimes left the team exposed because I was looking to get forward all the time. He was right. He wanted an all-round midfielder.

I had been getting away with playing in central midfield when we were a poor Division One side but he knew I wasn't what we needed there if we were going to try to press for promotion. He asked me where I wanted to play and I said that if I had a choice, it would be up front. So I started in attack against Spurs. I scored and I played really well. Rioch wasn't there because he had gone to scout another game but Hamilton was and when the new season started, I was up front.

I scored seven goals in the first eight league games and never played central midfield again. I was the name on everybody's lips for a while and Norwich moved quickly to head off interest from other clubs, including Spurs. They offered me another new contract, my third in a year. This time, I would be on £2,000 a week. It was a five-year deal that was structured so that, by the fifth year, I would be on £7,000 a week. I signed it straight away. No fuss this time.

And Claire and I went house-hunting. We went to look at a show house. It had four bedrooms and it had two garages. It was the kind of place I had never imagined that I would live in, not in my wildest dreams. We were both still teenagers and we were looking at a house that was miles better than the houses our parents lived in. It was a strange feeling.

Claire fell in love with that house but she thought it was beyond us. I didn't tell her but I went back to the estate agent and bought it. I took the keys home and pressed them into Ellis's hand and told him to go and toddle over to mummy on his walker. Claire looked at the keys and they had a tag with the address of the house on them. She thought I'd kept them from the appointment.

"You've got to go and give those keys back," she said.

"No, I haven't," I told her. "It's our bloody house."

To tell the truth, there was another house I'd liked better. When we first started looking, they took us to look at John Polston's place.

Polston's career had fallen into decline since the days when I used to clean his boots and watch him throw the tea I'd made for him down the sink. He'd only played a handful of games for Norwich in 1997-98 and now they were shipping him out to Reading, who were a league below Norwich in the old Division Two, on a free transfer. He wasn't there when I went round to look at his house. I don't think his wife enjoyed showing me around too much. She had probably heard a few stories about what an arrogant little prick I was. And now the arrogant little prick, who was only 19, was coming round to look at the house Polston had grafted his whole career for.

I liked that house. I was going to buy it. But then I decided against it. It was odd really but I did it out of respect for Polston, even though I felt he had shown me absolutely none. It felt like it would have been me laughing at him if I had bought his house and I didn't want to do that. I had no interest in trying to score points over him any more.

I thanked his wife and walked away.

6
—

Goulden Start

When I first started playing for Wales, it often felt as if I had stumbled into a black comedy. I was incredibly proud to be involved with the national team but when I joined up with the squad for the first time before a friendly against Jamaica at Ninian Park, I spent most of the days leading up to it in a state of wide-eyed bemusement.

It was well-known that there was friction between the manager, Bobby Gould, and John Hartson, who I had got to know quite well from playing with the Wales Under-21s. At my first training camp, Gould got everyone to form a big circle and then told us all that he and Harts were going to go in the centre of the circle and wrestle each other.

He told Harts that he wanted him to use it to vent all his

frustration, to rid himself of the resentment he was feeling by expressing himself in the wrestling. I suppose it was the equivalent of getting a kid to hit a punchbag, except in this case the punchbag was the manager of the national team.

Harts was reluctant. He felt awkward about it. For obvious reasons. But the rest of the players were urging him on and telling him he had to do it and that he couldn't back down. So in the end, Harts went to the middle of the circle. He's a big bloke and after a few seconds of grappling, he gripped Bobby Gould in a headlock and then flung him across the circle on to the floor.

Everyone was roaring and shouting. I almost had to pinch myself that this was happening. It was a bizarre sight. When Gould got to his feet, he was holding his nose and looking aggrieved. Blood was streaming out of it. He muttered to everyone that they should go for a jog so we set off around the pitch. I couldn't believe what had just happened.

I came to understand that it wasn't actually that unusual. I liked Bobby Gould. He was a well-respected man in the game and he was generous to me. I also understood that he was trying to bring new, young players in and that Wales at that time were a comparatively weak football nation but a lot of the new ideas he tried, on and off the pitch, didn't always work.

He would do things like organise games of charades in the evening. The players didn't like it. Footballers can be conservative, cautious people in a group and charades never went down particularly well. The only occasions it got animated were when Gould became the object of ridicule in some of the mimes. It was comical but it was heart-wrenching, too, because it was your country. The training, frankly, didn't impress me.

I made my debut against Jamaica at the ground where I had watched my first football match and seen Wales play for the first time. I was still only 18 and I felt I had achieved something special. At the end of the 1997-98 season, Wales played a couple of friendlies in Malta and Tunisia and I was included in the squads for those games, too.

I started the game against Malta. I played in a three-man midfield alongside Gary Speed and Mark Pembridge and scored my first international goal to put us 1-0 up in a game we went on to win 3-0. The next evening, we were allowed to go into the town for a night out and I went out with Chris Llewellyn and Simon Haworth. Bobby Gould had allowed it but he had asked us to be back at a certain time because we were 18.

We kept our distance a bit from the senior players. Harts was on the trip, too. He was five years older than me and he was out with the senior players. I always thought he was a great guy. He had been in the team when I made my Under-21 debut against San Marino and it was clear then that he was too good to be playing with us. He was at Arsenal and he should have been in the first team. In fact, he was better than three quarters of the first team.

His relationship with Bobby Gould was already poor back then. He scored against San Marino and then booted an advertising hoarding so hard in frustration that he broke it in half. Gould asked him why he had kicked the board, which started a big row about why he had been selected for the Under-21s instead of the senior team in the first place.

Harts is Welsh through and through. He's a hard boy and confident, too. He would always be on the karaoke and whenever we went out with him, he wouldn't let anyone else buy a drink. He got every round. Maybe one of the reasons for that was that few others seemed to drink at his pace.

There were a lot of Cardiff fans in Malta that night and there was tension between them and Harts because he was from Swansea. Even though he played for Wales, it sometimes felt there was a chance that the Wales fans might attack him if they bumped into him on a night out. To a lesser extent, it was the same with me. I come from Cardiff but had never played for Cardiff and there were one or two who tried to take me to task because I had left the city to play for Norwich.

I was only a kid and I said something back. Suddenly, there were two or three blokes coming at me and swinging punches. Simon Haworth dragged me into a taxi but I was very close to getting into trouble. It was my first away trip with Wales and it made me realise how careful you have to be, even with your national team. I thought because we were all Welsh, we would all get on but it wasn't like that. It caught me by surprise.

The next day, we travelled to Tunis. When we arrived at the hotel in Tunis, it was a shocker. Gary Speed said it wasn't good enough. Bobby Gould agreed and we were moved to another place. It wasn't the ideal start. Everything seemed to be done on a shoestring with Wales. There was a lot of penny-pinching. Rows like that were not uncommon.

Tunisia had been in England's group in the 1998 World Cup that was beginning a few days later and they thought British opposition like us would provide them with the perfect test. But I'm afraid we weren't much of a challenge for them. We had one or two players who weren't in good shape. They hadn't ended the season well for their clubs and then they had ne-glected their fitness before they joined up for international duty.

Those summer games can be difficult. They can be treated as an afterthought. Ryan Giggs and Mark Hughes weren't there, but there were a few of the younger players who knew we had Italy in the first qualifier for Euro 2000 at the start of the next season and wanted to put themselves in the frame for that. They were hungry to do well – but they were in the minority.

The game kicked off at 3pm in Tunis, so you can imagine the heat. Tunisia gave us a hiding. We played one up front with Harts, who was out of shape and was suffering so much in the heat he could barely move. To make matters worse, we played in this garish green Lotto kit that has never been seen since. I don't even know where it came from. It was a little bit too small for Harts. None of us looked good in it but he looked worse.

It was a grim afternoon. We were beaten comfortably. Harts and Dean Saunders were substituted midway through the second half and then I got subbed in the last ten minutes.

On the bench, Saunders started moaning about Gould. "What's he doing, bringing us off? We were the best players," he said.

Saunders was like that. He liked to start the ball rolling and then sit back. He never said anything to Gould's face. Deano was always the one at the back of the bus, moaning and chipping away. Gary Speed was the opposite. He would always do it in the open. I loved Speedo for moments like that. He wouldn't bitch. He said his bit – and he was correct – and then he went quiet. I knew the people who I admired and why.

To be fair to Saunders, a lot of players were unhappy with Bobby Gould before that anyway. After the game, Speedo went ballistic. He said we were a pub team, we were a disorganised rabble who hadn't got a clue what we were doing. He turned on Gould, too. He told him he had set us back years, that we had been a decent team and now we couldn't even give sides like Tunisia a game. Gould was reeling. He said Tunisia were a decent team but Speedo went into one. He said England would batter Tunisia and that we should all be ashamed.

I sat there in the dressing room with my head down. I was only 18 and this kind of stuff was new to me in football. 'This is going to be a tough, tough living,' I thought to myself. Then the black comedy started again. Gould looked at Chris Coleman.

"There are too many players in this dressing room who think they are better than they are," he said.

"What are you looking at me for, Bob?" Chris Coleman said.

"I don't mean you," Gould said. "I just mean in general."

The balloon went up again then. All the players were annoyed now and everyone started having a go.

Harts sensed an opportunity to salvage something from a pretty dire afternoon and had a go, too.

"Why did you take me off, by the way?" he said.

"Because you looked overweight, the sun was way too much for you and I thought I was doing you a big, big favour," Gould said. Harts just looked at him. There wasn't much of an answer to that and he knew it.

"Okay," he said.

At least it was never dull with Wales. The following season, I found myself sent back down to the Under-21s squad when the qualifying tie against Italy came around at the beginning of September, 1998. That was fair enough. All the top players who had missed the summer friendlies were back and this was Italy. It was a glamour game. Even the Under-21 match had a smattering of superstars.

We lost 2-1 to our Italian counterparts but that was hardly a disgrace. They had Andrea Pirlo, Gianluigi Buffon and Massimo Ambrosini in their ranks, so they weren't too shabby. I scored the Wales goal and after the game I was drafted into the senior squad for the match at Anfield the following evening.

We were staying at the Carden Park Hotel, south of Chester, and when I went into the team meeting at 10am, I noticed that Robbie Savage wasn't there. That didn't make me particularly observant, by the way. Sav was such a loud presence that you noticed when he was absent. I thought maybe he had been injured in training the previous day.

I have always liked Sav. Behind all the bluster, he's actually a pretty insecure guy. Because I'd been playing well for the Under-21s and I was creeping closer to a place in the first team, I could tell he was threatened. I wore the number 4 shirt during the friendly in Tunisia and Sav collared me soon afterwards. "Don't worry," he said. "You'll be giving that back to me soon enough." That was typical Sav. He knew I was a better player than him and he knew he was going to be under the cosh for his place.

Bobby Gould walked into the meeting room and went straight into a rant about how he had been watching television the previous evening when he saw Sav doing an interview with Sky. Sav was holding an Italy number 3 shirt, Paolo Maldini's shirt, and then he scrumpled it up for the benefit of the camera and threw it away. Bobby Gould was appalled by that. He said it showed a complete lack of respect for one of the world's greatest players.

He told us what he had done. He had rung Sav in his room in the middle of the night and told him to leave the hotel and that he would not be playing any part in the Italy match. He had sent him home. Sav himself said later that the call came at 5am and that Bobby Gould had threatened to call the police if Sav refused to leave. Sav was insistent it was just a prank and he thought Gould was overreacting. Once again, we were lurching into farce.

Speedo spoke up straight away. He asked Gould what he had sent him home for. He said we needed him for the game.

"What can I do?" Gould said. "I've sent him home and the media knows I've sent him home."

"Well, then go and get him back," Speedo said. "Ring him. We need him back in the squad."

Chris Coleman backed Speedo up and Bobby Gould began to retreat. It didn't make him look very clever. It was another fuss about nothing and it was overshadowing a massive game. It was obvious to me, obvious to everybody, that Sav respected Maldini. It was just Sav's idea of a joke, his tongue-in-cheek effort at saying the Italians didn't scare us. It was obvious it was meant to be funny, not derogatory, but now we had made a big drama out of it.

By then, Gould had already given a television interview explaining why he had sent Sav home. "Players must realise that they have a duty to put-up on the field of play and shut-up off it," he said. "This type of 'set-up' interview has caused problems in the past and is totally alien to the true spirit of the game which was so epitomised in the classic picture of Pele and Bobby Moore embracing and exchanging shirts in the Mexico World Cup of 1970. That was true sporting comradeship and what I saw last evening certainly was not, and I have a duty to uphold the good name of Welsh international football."

It was a total mess. All sorts of rumours started flying around. Sav was still at home. Sav would be on the bench. Sav would be in the first team. Sav would never play for Wales again. Nobody knew what was happening. Everyone was talking about the row, not the fact that we were about to face a team that included Alessandro Del Piero, Fabio Cannavaro and Christian Vieri.

When we arrived at Anfield, Sav was there like a puppy with big eyes. He was very emotional. He was upset about what had happened. It turned out that Gould had backed down up to a point and had put him on the bench. He gave a debut to Nottingham Forest midfielder Andy Johnson instead and Johnson played superbly.

In fact, we did not disgrace ourselves. Giggs was absolutely outstanding up front and he started off by going on this blistering run that took out most of the Italian defence before he was denied by a last-ditch tackle. The crowd was roaring us on, the atmosphere was brilliant and for 20 minutes, everyone was dreaming of an upset.

But then we conceded a silly goal when there was a mix-up between Chris Coleman and the goalkeeper, Paul Jones, and Diego Fuser slid the ball into the net. Giggs hit the bar with a free-kick just before half-time and Cannavaro defended brilliantly in the second half before Roberto Baggio came off the bench and set up Italy's second for Vieri 14 minutes from the end. By the end of the match, the crowd had begun to turn on Gould. "We want Bobby out," they sang.

Sav came on for the last 10 minutes but the game was lost by then. I didn't make it off the bench but I still got a lot out of the game. I looked at some of their players, their attitude, their professionalism, their talent, the way they carried themselves, and it spurred me on. I wanted to get to their level. It made me determined to keep working and keep trying to improve myself.

A month later, we travelled to Copenhagen to play Denmark in the next qualifier and it was billed as Gould's last game. The press were after him, the fans had lost patience and the players had largely lost faith in him. Most people expected us to get beaten heavily. We were in freefall.

I was on the bench. I had a good view of Denmark battering us in the first half. They finally got the goal they deserved in the 57th minute when Soren Frederiksen put them ahead with a scrappy shot after we failed to clear a corner. But a minute later, we equalised when the Denmark keeper, Mogens Krogh, who was standing in for Peter Schmeichel, somehow let a header from Adrian Williams squirm through his hands.

With 21 minutes remaining, Gould brought me on in place of Nathan Blake. Four minutes from the end, Darren Barnard swung a long cross over from the left, their centre half missed it and I headed it past the goalkeeper and into the corner of the net. I wheeled away, ecstatic, before Sav grabbed me to celebrate. I might have scored against Malta earlier in the year but this felt like my first proper international goal. It was a big game against a decent side and my goal won the game. I was Wales' new hero.

Not with everybody, though. After the match, Dean Saunders came up to me. "You do realise you've just saved this guy's job," he said. I didn't know whether to laugh or cry.

When we got home, I felt like a big star for the first time in my career. And when I got back to Norwich, I was feeling so pleased with myself that my attitude was slack in the next match against Crystal Palace. Bruce Rioch had to have a word with me and remind me that the best players never rest on their laurels or celebrate their achievements for long.

Four days later, we won again, beating Belarus at home. We nearly blew it, going 2-1 down early in the second half. But we equalised and then Kit Symons got the winner five minutes from the end. For a few months, there was an unfamiliar feeling of optimism about our fortunes but that was punctured the following March when we lost 2-0 to Switzerland in Zurich. Next up was Italy in Bologna in June. That was when the fun and games started again.

We prepared for the game in Rimini on the Adriatic coast, about 80 miles away from Bologna. Gould tried to change his approach. He let us do what we wanted to, basically. He abandoned the playing of charades. Even he had begun to realise that wasn't working. You'd see boys trying to sneak out of the door while it was going on. In Rimini, we were out most nights.

It was hot in training. When the sessions started to get serious, it began to look as though the front line would be Giggs on the left, Hughes in the centre and me on the right. That meant Mark Pembridge, Saunders and Harts would miss out. All three of them had probably been expecting to play. They weren't impressed and they weren't shy about showing it.

There was one full-scale training match where one or two disaffected players got the ball and then just booted it into touch. They spat their dummies, basically. I'm not judging them. It was just a way of showing their frustration. I wasn't going to say anything because I was a 19-year-old kid but I knew things were going to get interesting.

Gould caved in. He moved things around to accommodate the established players and now it looked as if I was out. It didn't bother me too much but it upset a few other people. So now the ones who felt they were being discriminated against started not to try in training. Gould had had enough of it. So he called everyone in.

"I tell you what, you lot can pick the team," he said, "and when you've done it, come and let me know what it is."

"You're paid to pick the team, not us," Speedo said.

"I've just picked it," Gould said, "and nobody listened to me."

People started laughing. Maybe Gould was trying to play a mind game but it felt like we were in chaos.

I went back to my room and before long, there was a knock on my door and Gould came in. Neville Southall, who was his assistant, had seen me play in central midfield in a game for Norwich when we had gone down to 10 men and I had run the game. He had mentioned that to Gould, who had now decided he was going to play me in central midfield.

We travelled to Bologna. The day before the game, he sat us all down, got a clipboard out, flicked over a page and showed us the team. Sure enough, I was in a three-man midfield with John Robinson and Speedo. Giggs, Hughes and Saunders were up front. I felt excited. I was going to play against Italy, one of the best teams in the world. I felt quite good about myself.

Then Gould flicked over another page. It was a diagram of the Italy team. Except it wasn't just their names. Underneath every Italy player, he had written their age and the amount of caps they had won. When he came to Christian Panucci, he mentioned that he had won the Champions League with Real Madrid the previous summer. He also mentioned that he had won it with AC Milan in 1994, too.

Then he moved on to Cannavaro and the goalkeeper, Buffon,

and what unbelievably good players they were. He pointed up to the roof. "Cannavaro could jump as high as this ceiling," he said. Then he got around to Maldini. "Paolo Maldini," he said, reverently. "Need I say any more?" It went on and on and on like that. He went through every single Italy player.

I was an admirer of the Italians, too, but I started thinking 'how on earth am I going to make any sort of impression at all against this lot, we're going to get murdered'. I hardly slept all night.

We got to the stadium the next day and the pitch was beautiful. They were a great team. They even looked incredible in the warm-up. I looked at them in the tunnel with their immaculate hair and their blue kit. I started thinking about everything Gould had said about them.

Soon, it was 'bang' and they had scored. Vieri put them ahead after seven minutes. He jumped higher than the crossbar to get to it. Filippo Inzaghi and Maldini added another couple before half-time and the game was over. Their movement was on a different level to anything our defenders had ever seen before.

Gould took Saunders off at half-time. That went down well. Harts played the second half but things didn't get much better. We stopped shipping goals until Enrico Chiesa added a fourth in the last minute. It was just a bad, bad day. Not being able to compete was difficult. They could have won by as many as they wanted.

"Boys," Bobby Gould said in the dressing room after the match, "I think I have taken you as far as I can."

"What," Speedo said, "you mean as far down the world rankings as you can? We were 27th before you took over."

Gould said he was going to resign. He said he would not travel on the plane back home with us because we had a game against

Denmark at Anfield a few days later and he did not want his presence to be a distraction for whoever took charge (it was Neville Southall, as it happens, and we lost 2-0). A lot of the players seemed relieved Gould had gone but the chaos of it all was making my head swim.

We got to the airport the next day and the first person we saw was Bobby Gould. It turned out there weren't any other flights. He had to come back with us after all. It was the final indignity.

7

Hell And Back

There were still ups and downs at Norwich, too. I made that great start to the 1998-99 season but a couple of months after the high of scoring the winner for Wales against Denmark in Copenhagen, I suffered the first bad injury of my career. Like a few other victims before and after me, I came up against Kevin Muscat and suffered the consequences.

In those days, a lot of players at that level talked a lot. They yapped. At the top, players are so confident in their own ability that they don't need to talk but in the Championship, it was common for players to threaten to break your legs. It might be before a game or during it.

Threatening a player was a way of testing whether they could deal with it mentally. It might give an ordinary defender an advantage over a clever attacker he would not otherwise have enjoyed.

It happened to me a few times. In February, 1999, we played Bury at Gigg Lane and when I wandered out for the warm-up before the game, a guy called Darren Bullock was loitering in the tunnel. He had some skinhead sidekick standing next to him and they were both getting lairy. "Oi, Bellamy," I heard one of them say as I went past, "you're going to get your legs broken today."

It seemed like the two of them were sent out there to cause trouble, basically. Luckily for me, Bullock didn't hang around long enough to do me any damage. He got sent off after 11 minutes for dancing on Peter Grant's head. I have never felt so relieved in my life. It was Bullock's home debut, too. Nothing like making a good first impression.

The skinhead was still around but he wasn't so brave without his mate. I scored a quarter of an hour later. I wasn't going to be intimidated. I wouldn't go into my shell. I didn't need much encouragement to get lippy myself in those days but I knew what I was up against and that was one way to combat it. I spoke to them as they spoke to me. I might have been small and new on the scene but I wasn't going to take any shit.

I had already made my acquaintance with Muscat by then, anyway. He was the real McCoy. Once you'd run into him, other players didn't hold quite the same fear. He was playing for Wolves at that time and we went to Molineux to play them in the middle of December, 1998. We started off well and took the lead. The crowd became hostile and restless and the Wolves players reacted badly.

Muscat was already notorious by then. Ten months earlier, he had effectively ended the career of Charlton's Matty Holmes with a foul that injured him so severely his surgeon told him he had been fortunate not to have had his leg amputated. Holmes underwent a series of operations but was unable to return to top flight football. Holmes subsequently won £250,000 in damages from Muscat at the High Court.

And a few years later, in an uncanny echo of what happened to me at Gigg Lane, Muscat told Watford's Ashley Young, who was warming up as he waited to come on to make his debut, that he would break his legs if he took the ball past him. Like Bullock, Muscat was sent off for stamping on someone before he had the chance to turn his attentions to a kid trying to make his way in the game.

Muscat had compiled a long, long rap sheet by the time he finished his career in Australia by earning himself an eight-game ban for a grotesque knee-high tackle on Melbourne Heart's Adrian Zahra. That was in 2011, 13 years of crazed challenges away from the one he inflicted on me at Molineux. "He is probably the most hated man in the game," Birmingham's Martin Grainger said somewhere in the interim.

I got an early warning in the Wolves game when Muscat flew at me with his studs up. I managed to avoid his lunge and stared at the referee to suggest that maybe he ought to be doing something about that kind of challenge, but the referee did nothing. He knew the crowd was on his back by then because we were winning and a couple of decisions had gone against Wolves and he did not want to provoke any more jeers or boos.

People like Muscat are clever. They know in a situation like that that they can get away with anything because the ref is scared. After I avoided him the first time, Muscat told me I was going to get it. He was as good as his word. In the second half, I went to close him down when he was on the ball in his own area and as we came together, his foot went over the ball and he stamped on my knee. My knee hyper-extended and I knew I was in trouble.

Everyone stopped but the referee panicked. He didn't know what to give because he would have had to have given a penalty, so he let play continue. Bruce Rioch, who had been a hard player in his day, was so horrified by the challenge that he ran on to the pitch to try to get play stopped and remonstrate with the linesman. He had to be restrained by our backroom staff.

They took me to the Wolves medical room. After the game, Wolves players Carl Robinson and Keith Curle came to see me. Muscat didn't. Some players have reputations of being hard players. Some players will give you a kick and you can take kicks. You get that in most games. But when someone seems to get in trouble as regularly as he has, it makes you a breed apart, a different category.

I hear he is a nice guy off the pitch. Maybe he is but if he is a man who has any kind of self-knowledge, the consequences of what he has done will hit him one day. I was very lucky. I had an operation and a couple of months out. I had a puncture wound to my knee-cap where the stud on Muscat's boot drilled into it but compared to Matty Holmes, I was very fortunate.

It was still the most painful recuperation from an injury I've ever had. I was in agony afterwards. The operation was to get in and clean it out because of the danger of infection. I had a few months out. My rehab was very ordinary. I wasn't allowed to do too much straight away. It was my first real injury and I lost a lot of muscle in my leg.

I was rushed back. A couple of months later, one of the usual suspects was offering to break my legs for me at Bury. I did okay but my knee didn't feel right. I pulled my thigh a few weeks later and still kept playing. I was limping around but if you are told you have to go and play when you are that age, you go and play. But I was an accident waiting to happen.

I finished off that season with one or two goals and 19 overall but I wasn't in a good condition. We finished just outside the play-offs and, after I got back home to Cardiff from the debacle with Wales in Italy and the subsequent defeat to Denmark, I thought the summer would allow my leg to recover and that I would get back to Norwich as good as new.

When pre-season began, my knee was still sore. I was dismayed. There was a lot of talk around that time that Spurs, who were being managed by George Graham, were about to make a bid for me and even though I knew my knee wasn't right, I still felt flattered that a Premier League team was keen on signing me.

I got on with pre-season. We played a friendly against Southend United at Roots Hall and it was all fairly routine. I spent a lot of the game on the fringes. Then somebody played a ball long for me and I chased it down into the corner. I remember that my feet were sore. I remember thinking about my blisters as I ran after the ball.

Out of the corner of my eye, I saw a lad coming with me to my left and I thought I could hold him off. I was marginally ahead of him and I was favourite to get the ball but then he did something I didn't expect. Instead of jockeying for the ball, he tried to tackle me. It wasn't really a bad challenge and it wasn't his fault but it was a foul and it was needless.

Because it caught me by surprise, my left leg was planted and, as we made contact, I heard a click in my knee. His weight shoved my leg forward and I hit the floor. I was in pain straight away. It was my left knee, the one I had experienced problems with after Muscat's tackle, and I wonder now whether, if the muscle had been properly built up around it, I might have avoided the injury at Southend. I'll never know.

The club wanted me to get a scan so the Norwich physio, Tim Sheppard, took me to Southend University Hospital, which is only about a mile from the ground. It was Friday night, the drunks were in and I was sitting there with my knee swelling and my Norwich City kit on. You can imagine the scene. It wasn't pretty. I had an x-ray but it did not show anything definitive. I thought I was probably okay.

My knee blew up even more during the night but I still didn't think too much of it. That day, I went to see the specialist at a private clinic in Norwich and they had a look at my knee movements. I heard them talking and one of them mentioned something about 'six to eight'. I thought 'oh, no, I can't be out for six to eight weeks'. My mind flitted straight to the Tottenham interest. Six to eight weeks out would ruin any move.

Then they said I had ruptured my cruciate ligaments. It wasn't six to eight weeks. It was six to eight months. It hit me really hard then.

Claire and Ellis came to pick me up at the clinic and they didn't know what to do or say. We got into the car with Tim Sheppard so I could be driven back home. I was distraught.

"I know what a blow it must be," Tim said, "but look in the back. That's what's important."

Ellis was sitting there in his baby seat and even though I didn't

Home where the heart is: I'm back living in Cardiff where I grew up.
I've never been more contented than I was in my childhood

Happy days: A family photo with my mum, dad and two brothers. Left (from top): An early picture of me; my grandparents on my mum's side Nan and Grampy Pace and (bottom) with Nana Mary and Grampy David

Trowbridge Junior School 1990

Learning game: It all started with the school team. I was picked to play with boys who were older than me. I'm on the second row, second from the right

Sunday best: Lining up for Caer Castell. I'm pictured next to my dad (far left, back row), who helped me get enough players together for a team

Step on the ladder: Playing in youth tournaments with Norwich like the Dana Cup in Denmark gave me my first glimpse into what it might be like to be a professional footballer

My country calls: Wearing my first Wales cap at the age of 14

Eyes on the prize: After I became a father, I was determined to be a success at Norwich and give my family the best possible life

Down and out: In pain after the horror tackle by Wolves' Kevin Muscat that could have ended my football career before it had even started. It was my first real injury and a tough road to recovery

Striking Gould: This goal for Wales against Denmark in October, 1998, really got me noticed. I came off the bench to score the late winner – and probably save Bobby Gould's job

Where it all started: Making my debut for Wales against Jamaica at Ninian Park – the stadium where I also saw my first match

End of an era: (Below) Ready to face Italy in 1999. We gave them too much respect and paid the price

Early bosses: (Clockwise, from top left) Martin O'Neill, Gary Megson, Mike Walker, Bruce Rioch, Bryan Hamilton and Coventry manager Gordon Strachan. I was so impressed by Strachan that I signed for him straight away

Big time: One of my first Premiership goals, against Manchester City in a 2-1 win in August, 2000. We got off to a decent start but then I struggled to score as often as I would have liked

Friends and rivals: I must have done something to upset my Wales team-mate Robbie Savage here during a game against Leicester City. I scored the only goal in a 1-0 win (right)

On the run: Trying to get an attack started against Derby County in March, 2001. Playing at the top level was so different from the standard of football I'd been used to in the Championship

Shattered: The moment I knew we were relegated after losing 3-2 to Aston Villa

Role model: Lining up with Gary Speed for a Wales game in 2001. We would soon be club team-mates, too, as I joined Newcastle at the second time of asking

Calling the Toon: Celebrating a goal in the Intertoto Cup at the start of the 2001-2002 season. Gary set the standards for us all to follow

acknowledge what Tim said at the time, I knew he was right. I didn't want to hear anything anybody said then, though. On the drive back, I was just silent. I thought it might be the end of my career. I didn't know whether I was going to come back. I knew that Alan Shearer and Dean Saunders had both had cruciate injuries and come back. That gave me a bit of comfort.

I had to wait about a week before the knee was operated on and I was feeling sorry for myself. I rang people up and they didn't know what to say. I worried that I would wake up after the operation and a surgeon would come and stand at my bedside and say that it had not gone as well as they had hoped and that I would never be able to play football again.

But that didn't happen. They operated on me and the surgeon, David Dandy, said that, with the right rehabilitation, I would be able to resume my career. That was perfect for me. I made up my mind I'd come back better. There were loads of things I could work on almost straight away, like my upper body, and when I came out of hospital five days later, I vowed I would be the perfect patient.

I started off doing my rehab in Norwich but we only had one physio and Tim Sheppard had an entire squad of footballers to look after. I knew I needed work. I needed to be pushed and at the beginning of my rehab, I was left on my own a lot. I sunk into a depression. I felt nobody cared about me any more. I wasn't a player any more. I felt I didn't matter to anyone.

When the players had some sort of evening out, I'd go along but I was on crutches and I didn't feel I could really be part of anything. It got to the point where I didn't want to go to the training ground when the other fit players were there. So I started coming in to do my work after they had gone home.

Sometimes, players could be tactless. Sometimes they could be insensitive. Sometimes, they could be spiteful. I was out with the players one night and one of the senior lads, Neil Adams, had had one or two drinks. He turned to me at one point.

"That's you done," he said. "You're finished. Your career's over. You aren't going to come back the same player."

He might have thought he was taking the piss and being funny but I still remember it now. I thought 'all right, good one, we'll see about that'. I shut myself off from everyone. Even Claire and Ellis. Everything was a blur. Paul Gascoigne had undergone the same operation and he never looked the same after it. All sorts of dark thoughts crowded in on me.

I consoled myself with the fact that I was young. I was desperate for all the rehabilitation work I was doing not to be a waste. I persuaded myself I could come back quicker. I was determined to think only positive things. But I also needed the sacrifice of shutting myself off from everyone else. I needed that single-minded approach, or else I thought I wouldn't get through it.

After some time, I bought a Technogym leg presser and put that in my garage at our home in Norwich. I did leg presses every night before I went to bed. Building my leg muscles all the time, trying to make sure there would never be any kind of weakness there, trying to do everything I could to protect myself from having to go through this again.

I even went into the garage to do my leg presses on Christmas Eve. I thought I'd remember doing that for the rest of my career and it would make the sacrifice worthwhile. But after Christmas, I still felt I wasn't getting the attention I needed in

Norwich. I wanted to step my recovery up. I wanted to shut up people like Neil Adams as soon as I came back. I wanted to show everyone straight away that I was just as good as I had ever been.

So I went to Cardiff and saw an eminent surgeon called Professor John Fairclough, who had worked with the Welsh rugby squad and was based at the Cardiff and Vale Orthopaedic Centre at Llandough Hospital. I had a check-up and he said things were good but they could be better. He recommended a guy called Tim Atter, who went on to become the physio for the Cardiff Blues rugby team.

We began working three times a day and even though Norwich were reluctant to let me move back to Cardiff to begin with, they soon came round when they realised how focused I was. I worked with Tim for a couple of months and as soon as I was able to run and work outside, I went straight back to Norwich to begin the next phase of rehab.

I didn't watch Norwich as much as I should have done because it hurt not to be playing. They weren't doing too well and that made me feel even more guilty. Every time I went to a game at Carrow Road, people were asking when I'd be back. That kind of tortured me.

There was another reason, too. I just don't like going to watch matches. It's one thing preparing for a game when you're in the dressing room and cocooned inside the bubble that players live in. You can be single-minded about what you do and not worry as much about everything that surrounds the game. But when you take yourself out of that bubble, when you sit in the stand and hear the crowd and realise the expectations they have, it can feel daunting.

You sit with the fans and you realise what a responsibility you have. There's no escape from the fact that what happens out there on the pitch is very important to them and that they are relying on you to deliver. I felt that if I saw too much of that side of things, the pressure might start to get to me, so I ended up rationing the amount of games I watched.

When I got back to Norwich after working with Tim Atter, I started to join in a few training sessions. I noticed a difference with my knee. It wasn't exactly as good as new. But it was appreciably better than it had been after the injury Muscat inflicted on it. I could feel it was stronger. I could feel that the work I had put in had paid off.

I had missed football. It had been taken away from me and now that I was close to a return, I had even more determination to try to succeed. I didn't feel vulnerable. I played a reserve team game in April against Cambridge United that felt like a huge step forward. My dad came to watch and some Norwich fans turned up too, which meant a lot to me.

I made a couple of tackles and went in hard. I wanted to show people I wasn't going to try and hop out of it. I only played a half but I felt great. Phil Mulryne, one of my Norwich team-mates, had suffered a double leg break a few months after I was injured at Southend and we both made our comebacks at the same time. We'd become good friends during our rehabilitations. We helped each other pull through. I could sense that the same sort of relief I felt was coursing through him, too.

Some of the reserve team players held a party for Phil and me after the game and it felt like a great triumph for both of us. Injury is every footballer's secret struggle and the fight is made harder because it is conducted away from the limelight.

Nobody sees the work you are doing, nobody knows how hard you are trying, nobody knows the fears that are stalking you.

I had been out for so long that by the time I was fit again, Bruce Rioch had left the club. We had had another disappointing season, getting nowhere near the pace set by clubs like Charlton and Manchester City and Rioch resigned in March. Bryan Hamilton took his place on a temporary basis so he was in charge when, after nine months out, I made my first team comeback against Port Vale on April 22, 2000.

I came off the bench against Barnsley at Oakwell in the next game and scored. And then, in the last home game of the season against Sheffield United, I got my first start. After about a quarter of an hour, I found myself one on one with the goalkeeper. I took it round him but he dragged me out wide and I thought my chance might have gone but I drilled it in from a tight angle.

That goal meant a hell of a lot to me. More than almost any other goal I've scored. After everything I had been through, it was a symbol of recovery, a sign that everything was going to be okay. To people like Neil Adams, to the fans, to Premier League managers who might want to sign me, it sent out the message that I was back.

8

Signing Off

I didn't want the season to end. I was fit again and I wanted
to keep on playing. I would have played all summer if I could.
I did get a bit of an extension when the new Wales manager,
Mark Hughes, called me into the squad for the June friendlies
against Brazil and Portugal.

I'd missed the first ever game at the Millennium Stadium, a
2-1 defeat to Finland in March when Jari Litmanen had run
the show. But Sparky called me up for that game just so I could
be part of the occasion, which was something I really appreciated. Then I came on for about 20 minutes against Brazil, who
included Rivaldo and Cafu. And then I started against Portugal
in Chaves against stars like Figo and Rui Costa. I'd worked hard
to fulfil the dream of playing against great talents like them.

I went on holiday for a few weeks but I never stopped training. I couldn't wait for the new season to start. And the closer it came, the more phone calls I started to get telling me that other clubs were interested. I wasn't even back in pre-season training when I got a call from an agent who said that Newcastle wanted to sign me. He asked if I would like to go there. "Of course I would," I told him.

But before the season began, I was told that Wimbledon had bid £3.5m for me. Bryan Hamilton called me in and said it had been knocked back. He said going to Wimbledon was no good for me or for Norwich. They had just been relegated so it wasn't as if they could offer me Premier League football, and Norwich wanted more than £3.5m.

Hamilton was aware of Newcastle's interest. Bobby Robson was the boss at St James' Park and he and our manager were friends because of their Ipswich connection. Norwich kept waiting for the Newcastle bid to come but Newcastle kept stalling. They wanted to get Duncan Ferguson out and they knew Everton wanted him. But they needed the money from that deal to sign me.

I felt very unsettled. I was a young kid who had just done my cruciate and I wanted to sort the situation out. I played in the first game of the season against Barnsley and then the following Monday, Hamilton called me. He asked me where I was. I told him I was at home. He said he was coming round. When he arrived, he sat down and made a bit of small talk. Then he said Norwich had accepted an offer of £6m from Coventry.

He asked me what I wanted to do. He said Norwich would offer me a new contract, although the terms wouldn't match what Coventry had offered. I was a naïve kid back then so I asked him why they were offering me a new contract if they had accepted a bid from another club. Hamilton was straight with me. He said it was too much money for them to turn down. I guess they had to be seen to be offering me a new contract to try to save face with the fans. They were making me look like the bad guy.

I said it was unfair. Hamilton said it was just politics. I told him I didn't want to go to Coventry. He said he realised that. He said he knew I wanted to go to Newcastle but Norwich still hadn't received a bid from them yet. I was almost pleading by then. I asked him if we could wait for a while to see if the New-castle bid materialised.

He said that was one option. But he also said that Norwich had given Coventry permission to talk to me and that the man-ager, Gordon Strachan, and the chairman, Bryan Richardson, were driving down to meet me as we were speaking. He asked me to go and hear what they had to say. He said there was no pressure on me to make a decision and that if I didn't like their offer, we could wait and see what Newcastle came up with.

I didn't know what to do. The club said Strachan and Rich-ardson were going to meet me at a place called Dunston Hall, a country house hotel in an Elizabethan-style mansion a few miles south of Norwich. It was all in motion already. It felt like I was being rail-roaded into something. I kept thinking that I didn't want to sign for Coventry. I wanted to sign for Newcastle. This wasn't what I had envisaged.

I felt I couldn't refuse to meet them. I thought I'd just listen and then walk away. I didn't have an agent at that time. I had a financial adviser called Jonathan, so I rang him and asked his advice. He was just as nervous about it as me. He didn't know what to do. He just dealt with my financial stuff. Jon said he would get straight up there and would make sure I didn't get stitched up.

I set off for Dunston Hall. While I was in the car, my phone rang. It was Bobby Robson.

"Speak to them by all means, son," he said, "but whatever you do don't sign. We'll have made our bid in the next 24 hours."

A couple of minutes later, the phone rang again. This time, it was David Stonehouse, the Newcastle chief executive. He said pretty much the same thing.

I got to the hotel and Strachan and Richardson were waiting for me. Strachan spoke brilliantly about football, his philosophy and his plans for the club. He was up front. He said Coventry weren't a top Premier League club but they worked hard. He said he would work night and day to help me become the player I wanted to become. He really impressed me but Coventry as a club didn't. I had set my heart on Newcastle.

Then things got messy. As I was talking to Strachan, Jon walked in with John Fashanu. I was open-mouthed. I had never met him before. I had no idea what he was doing suddenly presenting himself at the negotiations for my transfer deal. I took Jon aside and asked him what was going on. It turned out he had got to know Fashanu over the last few months.

When I had called Jon to tell him that I was going to the meeting at Dunston Hall, Jon had phoned Fashanu to ask for advice. And before he knew it, Fashanu had invited himself along as well. He said he would come along to make sure I didn't get taken for a ride and offered to look over the contract while we were at the hotel as well. Jon didn't really know what to do so he accepted his offer.

After they had been gone for a little while, Strachan marched over to where Jon and I were sitting.

"What's your arrangement with John Fashanu?" he asked.

"I haven't got a clue," I said.

"You know he might be trying to get paid money for this," Strachan said. "He could want a percentage."

I didn't know if this was true but I looked over at Jon and his face went white because I think he realised how embarrassing this was. He went to speak to Fashanu and left me with Strachan. "I'm sorry," I said "This is a mess. It's nothing to do with me."

My brain felt scrambled. Strachan was a decent bloke. I didn't want to appear like an idiot in front of him. But this all looked so amateurish. I felt guilty. I felt embarrassed. It was just a nightmare.

Strachan told me what they were offering me. It was a lot of money. Credit to Coventry. They were up front about it. Newcastle had told me they were going to offer me a straight five-year contract worth £12,000 a week. Coventry were offering me a five-year deal worth £18,000 a week to start with and going up to £25,000 a week by the final year.

It was a huge jump in salary for me and Strachan and Richardson pitched it well to me, too. They knew what I had gone through with my cruciate ligament injury. They knew how I would have been worried about my future. They pointed out to me that if I signed, I would never have to work again after football and my family would be taken care of for life. That struck a chord with me. It wasn't long ago when I feared I might not have a career any more.

They were persuasive. I also felt undermined by the mess with

Fashanu. I wanted to save face with Strachan. I felt stressed. My chest was tight because I'm asthmatic. I was struggling to breathe properly because I was so tense. I was in a state. So I did what everybody had told me not to do. I told Strachan I'd sign. I shook his hand. And then I went home.

I felt a sense of dread about what I'd done. I just didn't want to go to Coventry. I didn't feel comfortable. I felt that, with the players they had, Coventry were going to have a difficult season. They would look to me to lift them out of it but I wasn't sure I could do it. I had been out for a long, long time and I knew that I was bound to have ups and downs.

I knew I might be inconsistent and there would be times when I might need a rest. I still didn't know how my knee was going to react when I was back playing regular football week after week. At Newcastle, I would be around really good players and I would have space to be rested for a week if I needed it. That wouldn't happen at Coventry.

I knew at Coventry, not only would I be straight into the side but everybody would be looking to me. They would need me to score 20 goals that season or else they would be relegated. I looked through the team and I knew it was going to be hard work. They had lost Robbie Keane to Inter Milan and Gary McAllister to Liverpool. They were important players.

The next day, Jon picked me up and took me back to the Norwich training ground to get my boots. There were a few people there and I said goodbye to one or two of the reserve boys and to Steve Foley, who had been such a big influence on me and had helped my career so much. When we drove away, I knew I was never going to come back.

It felt sad. I knew I was going to leave Norwich at some time or another and I had been hoping for a move to a Premier League club for a while. But when it actually happens, it still catches you by surprise. I had been there since I was 11 years old. I had worked very hard but that didn't change the fact that I owed the club a lot.

They persevered with me as an individual. They could have got rid of me in the early days when I was so homesick that I was almost begging them to kick me out. But they didn't. They were different class. They brought me up right in football, with passing and keeping the ball on the deck. That was their philosophy on the game and that was how they wanted to produce young players and I was a beneficiary.

I was educated well in the game at Norwich. They shaped me. Even when I was in the youth team, we were doing step classes and other things that were thought curious then but turned out to be ahead of their time. As a club, they were open and innovative and I bought into that. It was a good grounding.

But I knew I needed to improve as a player and I knew I needed to move up to the Premier League to do that. I had just come back from a big injury and I didn't know if I would get the opportunity again. I was still in a dreadful quandary about Newcastle but it had started to seem as if their bid would never arrive. I should have been more patient.

After we left the Norwich training ground, I travelled down to Coventry as promised. I still had the feeling of dread in the pit of my stomach but it was like the move had gathered this momentum and I just couldn't stop it. Bobby Robson phoned again. He said the bid was coming in but I told him that unless it actually arrived with Norwich, there was nothing I could do. He told me he would phone back as soon as he could.

That conversation made me feel even worse. I didn't have a clue what to do. I had given my word to Strachan and I didn't want to go back on that. But when I parked at Highfield Road and got out of my car, I stood around for a while. I didn't want to go through the doors because I knew there would be no way back then. I stood there for half an hour, waiting for Bobby Robson to call me back but my phone didn't ring.

Eventually, I went inside. I met the directors who gave me a very warm welcome. Then I sat down and signed the contract. Even as I was signing it, I thought 'what am I doing?' but the die was cast. It was too late to back out. I was taken to the training ground then. My first thought was that it wasn't as good as Norwich's. I said hello to the players and then went to a hotel in Henley-in-Arden that would be my home for the next few weeks.

When I got to my room, I switched my phone back on. There was a message. I started to listen to it.

It was from Bobby Robson.

"Hello son," he said. "Good news. Our bid's in."

9

Down

I signed for Coventry four days before the start of the 2000-01 season. I didn't particularly like what I saw but then I hadn't really signed for the club, I had signed for Gordon Strachan. I believed in him but I didn't believe in the team. I looked around at training and realised it was pretty likely we were going to be in a relegation fight.

They had replaced Robbie Keane and Gary McAllister with me and David Thompson, a promising midfielder from Liverpool. They had good players, too, like Mustapha Hadji, Youssef Chippo and my old mate, John Hartson, who was signed during the season.

But there were plenty of others who struggled at Premier League level and that became evident very soon. Even Hadji and Chippo failed to get anywhere near the form of the previous season.

It's strange when you go to a new club. A lot of eyes are on you. A lot is expected of you. I could tell immediately that some of the Coventry players resented the money I was on. Some of them were probably looking at me and wondering who this little jerk was that the club had paid so much money for. Still, they were expecting a lot from me because they knew that if they had any chance of staying up, they needed a lot.

We were at home to Middlesbrough on the opening day of the season. It didn't go well. I got a good reception from the Coventry fans in the pre-match warm-up – they were always decent with me. There is not quite the intensity there as at some of the other clubs I've played for. It's not a football heartland because their support is diluted by having so many Midlands clubs in close proximity.

I was desperate to do well for them, though. I was excited about appearing in the Premier League and I was keen to make an impact straight away. It didn't happen. I was up against Gary Pallister and even though he was a veteran by then, he had a terrific game. It was a good early taste of the step up in quality I was going to have to make if I was to succeed at a higher level.

Middlesbrough had just signed Alen Boksic, the great Croatia forward, from Lazio and it would be fair to say that he made more of an impact on his debut than I did. He scored twice in a 3-1 win for our opponents. It wasn't a great day for Coventry. David Thompson marked his debut by getting sent off 20 minutes from the end.

The games came thick and fast. The following Wednesday, we played at Southampton and won 2-1. I scored a penalty in that game, my first goal in the Premier League. The next weekend, I scored again in a 2-1 win over Manchester City at Maine Road. I know this sounds like I was walking round with a cloud over my head but I knew it wouldn't last and it didn't. We won one in the next 13 and by mid-December, we were deep in relegation trouble.

The first game in that run was against Newcastle at Highfield Road. As the game approached, I kept thinking things could have been very different for me. I still couldn't get those conversations with Bobby Robson out of my head. We lost 2-0 and after the game, I bumped into Sir Bobby in the tunnel. "Work hard, son," he said. "All the best." I couldn't help but think of what might have been.

I was struggling to adapt to moving up a level. The game was quicker. You have to be fit in the Championship because it is helter-skelter stuff but the Premier League was more technically demanding. I noticed that straight away. Now you had to concentrate on receiving the ball at the right angle or a defender would read the pass and come and pick it off.

Playing against Tony Adams at Highbury was an education. No other word for it, really. It was in the middle of September, early in our descent towards the bottom and at a time when I was just beginning to realise how clever some of my new opponents were. Adams was just out of this world, the best I've ever played against.

I thought I knew all about him. I thought I might be able to exploit his lack of pace, in particular. Well, I might have been quicker than him in terms of raw speed but he was about five seconds ahead of me in terms of football intelligence. I hardly got a kick. He anticipated everything. He was playing one-twos round me, just having fun, taking me to school. He played me off the park. He was at another level.

I came off 27 minutes before the end. I think Strachan was showing me mercy. As I sat down on the bench, I knew I had a long way to go before I could compete with players like Adams. He was immense and he was playing in a terrific side. I was a month into my first season in the Premier League and the learning curve was getting steep.

Strachan was brilliant with me. He has got a quirky sense of humour and he rubbed some of the players up the wrong way. He could be harsh, too. When he fell out with someone, it wasn't pretty. Sometimes, he took things personally. I heard him tell people they would never play for the club again after arguments.

But he worked tirelessly to try to improve me. He talked to me about forward movements like coming off at the half angle. Sometimes I would come short to receive the ball and then spin to try to catch the defender out and run on to a pass that was played in behind him. But Strachan told me to forget about coming short sometimes.

"Just spin," he said. "If you come short, a defender's on his toes and he is ready for you to do something. But if you pretend you are not interested and then just go, you will catch him off guard. And with your pace, you'll be in."

Because I was unsure about my injury, sometimes I would just run with players rather than trying to go past them. Subconsciously, I was scared of getting wiped out and hurt again, I think, because that was how I had done my cruciate in the first place. Strachan told me to trust my pace, to run past players, not with them. He was correct. If you are looking to get past someone, they have to come in with a challenge. It commits them.

Strachan was full of tips and instructions for me. He was such a good coach but unfortunately for him and the club, they did not see the benefits of everything he was teaching me. I did, though. I could feel myself becoming a better player. I felt I was developing a greater awareness of the game. It was just that Coventry didn't see the effects of my improvement quickly enough.

I understand now that when you have been out for a while, it is very hard to play well consistently straight away. My movement was different. Everything was new. When you have had major surgery like that, you are finding yourself as well. I was in the gym all the time because for me to cope at that level, my body bulk needed to be bigger. The fitness people were trying to pile food down me non-stop to get my body weight up so I was adjusting a lot. I was still a bit of a scrawny kid, too fragile for the top level.

We were not a good side. Defensively, we lacked pace and offensively, we lacked creativity. And we had players who simply weren't playing well. I was one of them. Things improved a bit when we signed Harts and that gave me a new lease of life. I felt like I had an ally in the side at last, someone I knew, someone who looked out for me a bit. Players like Paul Williams and Paul Telfer, who had been there for a number of years, made it plain they didn't like me. Stephen Froggatt was the same. I was young and I'd come in on good money. Maybe they were bitter. It happens. It's part of the dynamic at clubs. I can usually defend myself but I felt I wasn't part of their gang. They behaved as though they held me responsible for Coventry's plight.

It even happened in training. Williams would try to give me the rough treatment. Because he was slow on the turn, I would often go past him quite comfortably and he would pull me back straight away. He came across as a bit of a bully. And like all bullies, they are not so brave when a bigger bloke turns up. Maybe I imagined it but when Harts arrived, all the rough stuff from Williams suddenly seemed to stop.

I wasn't particularly vocal during that period. My confidence was low. I knew I had to work and improve. These players had played at this level a lot longer than me and I didn't feel I could shout the odds with them. I felt responsible for the manager and the club after my fee. Sometimes, I even felt responsible for the other players as well.

It all got to me. I bought a house in Stratford-upon-Avon before Christmas. Claire was pregnant with our second child and Cameron was born in January in Cardiff. I went down there the day after the birth. I wasn't behaving particularly well. I was wrapped up in my own troubles and worries because I was so concerned about what was going on at Coventry. It was taking over my personal life, too.

Coventry was all I was thinking about. I was feeling down a lot. I shied away from Claire, too, even when she was pregnant. I found everything so difficult to cope with. Anyone who came to visit me couldn't get two words out of me during that period. I kept it all inside. So Claire and I weren't going through a great spell when Cameron was born.

I felt so much shame about what was going on in my career that I blanked everything else out, which was very selfish. Cameron's an incredible child but I was so wrapped up with everything that was going on at Coventry that I neglected him and

Claire. I was questioning myself as a player. I was asking myself whether I was good enough for the league. I thought I'd be back in the Championship.

My aspirations had always been to play at the top level but I began to think that perhaps I had been deluding myself to think I could make it, particularly after my injury. Maybe I wouldn't come back as good as new after all. I was still feeling pain in my knee. I kept thinking about what Neil Adams said about how I wouldn't be the same. I kept thinking maybe he was right.

I missed the odd game here and there but my knee felt better in the second half of the season and I started to come to terms with what the Premier League was about. But by then, it was a bit late. We had a good result against Everton at Goodison Park on Boxing Day but then we went on a run of 10 games without a win and things began to look grim.

I played some good football in the last quarter of the season and we got three wins in four games, beating Derby, Leicester and Sunderland either side of a defeat to Manchester United. Harts scored in all four of those games and I got one, too. We gave ourselves a glimmer of hope. Everyone started to believe that after struggling for so long down at the bottom we could get out of it.

But when we went to Aston Villa to play the penultimate game of the season, we knew that if we lost, we would be relegated. Bradford City were already down and Manchester City were scrapping with us in the relegation zone but we knew that if we beat Villa, we could still catch Derby and make a great escape. Two goals from Hadji put us 2-0 up but we couldn't hold on to our lead and Villa came back to win 3-2. We deserved to go down but it was still a desperate moment.

I felt all eyes were on me. A few members of the Coventry staff went round shaking people's hands to say hard luck and I noticed that three or four of them missed me out on purpose. I was a 20-year-old kid. I felt that was a bit harsh. They were trying to make the point I had let them down. They didn't have to do that. I knew it myself. I didn't need telling.

I didn't say anything because I felt the guilt. I had come with the price tag. I felt I hadn't lived up to expectations. I was the big money signing and I hadn't delivered what they needed. I might have been the club's joint top scorer in the league but I only got six goals. It wasn't enough. Hadji had a poor season and he got as many as me. Harts only arrived in February and he got as many as me, too.

I worked so hard that season and I felt that if we could just stay up, I would have shown Coventry fans what I could really do. But relegation ruined everything. I went back to Cardiff that summer and turned my phone off. I didn't want to see anyone. I didn't want to speak to anyone.

I had found a different representative by then, Steve Horner, who was David Thompson's agent, too. I have looked to him for advice and guidance ever since. He told me there were one or two clubs interested in bidding for me. You always get one or two rumours of interest from other clubs but I thought 'who's going to want to buy me after the season I've just had?' Coventry would want decent money back for the fee they had paid and I didn't think anyone would take a chance on me.

I was geared up for going back to the Championship and I was hoping I could make amends. I told myself that I was to blame for them going down and that the only way I could make myself feel any better would be if I was responsible for getting them back up. I was an improved player and I wanted to pay my debt to Gordon Strachan.

Then my dad rang. My agent had called him. He wanted me to phone him urgently. When I rang, he said Coventry had accepted a bid from Newcastle. They needed to slash their wage bill because of relegation and Newcastle had come back in for me. They wanted me to go straight up to Tyneside to have a medical. I couldn't believe it.

I had been given a lifeline. This was my big chance. The next day, I flew up from Cardiff to Newcastle. Straight away, I felt there was an aura about the place. Not just St James' Park but the city, too. I love the stadium, sitting there above the city, dominating it. I was going to be playing there every other weekend now. I was going to be part of this great institution.

It all felt right. It was important to me that Gary Speed was there. He was someone I looked up to and I knew he'd take care of me. I knew Kieron Dyer well, too, from the time when I was at Norwich and he was at Ipswich. And then there were players of the calibre of Alan Shearer and Rob Lee. It was quite a cast-list.

Harts rang me up from Coventry's pre-season trip because he had seen the news of my signing on the television. He was disappointed I was going. He said he would probably leave, too, and soon after, he joined Celtic.

Gordon Strachan rang, too. He said he knew I was disappointed about how the season had gone but that he was grateful for all the work I had done. He was as gracious and classy as anyone could be.

I got a call from Bobby Robson then. He hadn't been at my medical. He was away on holiday somewhere.

"I'm delighted you're here, son," he said. "Now I've finally got you, I want you to know I think you're an immense talent."

For someone of his stature to say that meant an awful lot to me. After all the strain of the past season, it gave me a huge boost in confidence. Generally, I felt like a great weight had been lifted from my shoulders.

Newcastle paid £6m to sign me. At least Coventry got their money back. And I was on a similar salary to the one I had been on at Highfield Road. Before I went back to Stratford, I went to the boardroom at St James' Park to meet the Newcastle chairman, Freddy Shepherd. He strode over to shake my hand.

"So this is the little shit that's cost me so much money," he said.

10

One Of The Greats

I am aware there are many people who believe that I had no respect for Bobby Robson. From a lot of the coverage of my time at Newcastle, you could be forgiven for thinking that I spent my years there trying to undermine him or, failing that, simply mocking him or refusing to do what he asked. The impression that was conveyed was that I was an unruly kid taunting a wise old teacher. Many people still seem to think I was responsible, either directly or indirectly, for his eventual exit from the club.

That is a million miles from the truth. The truth is that Bobby Robson was the best manager I ever worked with. The truth is that I had the utmost respect for him.

The truth is that I admired him and revered him and that I could never quite accept the way he was forced out of the club.

He was one of the greats. I was very, very lucky to have played for him.

When I was growing up, Bobby Robson was the manager of England but I always followed his career closely because he went on to become the manager of PSV Eindhoven and I loved Dutch football. Then he was the manager of Barcelona when the Brazilian Ronaldo played there and that lifted Sir Bobby even higher in my eyes.

So when I first found out he wanted to sign me, I thought of all the players he had signed and all the players who had played for him and I knew what an honour it was to be joining that number. What a huge compliment for a player. That was so important to me as an individual. It was huge. I was joining men like Ronaldo, Figo, Stoichkov, Muhren, Romario and Guardiola.

Another idea has been allowed to take hold that the players at Newcastle viewed him as a soft touch and took advantage of his kindness and his age. Again, that isn't true. He could be kind and he was the best man-manager I have ever come across but he had a ruthless streak, too. He wasn't soft. No one who lasts in management as long as he did can be weak.

He was clever. He could be really cute in the way he dealt with the media. When the cameras were out at the Newcastle training ground, he was coaching. When the cameras were gone, he would stand on the sidelines and watch. He was aware of the importance of image and appearance as well as reality. He knew all about media management.

Whether he was coaching or standing on the touchline, he was out there every day, no matter what the weather. He was 66 when he took the Newcastle job but he never took it easy.

He never put his feet up and handed over to others. He saw everything. People used to make fun about his recall of names but he had been doing that for 30 years.

It wasn't about him being old. If you have managed as many players as he had, you are going to get people mixed up. We didn't think of him as being old. We didn't really take his age into account. You knew he was switched on because he knew everything about the game there was to know. If you didn't do your job, he was on you straight away. He didn't miss a thing.

Maybe it is part of the British culture that we have this inflexibility about how everyone must be treated the same. If you are hard on one person for a failing, you must treat another person in exactly the same way. Robson wasn't like that. He had learned, he said, by being abroad to treat every individual differently. He was such a clever man. Way above any other manager I have worked with.

He judged you on how you were as a character and how you played on Saturday afternoon. If you didn't want to do a run at a certain time, you didn't have to. But you better make sure that if there's something he needs you to do during the game, you have to be able to do it. He trusted you like that and his trust was repaid.

I'll give you an example of his man-management skills. In March 2004, towards the end of my last full season at Newcastle, I had a well-publicised argument with Robson's assistant, John Carver, the day we were due to fly out to a Uefa Cup fourth round second leg match against Real Mallorca. At the time, it was seen as a symptom of Robson's loss of control over a troublesome squad but to me the episode proved the opposite: he was a master of control.

What people never quite grasped is that John Carver is one of my best friends. He was at my wedding. As a coach and player, we used to go out in the evenings together. I liked him a lot. The row before the Mallorca game had started at training a few hours earlier when I parked in his parking space at the training ground.

I was being mischievous really. A little provocative perhaps. I arrived at the training ground and he wasn't there. He's a coach. He should have been in before me so I parked in his space. I knew it would wind him up. I walked past him later that morning and said 'hiya', all proud of myself because of my little stunt, and he just walked straight past me without saying a word. It made me smile. I thought 'job done'.

My problem sometimes is that I don't know when to stop. So I kept winding him up. I wouldn't let it go. So by the time we got to Newcastle Airport to get the flight to Majorca, he was at snapping point and we had a confrontation. I was talking to someone else and I mentioned 'JC' loudly enough to make sure he heard me poking fun at him. He snapped and came marching over.

He had a real go at me. We had a shouting match. I thought he had turned it from a joke into a proper argument. People had to keep us apart. So, suddenly I convinced myself that I was the wronged party. I was fuming. All my light-heartedness disappeared and we got involved in a real row.

The reports said I threw a chair at him in the departure lounge that had been set aside for the players. That wasn't entirely true. I was angry and I threw a chair out of the way so I could go and argue with him. It nearly hit Shay Given, actually, but that was an accident.

A fight isn't just fists. It is what it is. Whatever you can get hold of, you get hold of. If you lose your temper, anything goes. But this wasn't a fight. This was just silly stuff. It was very childish from both of us. I was yelling at him and he was yelling at me but we were mates, basically, so were never going to start throwing punches at each other. We ended up wrestling stupidly on the floor. I didn't know at the time but Bobby was giving a press conference on the other side of the screens from where we were grappling and the press could hear that a kerfuffle was going on.

Someone went to get the manager and he came in and yelled at everyone to get out and get on the plane, which was waiting at the gate and was ready to board by now. I had lost my rag totally by that point. I was saying "I'm not going, I'm not getting on the plane, I'm going home to see my missus."

Bobby told Carver to get on the plane. He gave him a real rollicking and asked him what the hell he had been doing, confronting me like that. JC trudged off with his head down, like a naughty schoolboy who has just had a telling off. I was still saying I was going home. I was adamant. The manager put his arm round me. "Walk with me, son," he said.

So I walked with him and he started asking me about how my kids were, how they were doing at school, how was my missus. He phrased all the questions so I had to answer them even though I didn't feel like saying a word. The next thing I knew I was on the plane. I was thinking 'how the fuck did I get here?' If he'd told me straight that I had to get on the plane, if he'd ordered me to get on, I wouldn't have got on.

The news got out straight away. I could see some of the lads texting away furiously when we landed in Majorca.

That evening, I was in my room at the team hotel in Majorca and still not happy. It didn't take much in those days to put me on edge. So Bobby came round to my room and brought Carver and Alan Shearer with him.

I thought they had come to gang up on me so I was ready to have a right go back. I was building myself up for it. I was like a coiled spring, just waiting for the opportunity to get into another row and sure they were going to give me the prompt any second.

But then Sir Bobby sat us all down and started blaming everything on John Carver and made him apologise to me. JC started apologising profusely and saying how much he thought of me. He said he was my biggest fan. Then Sir Bobby told Alan what a great player I was and Alan had to agree. Alan had to say how much he rated me, too. I could tell Alan was saying that through gritted teeth. It was killing him. So Sir Bobby gave me no room to argue. I was just sitting there taking compliments. I had been desperate to have an argument but I had nothing to go against.

The next thing I know, I'm shaking everybody's hand and we're all friends. I ended up apologising to John Carver as well. Suddenly, everything was sweetness and light and we were all mates again. Sir Bobby put me on the bench for the game the next evening, I came on and scored with practically my first touch and we won 3-0.

So, yes, he was a great man. Soon after he died in July 2009, I read a newspaper interview that my friend Kieron Dyer had given about Sir Bobby's strength of character and his handling of the players, particularly me. It made me smile when I read it. It brought back a lot of happy memories. It went like this.

"There was a lot of talk about the brats, the likes of me and Craig Bellamy," Kieron told the interviewer, "but Sir Bobby knew how to put us in our place. He never lost the dressing room. We played Leeds at Elland Road once and Bellers was having a great game. We were 1-0 up at half-time and after about 60 minutes the manager put Craig's number up and Craig came off.

"We won the game 3-0 but when we got back to the changing room, Bellers was cursing and raving about how he did all the running, how everyone else profited from his efforts, how he needed goals, how he was judged on goals and so on and so on.

"The gaffer said 'will you shut up' but Bellers kept jabbering on. And then Sir Bobby went: 'I'll squash you, son, like an ant'. Bellers was a bit taken aback but he mumbled something else and this time the gaffer let him have it. 'Who are you?' he said. 'Ronaldo, Romario, Stoichkov, Hagi, Guardiola, Luis Enrique, Gascoigne. These are the people I deal with. Who are you?'

"The changing room went quiet and Bellers went quiet. And then Bellers looked over at me and said: 'He's got a point, hasn't he'."

I love that story. It exposes a lot of the myths about Bobby Robson as lies. It disproves this idea that he had lost the dressing room, that he could not cope with us, that he was out of touch, that he was weak, that we were running rings around him. He was very sharp and he had not lost his authority. Don't worry about that.

Kieron was the one who got most of the blame for the supposedly disrespectful attitude the players had towards Sir Bobby but in many ways, he was closer to him than any of us. Some of it was to do with their shared Ipswich connection. Sir Bobby had managed very successfully there and Kieron had grown up there. Sometimes, I felt they were too close. Because they were so comfortable with each other, they would have disagreements in front of everybody that others misinterpreted as serious differences.

Sir Bobby was a remarkable man. He could read characters very quickly and because he had been brought up in the area, because he was the son of a coal-miner from the village of Langley Park which is 15 miles south of Newcastle, because he had been taken to see Jackie Milburn when he was a kid, because he loved the city and the club, he knew exactly what the supporters wanted.

Freddy Shepherd knew that, too, which explains some of the buys Newcastle made when I was there. They seemed to me to be crowd-pleasing buys, signings that would take the heat off the board if things were not going well. They were not necessarily buys that served the best interests of the team in terms of getting the results we needed.

Sir Bobby knew the crowd, too. There were games when he attacked when we shouldn't have attacked. He would leave the defence bare at times in the name of attacking football. I felt for the back four at times but he knew what the public wanted. From his experience of being one of them, he knew how to build a team for them.

Maybe because of their shared affinity for the area, there was a kind of unspoken tension between Sir Bobby and Shearer. It wasn't that Alan worked against him or anything like that. But they were both local heroes and they were both idolised by the crowd. They were working towards the same goal but they were in competition, too.

Sir Bobby would put me in my place if needed but sometimes, if I was having a go at certain individuals, he would back me up.

Once, after a defeat, I expressed my irritation with a couple of the other players because of things I thought they had failed to do. He backed out of the argument and walked away. He wanted me to have a go.

He wanted an individual in the team to raise the issue because he knew it couldn't always come from him. I knew where I was with him. I knew he liked me as a player. I knew I fitted in to how he wanted the team to play. A fair number of my performances for Newcastle were exceptional and I put a lot of that down to him.

Before games, I made a point of coming out at the back of our team, the last man into the tunnel.

Sir Bobby had his own pre-match superstition which was to make sure he shook every player's hand. So before most games, we'd end up at the back of the tunnel together, having a chat about what lay ahead and the opponents we were facing. He'd stare at their players.

"He's shit scared of you already, that one, son," he'd say.

Or it might be: "Get him on the turn today, son, and you'll kill him."

Or: "Look at him, son, he's not even fit to be on the same pitch as you."

I felt like I was the quickest player going, I felt strong, I felt invincible because of him.

There is a lot to be said for managers who give you that kind of confidence, managers who build you up rather than try and hammer you all the time.

He would talk to me like I was the best player in the world and I went out at St James' Park feeling like I was going to play like the best player in the world.

I am 5ft 6 or 5ft 7ins tall but I am telling you this: when I put that kit on and I was standing in that tunnel with Bobby Robson, I felt like I was Didier Drogba.

11

Off To A Flier

My arrival in the north-east didn't exactly fire the imagination of the Geordie Nation. I had the radio on as I drove to St James' Park for my first day of training and the phone-in was discussing my signing. It was being interpreted as an indication that ambitions weren't high. I was a symbol, they were saying, of low expectations and a difficult season ahead.

My first job was to get in the team. If I could do that, I thought we had the players to do well. There was Alan Shearer up front, of course.

When I first met him, he managed a cursory 'hiya' and that was it. He struggled even to muster a handshake. I think Al's attitude was that you had to win his respect before he started being nice to you. He didn't acknowledge me that much. He probably didn't think that much of me as a player, which was fine. It didn't matter anyway.

There was a great bunch of lads at Newcastle. On the pitch, I hit it off with players like Nolberto Solano straight away. He was such a clever player and he made it so easy to play with him. He would put his head up and disguise the pass as if he was going to play it wide and then he'd play it in to your feet. He was always available for a pass but when he had the ball, he would always give it to you at the right time and he was always available to get it back off you.

If you wanted to make a run, he would pick you out even when you thought he hadn't seen you. He had that ability. His set-pieces were incredible. He was such an immense player. The movements I had learned from Gordon Strachan all came to fruition at Newcastle and stood me in good stead. Too late for Coventry, but in time for me to excel at my new club.

Then there was Gary Speed. Speedo set the standards at Newcastle, even in warm-ups. I wanted to copy him as much as I could. He would be at the front in warm-ups so I would be at the front too. He would go and do weights after training so I wanted to go and do weights too. He was a talented player but his attitude made him an even better player. He was the type of guy that if there were a war tomorrow, you would want him next to you because he would do anything for you. I admired his character immensely.

We had Shay Given in goal who was a terrific keeper. Kieron was a superb midfielder, at his best through the centre. Rob Lee was still there, although he was coming to the end of his time at the club. Carl Cort and Shola Ameobi were promising young forwards, Laurent Robert, the French winger, came in just before the start of the season, and Sylvain Distin arrived from PSG at the start of September to bolster a defence that had Nikos Dabizas and Andy O'Brien.

The previous season had been disappointing for Newcastle. They had finished 11th in the Premier League, 10 points away from qualifying for the Uefa Cup. So they had entered the Intertoto Cup to try to get into Europe by the back door. It meant that my pre-season was blissfully short and free of the hard running that had characterised many others. We were straight into matches.

First up was Belgian side Lokeren in the third round of the Intertoto. The first leg, my first game in a Newcastle shirt, was away. It was low-key, a summer's day in the middle of July that felt absurdly early to be playing competitive football. There were only 6,000 people there and Shearer was missing because he had just had an operation for tendinitis. I set up the first two goals for Wayne Quinn and Shola and we cruised to a 4-0 win.

A week later, we played them in the second leg at St James' Park. It was always going to be a formality but it was still special for me because it was the first time I'd played for Newcastle at the stadium and I felt like I had really arrived. There were nearly 30,000 people there for a game in late July when we already had a 4-0 lead. That tells you everything you need to know about Newcastle's support. I scored after an hour and we won the game 1-0. It was the perfect start.

The way Bobby wanted to play was perfect for me. He wanted the ball on the deck, for a start. He liked me dropping deep but he also wanted me to play on the shoulder. He wanted me to mix it up. He said an influential player like me should be on the ball as much as possible. That was music to my ears.

I felt at home straight away. And I felt privileged to be there. Until you settle into the area, you don't realise how big a club Newcastle actually is. It was a new level of scrutiny and a new level of expectation but after my troubles at Coventry, I wanted to seize the second chance I felt I had been given with both hands. I wanted to embrace the challenge.

I enjoyed working with John Carver too. He acted young and he was on the same wavelength as the players. He was the link between the manager and us and because he was a Geordie boy, he had a real feeling for the club. We had a good fitness coach, Paul Winsper, and everything felt as if it was geared to success. The first few weeks were brilliant. I loved every moment of it.

Sometimes in pre-season you are just concentrating on getting fit and staying out of trouble. Sometimes, a lack of match fitness can catch you out when you get to the first game of the league season. But the run in the Intertoto Cup solved that issue. After Lokeren, we beat 1860 Munich away and at home and that put us into the final against Troyes.

We under-estimated Troyes. I did, anyway. We drew 0-0 in the first leg in France but they were superb. They were managed by Alain Perrin, who had a brief spell in control of Portsmouth, and they played one-touch stuff. We were chasing shadows. They should have beaten us quite comfortably at their place but somehow we hung on for a draw.

We went 1-0 up in the second leg at St James' Park but then they took us apart. They were 4-1 up after an hour and although we dragged ourselves back into it and Aaron Hughes even scored a last minute equaliser, they deserved to go through. The supporters, of course, were disappointed because they wanted European football but it was probably the best thing that could have happened to us.

We had a good squad but we didn't have a big squad and now our playing resources wouldn't be quite so stretched. The six Intertoto games we had played had bedded everybody in and the players watching from the sidelines, like Shearer and Kieron, were thinking they were going to come back into a decent side. There was optimism around the place.

The first game of the league season was against Chelsea at Stamford Bridge. They had spent £32m on Frank Lampard, Emmanuel Petit, William Gallas and Boudewijn Zenden and they had ambitions of challenging for the title. But we matched them. We fell behind early but we finished strongly and Clarence Acuna equalised for us with 13 minutes to go. It was an early boost for our morale.

The next weekend, we were at home to Sunderland in the Tyne-Wear derby. I had sampled a few East Anglian derbies. In fact, I scored in one and the atmosphere was always brilliant. But it had nothing on that Newcastle-Sunderland game. I had never been involved in anything like it. It is on occasions like that when you realise why people talk about St James' Park as one of the great cathedrals of football.

Sunderland had a little bit of a hold over Newcastle at that time. A couple of years earlier, Ruud Gullit had decided to leave Shearer on the bench for a Tyne-Wear derby. It was widely interpreted as a power-play, an attempt to prove he could take on the Geordie hero on his own patch. It didn't work. In fact, many people interpreted the team sheet he handed in for that game as tantamount to a managerial suicide note. Sunderland won 2-1 and Gullit was out.

This time, we went a goal down after 20 minutes. Kevin Phillips had scored in Gullit's last game and now he scored again after about half an hour. But there were 52,000 fans inside the stadium and they kept up the support. Two minutes before half-time, Laurent Robert played me in and I slotted it past the Sunderland keeper. That gave me a lot of confidence and belief and helped establish me with the fans.

Shearer returned to the team for the next game against Middlesbrough and that felt like a big moment for me as well as the supporters. I knew what he was all about because I had watched him down the years, not just for England but for Southampton and Blackburn before his move back home. He was an incredible player. By the time I worked with him, he had dipped a little because of the number of injuries he had suffered but he was still a brilliant player. He could hit the ball like no one else I've ever seen. He was great at holding it up and he was magnificent in the air.

Sometimes people say 'be good with your left as well as your right, always work on ironing out imperfections' but Alan knew the time for that had come and gone. Alan just improved his strengths. If there were some things he couldn't do, he didn't try to do them. He worked hard, although pre-season, he wouldn't do any of the running that the rest of us did. He did his own stuff because he wasn't a runner. He wasn't quick. He didn't have those qualities. But he gave the team confidence. When you know Shearer's in your team...well, it can't help but give you a lift. He had something. He had stature. He had presence. The crowd adored him. When it was known he was coming back against Middlesbrough, the anticipation around the region was intense.

If you put the ball into the right area, Alan would always pick on the weakest defender. He had a sixth sense for sniffing out a defender's vulnerabilities. If that defender couldn't head the ball, he would be on him. He was just clever. When we started playing together, I did a lot of his running for him. I was coming short to receive passes and it was probably ideal for him. It allowed him to concentrate on being in the right areas.

I'm the kind of player who creates chances, too. I will be wide and crossing it or cutting the ball back. Sir Bobby Robson knew exactly what he was doing when he paired the two of us up. We hit it off straight away. We played together against Middlesbrough and he scored twice in a 4-1 win at the Riverside. We were very, very different personalities off the pitch, but on it, we clicked.

Early on in our partnership, the quality of his striking took me by surprise. Once, I made a run on the outside and Laurent Robert used my movement to slip the ball inside to Alan. I was watching and thinking he had time to take a touch but he hit it first time and it went straight in the top corner. I ran over to him and I was thinking 'that is something different to anything I have ever witnessed'. That was what made him different to every other player. When he hit the ball first time like that, nine times out of ten it would go in and if it didn't the keeper would have to make a very good save.

Newcastle was Alan's club. He was very strong within the club politically. Everybody was scared of going up against him. It wasn't thought of as a battle you would be able to win. I was just grateful to be playing with someone like him.

He wasn't a guy that went around giving people advice. There was no question that if you had a problem you would go and see him. He wasn't that type of character. I didn't mind about that because I had Speedo to go to.

Alan didn't want to know about other people's problems. He concentrated a lot on himself but then a lot of footballers do. That is probably what made him the player he was: he was very single minded. He did only think about himself. That was his only concern. Not the team, not the other players. It was about himself. That is probably his biggest strength.

Even when he got flak, it didn't bother him. He knew his own ability and if someone criticised him, he would set out to prove them wrong and succeed.

I got an extra-time hat-trick against Brentford in the League Cup the following week. I got three in the space of 12 minutes. The highlights were coming thick and fast. I had wanted to hit the ground running at Newcastle and those first few weeks were everything I'd hoped for. In fact, the best was still to come. We were at home to Manchester United next. It was one of the most dramatic games I've been involved in.

The atmosphere was electric. United were unbeaten. People were saying they might go the whole season without defeat. They had Juan Sebastian Veron, Ruud Van Nistelrooy, Paul Scholes, David Beckham, Laurent Blanc and, of course, Roy Keane. We were already full of confidence, though, and we tore into them.

We went 1-0 up. They equalised. Then Fabien Barthez made a mistake and Rob Lee put us back into the lead. Dabizas put us 3-1 up before they pegged us back to 3-3 with two goals in two minutes. It was breathless stuff. Seven minutes from the end, I managed to get away from Blanc and lay a pass out wide to Solano. His shot was saved by Barthez but it rebounded to

Alan and Wes Brown could only deflect his effort into the net. It turned out to be the winner.

I was substituted soon after that because I'd got a kick on the knee so I was watching when Alan and Roy Keane clashed on the far side of the pitch in the last minute. The ball went out for a throw-in and Keane, who was already wound up anyway, reacted to something Alan said and threw the ball at him. It hit him on the back of the head and Alan complained to the referee. The referee sent Keane off and Keane went absolutely nuts. He looked like he wanted to rip Alan's head off. It took about five of the United players to restrain him.

I adored Keane. He was one of the best players I ever played against. I idolised him, in fact, but I wouldn't have wanted to go up against him in those circumstances. I saw him waiting for Alan in the tunnel at the end of the game and Alan didn't seem to be hurrying off the pitch. He was one of the last to come off, actually, which we all made sure we remarked on when he finally made it back to the dressing room. Keane had had to be dragged back into the United dressing room by then. There was a lot of laughing and joking about it all. The spirit was good, United had been beaten, we were off to a flying start.

12

Party Tyne

There were two groups among the players. There were the more senior players, like Speedo, Shearer, Rob Lee and Warren Barton. When they socialised, they went out for meals with their wives. In the changing room before training, they'd talk about what they had done with their kids the day before or which restaurant they had eaten at.

Then there was the younger group: me, Carl Cort, Kieron, Wayne Quinn, Andy Griffin, Dabizas and Solano. We had a deal with each other. If we won, we would head out on the town, usually down to the pubs and clubs down on the Quayside on the banks of the River Tyne. If we lost, we'd stay in. If we drew? Well that was tricky. It depended on the performance. If we decided we'd played okay, we'd go out.

We only lost at home four times all season. So we went out quite a lot. If we wanted to win the next week, we had to keep up the tradition. That's what we told ourselves anyway. We had a team spirit and togetherness partly because we were all socialising.

On a Monday, the whole squad would go out for food and Sir Bobby encouraged that. He wanted that togetherness. I still look back on that with fondness. It would be called 'old school' now but it worked. We all enjoyed each other's company and we were treated like kings in the city. When you are winning and things are going well in Newcastle, you are loved like nowhere else.

It sounds outdated now, doesn't it? But the formula worked for us. I felt like part of a family within a few weeks of arriving. Sure, there were two separate groups – Shay Given belonged to both – but we all got on well. Underpinning it all was a belief that we had the potential to have a very successful season.

We suffered our first defeat at Upton Park against West Ham and lost twice at home, to Liverpool and Spurs. But after the defeat to Tottenham at the end of October, we won eight of our next 10 league games, a run that included back-to-back away wins at Arsenal and Leeds United. When we beat Derby at home in late November, it moved us joint top of the table.

We slipped back a little but when we won at Highbury a week before Christmas, we went top in our own right. It was a bittersweet moment for me. It was the first time I had ever been part of a team that was top of the league but I marked the occasion by being sent off by Graham Poll 20 minutes from time, supposedly for swinging my arm into Ashley Cole's face.

I didn't like Poll and he didn't like me. I thought that he was arrogant and rude. There was nothing worse than knowing you were about to play one of the big teams and finding out that he would be the ref because, in my opinion, if ever I came across a man who appeared star-struck, it was him. He loved David Beckham, for instance, absolutely loved him. I'd see him before games, shaking hands with Patrick Vieira, talking to the big players. He looked to me like he wanted to be around the cameras. He called some of the big stars by their Christian names, like he thought he was their mate.

In contrast, he seemed to hold me in contempt. I didn't show him any respect. I didn't want to be his friend and he used to book me given the slightest opportunity. I wasn't surprised when he booked the Croatian defender, Josip Simunic, three times during the 2006 World Cup because I didn't actually think he was that good a referee. There was an element of karma about that, too. He had that coming. I think he saw himself as a celebrity ref.

I don't have a problem with most referees. In fact, I think we are very fortunate with the standard of our officials. Mark Halsey is outstanding. So is Phil Dowd. I'm probably not the easiest player to manage on the pitch. I accept that. There are times when I can be very incorrect in what I say. I will appeal for something I am never going to get but during the game I'm convinced I'm right.

Some refs will know I'm talking rubbish and they'll tell me. I despise swearing at refs, believe it or not, but sometimes I can't help myself. Some refs tell me where to go straight away and swear back at me. That's fair enough. I haven't got a problem with that. I certainly don't take it personally.

Poll got a lot of stuff wrong, though. His decision to send me off against Arsenal was a joke. I might have brushed Cole with my arm but the contact was minimal and it was certainly accidental. Most people could see that but Poll would not change his mind so Newcastle appealed the decision and it went to an FA disciplinary commission. To no one's great surprise, Poll's decision was overturned and my three-match ban was wiped out.

We had real momentum by then. It had survived intact despite an episode in November that I suppose marked the beginning of the idea that people like me and Kieron were out of control during our time at Newcastle. We had beaten Aston Villa at home on the first Saturday in November and the next day the squad flew out to Malaga for a winter break.

We were staying at a resort called La Quenta in San Pedro Alcantara, a few miles from Marbella. The idea was to play some golf, relax and hopefully soak up a little sunshine. We had a friendly against Recreativo Huelva scheduled for Wednesday night. I didn't play golf back then so on Monday, which was a free day, Carl Cort, Andy Griffin, Kieron and I went for a bit of lunch at a place in Puerto Banus. We had nothing to do, it was pouring with rain and so we just stayed in the restaurant, eating and drinking. We were a bit bored, basically.

Early in the evening, about 6pm, Tony Toward, the team administrator, rang Kieron on his mobile. He told us we had to report back to the hotel at 7pm for an evening meal. We said we had just eaten but he told us we ought to show our faces and then we could go. Well, 7pm came and went and we were still in the restaurant. We made our way up to the hotel about half an hour later but we were oblivious of the time. We didn't think there was any particular urgency about the meal.

We got to the hotel but there was nobody there. They had

already gone in for dinner. We didn't want to just barge in because it would have created more of a scene. So we went to the bar for a bit. While we were there, we ordered four vodka Red Bulls and a cigar each and put them on Freddy Shepherd's room bill. Then we went back to our rooms to get changed so we could meet up with the rest of the squad when they came out of their dinner.

No one said anything except Speedo who was honest, as usual. He said we should have turned up. He said it was a dinner in honour of Newcastle's former chairman, Sir John Hall, and that it wouldn't have cost us anything just to put in an appearance as we had been asked to do. It was the first time anybody had told me it was in honour of Sir John Hall but anyway, after that everyone went their separate ways.

I woke up the next morning to a knock on my door. There was a guy from the club there with a sheet of paper that had an itinerary on it. He handed it to me.

"What's this?" I said.

"You've been sent home," he said.

I was astonished.

"What for?" I asked him.

"The taxi will be here to pick you up and take you to the airport," he said.

I rang Kieron, who was still recovering from a long-term injury at the time. They had nagged him to go on the trip and now they were sending him home.

That flight back from Malaga was not pleasant. We were all hungover, for a start. And the club hadn't booked us back to Newcastle. We had to get from Heathrow to King's Cross and then travel up on the train. I looked at one of the papers on the way up and saw a picture of me and a poorly child I had befriended. 'Everything I'm involved in now is news,' I thought.

I knew there would be more to come the next day. I knew we were going to get both barrels in the press after what happened in Spain. I knew it would get out and that we'd be crucified. It was about 18 months after the Leicester incident at La Manga when Stan Collymore let off the fire extinguisher. But this time, there was no incident.

Because we had been sent home, everyone believed something more must have happened. There was a hunt for the real story. Nobody believed that we had just missed a dinner. It was even on the 6pm news the night we arrived back in the north-east. I didn't realise it was going to be that serious. By the end of the week, all sorts of stories were flying around. One claimed the four of us had been in a brothel.

The four of us were summoned to a meeting at St James' Park in the chairman's office. We went in one by one to be greeted by Freddy Shepherd sitting there with his glasses on and behaving like a school headmaster. He said we had deliberately snubbed a meal for Sir John Hall but I said we hadn't been told anything about the nature of the meal.

Give us a fine, sure, a slap on the wrist, but he was hanging us out to dry. He had created a storm by sending us home. I apologised but there had been no malice in what I did. It was just the action of a young, stupid kid turning up late for a meal. Freddy wouldn't hear any of it. I just had to let him rant. I think what wound him up the most was that we'd put the drinks and the cigars on his room bill. If I was the chairman, I would have laughed my head off at that.

It all blew over quickly. The fans knew it was nothing and

treated it like that. Kieron came back into the side soon afterwards and he was such an outstanding footballer that it was like having a new multi-million pound signing in the team. Once things are going well and the team is clicking and that crowd in the north-east gets behind you, St James' Park is a difficult place for any opposition side to come and play football.

On the road, our fans came in great numbers to support us. And we were playing good football. We went in attacking and even if we did lose, we gave it a really good go. We would leave our defence open at times but that was the kind of team we were. All our training was about how we were going to win, not how we were going to avoid defeat. It wasn't about what the opposition was going to do to us. It was about what we were going to do to them.

Three days before Christmas, we played Leeds at Elland Road. They had reached the semi-finals of the Champions League the previous season under David O'Leary and they were still one of the top clubs in England but there was a sense that they might just be beginning to slide. The club had expended a lot of emotional energy on the trial that involved Lee Bowyer and Jonathan Woodgate, who had been accused of a racially-motivated assault.

The trial had ended the previous week but the club was exhausted by it and Woodgate, in particular, was a shell of the player he had once been. On the pitch, a couple of new signings, like Seth Johnson and Robbie Fowler, were struggling to make an impact and O'Leary was starting to feel the pressure.

We knew how important it was for us to beat them because we were similar sized clubs fighting for the same things with the same amount of revenue. We didn't know then quite what a financial mess they were getting themselves into but it was obvious to us that if we could get ourselves into the Champions League positions and deprive them of a top four spot at the same time, then they would be doubly damaged.

I overheard Sir Bobby saying that if we could overtake them, we might be able to get one or two of their players rather than have to listen about how they wanted to sign Kieron, which was a rumour doing the rounds at the time.

It was a terrific game at Elland Road. They had a fine team with players like Rio Ferdinand, Mark Viduka, David Batty, Harry Kewell and Fowler and it was an even game. I put us ahead before half-time after a great run from Kieron but Bowyer equalised straight away and then they went 3-1 up early in the second half.

But then Robbie Elliott got a goal back with a diving header, Shearer equalised with a penalty and Solano scored the winner in the last minute after more great work from Kieron. Sir Bobby said that the week could not have gone any better. The victory put us three points clear of Liverpool at the top of the table, four points ahead of Leeds, and six clear of Manchester United and Arsenal, who were fourth and fifth respectively.

Sometimes, I think that what Sir Bobby achieved at Newcastle just by getting us into that position in the first place has been too quickly forgotten. I know you don't get any prizes for being top at Christmas but this was a team playing the same kind of attractive football that Kevin Keegan's side had played a few years earlier, and I don't think Sir Bobby got the same kind of credit for it.

We lost twice at the end of the year, at home to Chelsea and away to United, but we were back on top of the table by the middle of January. We went on a run of five wins in six games but United were really starting to show their quality now and by the end of February, we were second, two points behind them but with a game in hand. Lots of teams weren't getting anywhere near us. Olivier Bernard had come into the side at left-back and he was refreshing because he was so attacking. We had pace, we had runners in the team with ability, we played quick one-twos, we were brimming with confidence.

Earlier that February, I had got myself into some trouble on a night out. We hit the headlines after the Malaga incident but this was my first proper taste of the attention you can get if you step out of line when you're in the limelight in a city that reveres its footballers like Newcastle does. It was a Monday night and Carl Cort, Wayne Quinn and I went out for a meal and then decided to have a few drinks.

We went to a club called Sea, which was on the Quayside. Carl and Wayne were single and they had a couple of girls with them by the time we wanted to head home. Kieron had been in Ipswich for the day and he phoned to say that he would pick us up on his way back and drop us off. So we all got in his car and we dropped Quinny off at his apartment.

Everybody got out except one girl, who said she wanted Kieron to drop her off at her house. I wanted to get back to my place in Jesmond but she insisted we had to drop her off first. Kieron said he wasn't running a taxi service and that she could order a car from Quinny's flat. She refused to get out of the car so it started to get a bit heated.

In the end, she gave up and got out. As she was getting out, I began to climb out of the back seat into the front for the journey back to my place. She was angry and she gave me a bit of a mouthful and then she got the door and slammed it against my leg. I got out, pushed her away and jumped back in the car. I went 'drive, drive, drive' to Kieron and we sped off.

She was a third-year student from Newcastle University. She said later I'd slapped her while we were arguing in the car. Then she said that after I'd pushed her over, I'd kicked her while she was lying on the ground. She chased after the car for a few seconds but then she gave up. It was a bit of a mad episode. I was worried about it but I hoped I wouldn't hear anything more about it. I was still naïve back then.

We trained the next day and then Wednesday was a day off. But in the early evening on Wednesday, Wayne Quinn called. He said Tony Toward had rung him and said a girl had been to the police and said she had been assaulted by a Newcastle United player. They had given her a team sheet with pictures of the players and she had picked out Wayne Quinn. Quinny sounded very nervous. He wasn't in the first team at the time. He felt vulnerable. "Bellers," he said, "they will probably sack me."

"Quinny," I said, "you're just going to have to bite the bullet on this one." He went quiet. There was a long silence. Then I put him out of his misery and told him not to be so stupid.

I phoned Tony Toward and told him it was nothing to do with Quinny. The next day, it was on the news and I had to go and see Freddy Shepherd in his office at St James' Park. He had been told what had happened. He seemed more angry about the girl slamming the door on my leg. He said the police wanted to speak to me to get my side of the story. He said I could fight it and I would win. But he said it would drag on and on and if I accepted a caution, it would all be forgotten about and I could concentrate on preparing for the next game. So on Thursday night, I went to the police station. They talked to me for about an hour, they cautioned me and I left. The next day, there were photographers outside my house and reporters climbing the fences around my house. It was horrible. It was the first time I had been at the centre of something like that.

Kieron came out of it well. The student said that he had behaved like 'a perfect gentleman'. But the papers said that I could wreck Newcastle's season. They said I could spoil everything, that I was the loose cannon that could throw the club off course. I was worried about the effect it would have on Claire but I had told her what had happened as soon as I got back the night it occurred and she was understanding about it.

I was very single-minded. I just wanted to get on with playing against Southampton that Saturday. Everything was going so well and I wasn't going to let an incident like that get in the way of it. A lot of the papers were speculating about what state of mind I was going to be in but I was fine. I didn't really feel I had anything to be ashamed of and certainly nothing to hide. The only thing I was concerned about was the reaction of the crowd but I got a great ovation when I came out for the warm-up at St James' Park and we won 3-1.

Gordon Strachan was the Southampton manager by then. He had been sacked five games into the new season at Coventry and taken over at St Mary's soon afterwards. He'd obviously read all about my nocturnal adventures because he smiled at me as I ran out on to the pitch.

"Know anywhere good to go out tonight, Bellers?" he asked.

13

Euro Class

I did some growing up in that first season at Newcastle, too, though. Sure, there were some things I did wrong and some things I wish I could take back. But even as our challenge for the title gathered strength, I assumed responsibilities I had not thought about shouldering before.

A couple of weeks before we went on the ill-fated trip to Marbella, one of the Newcastle press officers, Hazel Greener, asked me if I'd make a visit to the Royal Victoria Infirmary in Newcastle. She told me about a young boy there who was sick with kidney disease and whose father had asked if there was any chance of their son meeting me. The boy's name was Indie Singh. He was 14 years old.

It was only round the corner from where I lived. It was hardly even a diversion on my way home. It had been set up as a surprise for him so I went over there and met Indie and his dad, Bal. They were both avid Newcastle fans and Indie's face lit up when I walked in. I played a bit of PlayStation on the computer with him for a while and asked him about his favourite players, and whether he was a fan of mine because of the silver boots I was wearing at that time.

I really enjoyed it. He and his dad had season tickets just above the dug-outs at St James' Park so I told them that when we played Aston Villa the following Saturday, I would make sure to look up and give them a wave. Before the game, I thought I'd pop in and see him again. I gave him a Wales shirt and one of my Wales caps. I'd never given one of them away before because they're for my kids but it felt like the right thing to do.

The game felt big to me. I thought it might be one of the last times he watched me play because it was obvious he wasn't well at all. I wanted to try to make it memorable in some way. I got lucky. A few minutes before half-time, I hit a half-volley into the top corner and after I'd celebrated, I ran over and waved to Indie and his dad. I've still got the picture in my mind of him sitting there with his old man with a big smile plastered over his face.

We won the game 3-0 and I got the third that day, too, sliding it through Peter Schmeichel's legs. Indie came down to the dressing room after the game and I gave him my shirt and had my picture taken with him. I felt so good. It was one of the best feelings I'd ever had after a game. Whether there is a God or not I will never know but if there is, I thank him for that.

I don't know why it touched such a nerve with me. He was a lovely kid. That was part of the reason. He'd won some award for being a Child of Courage and had given the money he received straight to the hospital so they could buy presents for the other kids. But it was more than just that. I was a father, too, of course, and seeing what was happening was heartbreaking.

But I think it was a bit of an escape for me, too. It was getting increasingly hard for me to trust anybody and I could feel the spotlight increasing on me. When I went to spend time with Indie, I didn't have to worry about any of that. I find dealing with children so much easier than interacting with adults. With adults, I am worried that there is always a question behind the question. With young kids, they are blunt and truthful. They ask questions about things I am interested in like who is my favourite team and player.

Sometimes, I am a child and sometimes my love for the game is like a child's. I do have favourite players, I do remember things from a couple of weeks ago when a certain player did a trick or something. That's what kids remember, too. That's why I enjoy dealing with kids and that was part of the reason I loved being with Indie and his family. I could speak freely to him. Even with all the craziness surrounding me, it made me remember what was real.

Indie was sent home just before Christmas. His condition was deteriorating. He had a younger sister but he was his father's only son. If it was my child and that had been happening to him…well, I couldn't comprehend it. I spent quite a lot of time round at their house in Durham, just talking and playing on the PlayStation with Indie.

He was really ill this time. He began to lapse in and out of consciousness. I saw him as much as I could. One afternoon, I knocked on his door and his sister answered it. She didn't know what to say. Eventually, she told me that Indie had died that morning. I went in for a couple of hours and spent a bit of time with his family. I felt it probably wasn't my place to be there but they asked me to stay.

I am very fortunate to have met a boy like Indie but how many other boys are there in similar plights? That's one of the main reasons why I have an academy for kids in Sierra Leone now. So I can try to help a bit more. After Indie died, I went back for more visits to the Royal Victoria Infirmary. I saw a lot of doctors and nurses who used to deal with kids like Indie all the time. What a job they do.

It felt like, in a very small way, I was doing something worthwhile, something good. It stirred a few memories in me, too. When I was a young child and my asthma flared, there were quite a few occasions when I'd have to go and spend a week at Heath Hospital in Cardiff to recover. I'd always want my dad to stay with me overnight but that wasn't possible because I had brothers and they had to be looked after, too. I remembered how lonely those places can be for a child.

I'd like to say meeting Indie made me a little less self-absorbed but I'm not sure if that's true. I'm an obsessive. I was totally wrapped up in my career and in Newcastle's title challenge. We were still in the thick of the race at the end of February. When we beat Sunderland at the Stadium of Light on February 24, we moved to two points behind Manchester United with a game in hand.

Earlier in the month, I'd driven down to Cardiff with Gary Speed for a Wales game against Argentina. It was just after the Southampton game and the fracas with the Newcastle University student. Speedo had TalkSport on and there were a lot of phone calls about me coming in, about how well I had played after the week I'd just had.

Speedo turned the sound down and started talking. He talked about how different we were as characters in some ways but that he admired my attitude. He said I was one of the best players he had ever played with but he said it was time to cut the bullshit out. He knew I wasn't a bad kid, he said, but I had to understand I was becoming a player now and I needed to start acting like a player. I had to realise I was marked, he said.

There was so much I wanted to take on board, so much I knew I needed to improve. But there was so much coming at me, too. Playing in Newcastle, in a team that was top of the table, had exposed me to a whole new level of celebrity and attention. It was turning my head, to be honest. I was scoring a lot of goals and getting a lot of praise. I began to think I was invincible.

The title seemed in reach. We had a decent run-in, too. Our last six games were against Fulham, Derby, Charlton, Blackburn, West Ham and Southampton. Everybody was saying we had a real shot at it. We were right in the mix. It was all going so well. And then, during that win at Sunderland, my luck suddenly turned for the worse.

The Sunderland defender, Jody Craddock, went to hit a ball down the line and I scampered across and blocked it. As I broke to try to chase it, I felt a little click in the patella tendon in my right knee. It wasn't enough to make me come off but it got worse during the game and in the dressing room afterwards, it was really sore. I had a scan the next day and it showed I had a slight tear.

They said I would be out for four weeks. It was a hell of a

blow. It was such a crucial stage in the season. We had 11 games left. We thought if we won eight of them, that would probably be enough for the title. We were so tantalisingly close. The first two games I missed were tough ones, too. Home to Arsenal and then away to Liverpool. We lost them both without scoring a goal.

When we drew at home to Ipswich in the next game, we knew the league had gone. Almost in the blink of an eye. Suddenly, we were eight points behind United. Liverpool and Arsenal had opened a bit of a gap on us as well. We were even starting to worry about whether we would qualify for the Champions League because Chelsea were chasing us for fourth place.

When we could only draw at home with Fulham on April 8, our lead over Chelsea was down to a single point with five games to play. I had already missed six games and I was desperate to come back. I was training but my knee still wasn't right. It wasn't healing. But we rallied after the Fulham game. We won at Derby and rolled Charlton over at St James' Park. That meant that if we got a point or better against Blackburn at Ewood Park, fourth place would be safe.

I'd made the bench for the Charlton game and I came on against Blackburn. We came from behind twice as two goals from Shearer carried us to a 2-2 draw. It put us out of reach of Chelsea and it was my last involvement in the season. Sir Bobby left me out of the last two games. He knew that my knee wasn't right. There was no point risking me now that there was nothing left to play for.

In the end, we finished 16 points adrift of the title winners Arsenal, who had beaten Liverpool into second place. Behind us, Leeds pipped Chelsea to fifth place but they were about to disappear into the chasm. Nobody had expected us to finish fourth but we had done it. I had won the PFA Young Player of the Year along the way, voted for by my peers, and now I'd be playing in the Champions League the following season. The dream I had been chasing was coming true. I was part of football's elite.

I didn't have much chance to celebrate what we had achieved. Before the season was even over, I was on a plane to Colorado to see the surgeon, Richard Steadman. So I celebrated with a knee operation. He said I'd be out for four months, which would get me back almost for the start of the 2002-03 season and the beginning of our Champions League campaign.

I did very little rehab during the summer. My knee was in a brace, I kept out of trouble and I assumed everything was going to be fine. But on the first day of pre-season back up in the north-east, it still didn't feel right. The brace was off by then but I was in quite a lot of discomfort as soon as I even started jogging. I had to go back inside straight away. I was worried.

I wasn't ready for the start of the new season. I missed the Champions League qualifying round ties against the Bosnian side, Željezni, which we won 5-0 on aggregate, and I had to sit out the opening Premier League games against West Ham and Manchester City, too. We had let Sylvain Distin go in the summer, which was a mistake, but we had signed a decent Portuguese kid called Hugo Viana from Sporting Lisbon and even though expectations were much higher, I thought we'd have another decent season.

I came back on September 2. Sir Bobby brought me off the bench at Anfield when we were 2-0 down to Liverpool and I helped get us back into the game. Speedo and Shearer both scored in the last 10 minutes and we rescued a draw out of it. I played well and people were saying what a relief that I was back as good as new. But I knew I wasn't back. I knew my knee still wasn't feeling that great.

I wanted to play for Wales in a European Championship qualifier in Finland the following Saturday and Newcastle said I had to prove my fitness in a midweek reserve team match against Blackburn. The whole thing turned into a saga. I played in the reserve match but then my flight to Helsinki was cancelled. I rang the Wales manager, Mark Hughes, and told him what had happened.

Things had been a lot more professional under Sparky and he took this on as a test case. He asked the Welsh FA to charter a private plane to get me out there. He fought and fought for it and in the end they bowed to his demands. I was pleased. It showed we were getting serious at last and that we wanted to have a proper shot at qualifying. It sent a message. We won the game.

While I was waiting for that flight, I had a call from Eric Harrison, the guy who was the youth team manager at Manchester United when they won the FA Youth Cup in 1992 with that side that included Ryan Giggs, David Beckham, Nicky Butt and Gary Neville. Eric did some work with Wales, too, and now he was ringing to say that Sir Alex Ferguson had asked him to call me.

Eric wanted to know who my representative was so I told him and soon after, Steve Horner and Peter Robinson went to meet Ferguson at United's training ground. Ferguson told them he wanted to sign me but didn't think Newcastle would sell me.

I was flattered, obviously. But I was worried, too. I was unsure about my knee. It was constantly hurting. There were times when I couldn't do what I wanted to do when I was on the ball because the pain was getting in the way. I didn't want to make movements or runs that increased the pain. I knew that if I went to Manchester United, I would have to make an immediate impact and I didn't feel I was in the shape to do that.

There was also the small matter of the fact that I was very happy at Newcastle. I had just had a great season; we were in the Champions League; I was PFA Young Player of the Year and I had a brilliant manager who loved me. Everything seemed bright. It was nice to know United were interested but I thought perhaps it would be something that happened further down the line.

We made Newcastle fully aware that if they didn't meet my contract demands, I would run my existing deal down and go to United. I had a meeting with Freddy Shepherd about it. He asked me how much I wanted and I told him £50,000 a week. I knew what other players were getting. It was my market value at that time.

Freddy just got up from his seat and walked out of the room without saying a word. He didn't even have the decency to tell me to fuck off.

I didn't pay much attention. It was all in the future anyway and I was more concerned with the Champions League. We had been drawn in a tough group with Dynamo Kiev, Juventus and Feyenoord but I was still confident we could go through. I was excited, too. To be playing in the Champions League was another one of the targets I had set myself.

The first game was away in Kiev in the middle of September. Instead of playing in the Olympic Stadium, the match was at the Lobanovskiy Stadium, a beautiful old ground ringed by trees on a hill overlooking the River Dnieper. This was my first taste of the biggest stage of all. We walked out on to the pitch and the Champions League music was playing. This was football. This was where I wanted to be.

But Dynamo were a tough team, particularly in Kiev. They played three at the back and Alan and I were both man-marked. My marker, a defender called Tiberiu Ghioane, followed me absolutely everywhere, which was a new experience for me. They were two goals up after an hour and I began to get frustrated. My knee was hurting and Ghioane was trying to rough me up.

In the last few minutes, he cleared the ball upfield and followed through so he made sure he kicked me. The game was already lost but he was getting to me. In stoppage time, he gave me a nudge in the back and I turned around to confront him. As I squared up to him, I head-butted him. It was a pathetic thing to do but I thought I might have got away with it. The referee didn't see it and nor did the linesman. It wasn't the best head-butt and to the fella's credit, he didn't even go down.

I played in the next match against Feyenoord at St James' Park the following week. I hit the bar and had a shot cleared off the line by Brett Emerton but we lost 1-0 and everybody said that was the end of our chances of making it through to the next stage. Things got worse the next day when Uefa announced that they had reviewed television footage of my incident with Ghioane.

They released a statement. It said: 'In the 91st minute, Craig Bellamy deliberately head-butted an opponent in the face. Since the referee did not see the incident, the decision was rendered on the basis of video evidence.' I was given a three-game ban for violent conduct, which was heartbreaking. I had worked so hard to play in the Champions League and now I was going to miss out on two games against Juventus and the return against Kiev.

I'd be back for Feyenoord away but I thought we'd probably only have pride to play for by then. While I was suspended, we lost the next game to Juventus 2-0, courtesy of two goals from Alessandro Del Piero. We had lost our first three games. Our Champions League campaign was turning into an embarrassment.

The only positive was that the ban gave me a chance to go back to Colorado to see Richard Steadman again. I was worried that the operation on my knee had not been a success. I needed to have a check-up. Dr Steadman said he didn't want to operate again. The patella tendon was healing, he said, but he gave me very specific instructions about my continued rehabilitation.

He said I needed to do less shooting and no double sessions. As far as I was concerned, they were the kind of instructions that meant I wouldn't be able to play football again. 'You can't tell me to do this,' I thought, 'I'm a striker.' Part of the manic drive I had stemmed from wanting to improve and training was where I did that. I always wanted to stay to the last second of every session. I loved being out there until the last kick. Now I was being told I couldn't do that any more.

I hated leaving training and seeing the others doing extra finishing. I resented it. I grew bitter about it. I knew I needed to improve but I couldn't do it unless I was practising and I couldn't practise because I would put more stress on my tendon

and then feel the effects a day later. I became a miserable bastard. I was horrible to be around. This was my career on the
line and I became consumed by anxiety and anger.

I was playing off and on. I scored a few goals in the Premier
League but I felt like I was getting away with it, not excelling.
Some games I was brilliant but the next week I couldn't do
it again because my knee was suffering from the week before.
There was one ray of light. We had beaten Juventus at St James'
Park and then we beat Kiev in the penultimate match of the
group, too. That meant that if we beat Feyenoord at De Kuip
and Kiev lost to Juventus, we would finish second in the group.
It was an unlikely scenario but I was available for the Feyenoord
game. It gave me something to aim for.

I love De Kuip. I love that stadium. It's a beautiful ground, a
real proper football ground. We trained there the night before
the game and it was cold and crisp. It felt like a proper European night. I could tell it was going to be a great occasion. The
next day, we got on the coach to go to the ground and there
were loads of Feyenoord fans around our coach, banging and
shouting. It was hostile but it was great.

Both teams had so much to play for because we could both
qualify if we won. The warm-up was as hostile as anything,
which is right up my street. If I need any extra motivation,
that's it. I love it when fans scream at me. It puts me right in
the mood. For once, my knee felt great, too. I missed one good
chance but then Alan flicked one on from a kick out by Shay
Given just before half-time and I ran through and scored.

Four minutes after the break, Hugo Viana made it 2-0. We
still thought it was unlikely we'd get through to the next phase
of the competition because most people expected Kiev to beat

a weakened Juventus side in Ukraine. Our main focus, really, was on finishing third and getting into the Uefa Cup, rather than finishing bottom of the group and going back home with nothing.

They sent on a big forward called Mariano Bombarda midway through the second half and he pulled one back. Then, with 20 minutes to go, they equalised. We were right under the cosh but every time we broke we looked like scoring. It was a brilliant game. A few minutes from the end, I thought it was all over. Paul Bosvelt shot from the edge of the box and I thought it was in. Time stood still, Shay didn't even dive. But the shot flew a few inches wide.

We were holding on but then, in the last minute, we pumped a free-kick forward towards Alan. He won it in the air and suddenly Kieron was bursting into the box. He hit his shot low and to the keeper's left and when he palmed it out, I ran on to it. It was almost on the byline by the time I got to it but I just thought 'hit the target'. I hit it hard and true and even though the keeper got his body behind it, he couldn't keep it out. "Extraordinary," the television commentator bellowed when it went in.

It was extraordinary, too. It was a brilliant, brilliant night. I thought I'd salvaged a Uefa Cup place for us. I was delighted. The home crowd went silent. Sir Bobby was telling us to concentrate. Then the whistle went and next thing I knew someone said Juventus had beaten Kiev and we were into the next round of the Champions League. What a moment.

To be back on that stage after missing three games felt great. And to qualify in the dramatic way we did made it even better. No one had ever done that before: lost the first three games and then won the last three to qualify. It was a great thing for the city and the club. We were all on a high. I signed a new contract with Newcastle around that time. I got what I wanted. I don't think Sir Alex Ferguson was too happy with me but it was the best thing for my career at that time.

The Champions League format that year meant the second round was another group stage and we were drawn with Inter Milan, Barcelona and Bayer Leverkusen. That sent the excitement soaring even higher on Tyneside. We were doing okay in the league – we were ninth in mid-November – but this season the focus was more on Europe.

Two weeks after the drama of the victory over Feyenoord in Rotterdam, we were lining up to face Inter at St James' Park. It felt as though it would be another special night. I was going to be up against players of the calibre of Fabio Cannavaro, Javier Zanetti and Hernan Crespo. And I was about to make history. Just not the kind I hoped for.

I wandered down the tunnel to go out for the warm-up and Marco Materazzi was standing there with a teammate. I didn't know that much about him then although he had already played for a season with Everton. He was later to gain notoriety for his ability to wind people up. He provoked Zinedine Zidane into head-butting him with taunts about Zidane's sister in the 2006 World Cup final.

Materazzi stared at me as I walked down the tunnel. He never took his eyes off me. I thought the guy realised he was in for a hell of a game against me that night. Nothing could have been further from the truth, sadly. Inter went a goal up in the second minute when Domenico Morfeo turned in a cross from Zanetti. It was a terrible start but worse was to come.

Four minutes later, I ran after a ball down in the corner. As it went out of play, Materazzi grabbed at me and pinched me. It's very rare in our game we get pinched. Well it is in my experience, anyway. I swung my arm round to say 'fuck off' and it caught him around his midriff. He hit the deck and he was rolling round. I thought 'shit, this doesn't look good'. I saw the linesman flagging and I knew straight away I was off. I felt sick to my stomach.

I didn't mean to hit him. I'm not exactly Mike Tyson. I couldn't deck someone of his size with a punch. He had reeled me in beautifully. I suppose you have to give him credit for that. I bet he was surprised how quickly I bit. It must have been the easiest night's winding up he'd had for a long time. The referee showed me the red card. It was the fastest sending-off in Champions League history. I was out for another three games.

I felt terrible. I was desperately disappointed with myself. I couldn't believe I had been so stupid. We lost the game 4-1 and I felt totally responsible. Most of the other players were brilliant with me. Alan didn't say anything but then Alan never really did. I just felt I'd let everyone down. I walked through the mixed zone where the players speak to reporters after the game and I took the blame. Not that I had much choice.

I wasn't going to ask for forgiveness or make excuses. But I thought it was right for me to take the brunt of it. I didn't want to hide because I had let everyone down. After the Inter game, I had to face up to everything. It was a tough period but it was my own fault. One of the local radio stations gave me a lot of stick, the local paper ran a page of texts about what an idiot I had been. I had to swallow it. I had had enough praise in the good times.

My form in the league was okay and by Christmas we had

crept up to sixth but I felt sick about being suspended for the Champions League game against Barcelona in the Nou Camp. What a missed opportunity that was. Again, all my own fault. We lost that match but then we beat Leverkusen home and away to give ourselves a chance of qualifying.

I played against Inter in the San Siro and we drew 2-2. My pal Materazzi wasn't playing this time and I managed to avoid getting sent off. I set up our first for Alan and we went into the last game at home to Barcelona with an outside chance of making it into the quarter-finals. I missed a couple of good chances early on and when I did get a shot on target, Victor Valdes pushed it on to the post.

We pressed and pressed but Xavi and Gaizka Mendieta began to take control and Patrick Kluivert put them ahead after an hour. I missed a chance to equalise, then hit the bar before Thiago Motta put the game out of reach 15 minutes from the end. Nothing had gone my way but then perhaps I didn't really deserve any luck. It felt like karma. I was being punished for my two red cards. The adventure was over.

14

Club And Country

By the time we were knocked out of the Champions League, I had become consumed with worry about the state of my knees. Sometimes, I think people simply don't understand how an injury can take over a player's life and dominate everything. That's what it did to me. It even got to the point where the pain was so bad I felt I had to make a choice between Newcastle and Wales.

My mental state was up and down non-stop. I wasn't sure how much time I had left in my career so I didn't feel like I could look ahead. Tendinitis in the patella tendon is difficult to cope with. One minute you feel good and the next day you feel you can't decelerate.

It feels like someone is digging a needle into your knee when you run. Because I am an explosive player and I decelerate fast and twist and turn, it was the worst thing for me. Closing players down is a big part of my game but my confidence about my ability to do that was shot to pieces.

In many ways, it happened at the worst time for me, too. For the first time since I had been involved with the Wales team, it felt as if we had a genuine chance of qualifying for a major tournament. Things had improved beyond measure since Mark Hughes took over from Bobby Gould in 1999 and even though we had struggled to make any impression in qualifying for the 2002 World Cup, we felt we had the players and the belief to make it to Portugal in 2004.

Sparky went out on a limb to get me flown out to Finland for the first of those Euro 2004 qualifiers and it paid off. We won the game 2-0 and even though I only came off the bench for the last 15 minutes, the fact that I was there at all was the final proof that the days of farce and amateurism under Bobby Gould were over. We were serious now and that fed into our performances.

A month after we won in Helsinki, we played Italy at the Millennium Stadium in front of a capacity crowd of 70,000 fans. It was an amazing atmosphere and the Italy team was every bit as impressive as it was when I had been dazzled by them a few years earlier in Bologna. It was still full of football gods: Buffon, Cannavaro, Nesta, Del Piero and Pirlo. What a team.

But this time, we were prepared. We weren't in chaos. Nobody had been banished from the team hotel. We didn't play charades any more. Sparky didn't have wrestling matches with the centre forward. We prepared well and we had good players and we set about Italy with real purpose and verve.

We took the lead early. I made a bit of a break down the right after a nice pass from Simon Davies. I turned inside my man and slipped a ball back to Davies, who had timed his run well. He ran on to it and it sat up nicely for him. Buffon may have been expecting him to cross it but he took it early and lashed it past him into the far corner.

The stadium went wild but they equalised after half an hour. They won a free-kick on the edge of the box and every time that happened, we knew it spelt danger because of Del Piero's excellence with the dead ball. I was so angry about the decision to award the free-kick that I was booked for protesting. It was utterly pointless. It wasn't a Del Piero masterpiece this time but it deflected off Mark Delaney's head and looped over Paul Jones into the net.

But we didn't fade. Our heads didn't go down. We kept going. Ryan Giggs hit the underside of the Italy bar with a brilliant free-kick and then, 20 minutes from the end, John Hartson played me in on Buffon with a clever pass that dissected Cannavaro and Nesta. My pace took me away from them and as Buffon rushed out, I nudged the ball around him. I took one touch, slid the ball into the net and then let the mayhem wash over me.

That was one of the best nights of my career. Not just because I scored the winner and it was the first time Wales had beaten a leading nation in a competitive match for a long while but because we deserved it, too. Probably 90 per cent of the games I won with Wales, our keeper had had a great night. But the victory over Italy wasn't like that. Giovanni Trapattoni, the Italy manager, said afterwards that they were lucky they only lost 2-1.

I missed the next qualifier, a 2-0 win over Azerbaijan in Baku at the end of November, because of my knee problems. I had just scored the winner against Feyenoord but Sir Bobby knew how much I was struggling and he kept me out. It was billed as a club versus country row but I couldn't have played. I was in too much pain. After the high of the victory over Italy, Wales fans were not happy.

"I've had some unbelievably rude faxes from Wales," Sir Bobby said at the time. "I understand their frustration but they don't know the facts and they shouldn't waste our time. They're crucifying us for not letting Craig go, but he's been out for seven months.

"He wasn't fit at the start of the season, he's played and had a reaction, and he's been away for three weeks getting right again. I would have loved Mark Hughes to have Craig available. He played against Feyenoord but he would have told you himself that he couldn't have played against Azerbaijan."

Still, we had three victories from three games. It was great to be involved in a national sct-up surrounded by optimism at last. The next competitive fixture was in March 2003, at home to Azerbaijan, but by the time it arrived, I was battling with new issues.

My nan had just died suddenly and even though I'd driven down to Cardiff through the night in the immediate aftermath, I'd never had a chance to grieve properly. The games were coming thick and fast. Football doesn't stop. I didn't even go to her funeral because my dad thought I would become the centre of attention and it might turn into a bit of a circus.

I was really cut up about my nan. I'd been really close to her. She was a big part of my childhood. Sometimes, a football pitch can be an escape from that sort of grief but sometimes it can be a cruel place, too. Newcastle played Charlton at The Valley soon after she died that March and there was a point in the match where we were leading 2-0 and I ran on to a through ball but was flagged for being offside. The Charlton goalkeeper, Dean Kiely, seemed to think I was going to kick the ball back to him but I left it so I could get back in position.

"I hope your fucking mum dies of cancer," he blurted out as he ran past.

I've heard that kind of stuff from fans before but I had never had it from an opposing player. I had to turn around to make sure he had said it.

"You wait," I mouthed at him.

My head had totally gone. It was all I was thinking about. I went straight over to him at the final whistle. He wouldn't even look at me. He tried to get out of my way. John Carver tried to get in between us but I followed him down to the tunnel and he went out of sight.

The following Monday, I read some interviews he'd done in the papers where he was talking about how I was always mouthy and lippy but Shearer was the complete gentleman. I knew what he was doing. He was trying to cover himself in case I told everybody what he had said. Nobody knew what he had said to me at that point but he made an oblique reference to it.

"He's a fantastic player but he's not shy and likes to wind people up," Kiely said in his interviews. "But I'm not going to go home worrying what people call my mum or whatever. Maybe he thrives on that sort of thing but it seems to work both ways because you only have to look back to Newcastle's Champions League game against Inter Milan when he got himself sent off.

"I truly believe in karma and if you live doing that sort of thing, the other side will eventually get you back. You've got both ends of the spectrum at Newcastle. On the one hand there's Alan Shearer, who is rightly regarded as an ambassador for the game. And then there's Craig Bellamy."

Karma? What kind of karma do you get from saying you hope someone's mum dies of cancer? I got a number for Kiely from Shay Given.

I rang him in front of a few of the boys when we were in the changing rooms at the Newcastle training ground. I switched it to loud speaker so everyone could hear.

He answered. I got straight into it.

"How dare you say that to me about my mum," I said, "and then try to start covering yourself in case I came out and said something."

"Look, I apologise," Kiely said. "I was up all night thinking about it. I can't believe I said it to you. My auntie died of cancer. I'm in shock I said it to you. All I can do is apologise."

"Yeah, all right," I said. I pressed the red button.

Even now, I can't look at him. Prick. People have him down as this nice guy but what kind of person says that? I was just burying my nan. He wasn't to know that but it doesn't change what he said.

So I was ready to unravel when I got down to Cardiff for the week's build-up to that Azerbaijan game. It was the first proper stay I'd had down there since she died. I went out with Speedo on the Sunday evening. We had earmarked it as our night out before training began in earnest the next day. I drank quite heavily. I started to let it all out, all the grief about my nan. It wasn't the time or the place but it was the first chance

I'd had. We drank on until after midnight and then Speedo said we should get a taxi back to the team hotel at the Vale of Glamorgan.

We were driving through Cardiff city centre on the way back when I saw a crowd of people outside a bar called Jumpin Jaks. I thought there was a place open. I told the cab to stop and opened the door to get out. Speedo told me to get back in but I was gone by then. I wouldn't listen to him. I went to go in and the bouncers said they were shut.

I wouldn't hear it, of course. I insisted there were people in there and that it was my right to go in. The bouncers said again that it was shut. I kept arguing. At that point, one of the bouncers grabbed me and threw me down the stairs leading to the bar. I know Cardiff. That happens. In fact, I was lucky I just got pushed.

Speedo saw what was going on and came and got me. He told me to get back in the cab. But by then, there was no chance of me doing that. I was fuming. I wanted an argument. Speedo knew what I was like. He saw there was no way he was going to convince me, so he got back in the cab and left.

I started having a go at the bouncers. One or two kids who were outside the place started slagging me off. I don't blame them, really. I was acting like an idiot. Anyway, I told one of the kids to fuck off and things looked like they were going to get totally out of hand. At that point, a couple of other lads appeared and said they were staying in my hotel. They said they had a cab waiting and they'd give me a lift.

I'd had enough by then. I'd reached my limit. I didn't want any more hassle. I felt weary all of a sudden. So I got in their cab. I had never met those lads before and I have never met them again to this day but in the cab on the way back to the hotel, I started crying. I was wailing about what the hell I was doing down there when I should be with my kids and my girl-friend. It was all coming out. Those lads must have wondered what the hell was happening. We arrived back at the hotel and they helped me into reception and said goodbye.

I went back to my room and I got it into my head that I was going back to Newcastle and that I didn't want to play for Wales on Saturday. I was not in a fit state of mind, my knees weren't great, I didn't want to play. I rang Speedo and he told me to meet him in reception. Soon, Mark Hughes and his assistant, Mark Bowen, were there, too. It was 2am by now and they were all trying to convince me to stay.

But I was adamant I was going home. I rang my dad and told him to come and pick me up and take me up to Newcastle. I told him I didn't want to play for Wales again. It was like a drunk stream of consciousness. Sparky told me to go to bed and sleep on it. He said if I still wanted to go back to Newcastle tomorrow, he would drive me up himself. He knew I'd change my mind in the morning. They all knew what had happened with my nan and they knew the state I was in.

Speedo was begging me. He said I could sleep in his room but I wouldn't have any of it. My dad arrived and he told me to listen to them. But I refused and in the end, he agreed to take me. So we drove all the way back to Newcastle. I slept most of the way. We got there at dawn. Claire was astonished to see me.

I was still half drunk. I was warbling on about my knee and concentrating on Newcastle, which was what Bobby Robson always used to say I should do. I went to bed for a few hours, woke up about 11am and thought 'what the hell have I done?'

I rang Bobby Robson and went to see him at the training ground. At first, he was saying 'you can stay here, son'. But in the end he saw that I was full of remorse and that I was worried about what I'd done.

"You better get your arse back down there then, son," he said.

I knew I had to go back. I apologised to Sir Bobby and then I rang Sparky and apologised to him, too. He just laughed.

"I knew this was going to happen," he said. "See you tonight."

But it wasn't over. If only it had been that simple. My dad drove me back down to Cardiff and during the journey, the radio news was reporting that the police were looking to question me over an incident that happened outside a nightclub in the early hours of the morning in Cardiff.

I was puzzled as well as concerned. I could remember getting pushed down the stairs but not much else. I knew I hadn't been in a fight. When I got back to the Vale of Glamorgan, Sparky said the police wanted to speak to me and the next day I went to be interviewed at the police station.

They started asking me how much I earned and stuff like that. I had a solicitor down from London. They said a complaint had been made that I racially abused a young teenager. That was news to me. I denied it. I gave my side of the story and the police guy said to me afterwards that a kid had made a complaint but that he hadn't been particularly convincing.

"Good luck on Saturday," he said, as I was leaving.

I thought it was over and done with but in the next couple of days, it was claimed I had called the kid a 'fucking Paki'. That wasn't true but the allegations dragged on until the case went to court more than six months later. Newcastle defended me, up to a point. They said I was 'a rascal, not a racist'. When it came to court, the kid didn't even turn up but because I had admitted I had sworn, I was convicted of using foul and abusive language and fined £750.

So this time, I suppose it was me who injected the element of farce into the preparation for a Wales game. Thankfully, it didn't have any lasting effect. There was a brilliant atmosphere at the Millennium again, 70,000 for a game against Azerbaijan. We were 3-0 up at half-time and 4-0 up after an hour. I got a nasty kick on the knee early in the second half but we had already made one substitution and so I had to stay on for as long as possible. It was frustrating because there were goals to be had but I could hardly run, let alone shoot.

By the time I got back to Newcastle I was a bit of a wreck. My tendinitis was bad and now I had a heavy knock, too. I had heavy strapping on for the game against Everton at Goodison Park the following weekend. I was desperate to play in that, too, because we had won nine of our last 12 games in the Premier League and moved up to third place, five points behind Arsenal and three behind Manchester United.

But we lost at Everton, beaten by a header from a young Wayne Rooney and a David Unsworth penalty. The next weekend, we were battered 6-2 by United at St James' Park and the weekend after that, we lost to Fulham at Craven Cottage. Any faint hope we had had of snatching the title had gone but we went unbeaten in our last four games and held off Chelsea to finish third.

Newcastle were very aware of the fact that I was struggling with knee problems. I thought I needed an operation on both of them. But Wales had crucial matches against Serbia and Montenegro, at the end of August, and Italy at the beginning of September that would decide whether we qualified for the Euros. I knew that if I had knee operations at the end of the Premier League season, I would miss those games. I wanted to play those Wales matches and then go for surgery.

That would mean I would miss most of the 2003-04 Premier League season but it also meant I'd be fit for the Euros in Portugal in the summer of 2004. I was so close to playing in the European Championships and I didn't know if I'd ever get as good a chance to get Wales to a major tournament again.

It meant I would be putting Newcastle second, which ate away at me, but that was the sacrifice I was prepared to make. Newcastle told me I needed the operation on my knees straight away. I told them I was fine. They knew what the score was, I think. They knew I was looking at the bigger picture.

I went to Malaysia on pre-season tour with Newcastle and played a game against Birmingham City. I was in almighty pain after that game. I couldn't even sleep. Both patella tendons were killing me. All that was going through my head was that I would have to retire. I just thought maybe I could have one big game against Italy and then play in the Euros and that would be the end for me. I knew I was becoming a shadow of the player I once was.

We lost 1-0 to Serbia and Montenegro in Red Star's stadium in Belgrade. It was a blow but Serbia were not a danger to us by then. It was all about the Italy game for me. When the Premier League season started, I played in the opening game against Leeds and had little impact. I had bandages around both knees. I was a mess. It was obvious I wasn't right and, once again, I was in agony after the game.

I needed the operation straight away but I wanted to hold

out for another few weeks. We played Partizan Belgrade in the qualifying round of the Champions League and beat them 1-0. I didn't think they had any chance of beating us back at St James' Park. I thought we'd be way too strong. So I pulled out of the second leg. We lost the game 1-0 and then went out on penalties. 'What the fuck have I done?' I thought.

Wales' defeat to Serbia and Montenegro was on August 20. The crunch game against Italy was set for September 6 at the San Siro in Milan. I knew that if I had any chance of being even close to my best for the Italy game, I couldn't play again in the build-up to it. So I missed the second leg against Partizan and the home Premier League games against Manchester United and Birmingham City. We lost them all. By the time the Italy game came around, we were out of the Champions League and bottom of the Premier League.

Freddy Shepherd, understandably, was not particularly happy. He moaned at me about my involvement with Wales. He said it was obvious that I needed an operation and that I could not join up with the national team again until I had played for Newcastle. He said now that we had been eliminated from the Champions League, it was the ideal time to go and get my knees cleaned up.

But I was solely focused on my country. I knew what I was doing was essentially unfair to Newcastle, but I was desperate to play in the Euros. So I tried to appease Newcastle by starting to train again. But the club insisted I couldn't play for Wales unless I played for Newcastle first and I knew that if I played in the game against Birmingham, I would be in too much pain to play against Italy. My knees had got so bad, I needed more than a week's recovery time after every match.

Newcastle banned me from playing and got a solicitor to write to the Welsh FA. They warned Wales that if I joined up with them, they would sue the Welsh FA. I joined up anyway and Wales sent me to see an independent surgeon. The surgeon barely looked at me and gave me the okay. Wales said I was fine. Freddy Shepherd was furious. He said I'd never play for Newcastle again. It was a fraught situation.

Once the independent surgeon had passed me fit, there was not a lot Newcastle could do. I flew to Milan with Wales to prepare for the biggest international match of my career. My knees felt okay. They'd had a decent amount of rest. I knew it would be tough in the San Siro but our confidence was high. We knew how much was riding on it. Even for a player like Ryan Giggs, it was probably the best chance he was ever going to have of playing in a major tournament.

Giggs nearly scored early on but Buffon saved his volley after he had intercepted a poor headed backpass from Panucci. We fought hard in the first half, literally in my case. I got involved in a bit of a shoving match with Buffon after he reacted angrily to a tackle from John Hartson and we both got booked. It meant I'd be suspended for the following Wednesday's game against Finland in Cardiff.

There was still everything to play for at half-time. They had hit the woodwork a couple of times and we were riding our luck but the prize was still there. But 13 minutes into the second half, Del Piero headed towards goal, Vieri volleyed against the crossbar and Filippo Inzaghi swept the rebound into the open goal. Then the floodgates opened.

Inzaghi scored again with a close-range volley four minutes later and completed an 11-minute hat-trick with a superb turn and finish. Del Piero finished us off with a penalty. It was a bad night. Italy were top of the group now. Yellow cards meant Robbie Savage, Mark Delaney and I would all miss the Finland game. We realised we were probably playing for a place in the play-offs now.

I felt crushed. I had been building everything towards that night, sacrificing everything in the hope that we could get a result against Italy and now we had been beaten out of sight. I didn't have much impact, either. Not really. I felt like I'd let everybody down in the end.

Italy could only manage a draw against Serbia in Belgrade four days later, which meant that victory for us over Finland the same night would put us back in control of the group. Simon Davies put us ahead very early in front of yet another capacity crowd but we could not hang on. Eleven minutes from time, Mikael Forssell grabbed an equaliser. It was heartbreaking. It was out of our hands.

I held on for another month until the game against Serbia and Montenegro in Cardiff in mid-October. I played for Newcastle against Everton at Goodison and we finally got our first point of the season. Despite the result we were bottom of the table and Sir Bobby Robson was forced to deny rumours that he had resigned. We drew at home to Bolton and lost at Arsenal and then, a week before the Serbia tie, we finally got our first win of the season with a 1-0 win over Southampton.

Then it was Serbia. It felt like I had to make one last push to play in that game and hope beyond hope that we won and Italy slipped up at home to Azerbaijan. It didn't work out like that. There was no pressure on the Serbs because they knew they could not qualify and so they played with freedom. We lost a silly early goal when a free-kick squirmed past Paul Jones but then Harts equalised with a penalty.

By the second half, though, we knew that the Italians were 2-0 up against the Azeris and we faded away. Savo Milosevic put the Serbs ahead eight minutes from the end and they scored a third before Rob Earnshaw got a consolation for us with a header. But that was it. We had finished second in the group, four points behind Italy, who had beaten Azerbaijan 4-0.

We drew Russia in the play-offs but they were a month away and I knew I couldn't make it. I couldn't go on playing any more. Every time I played, it was like torture. In my absence, Wales drew 0-0 with Russia in Moscow and then fell to a 1-0 defeat in the second leg in Cardiff. I didn't go to the game. I probably should have done but I was so down and depressed that I didn't want to risk visiting my mood on any of the other lads. I watched it at home in Newcastle. When the final whistle went, it was heart-wrenching.

There was a late chance of a reprieve when it emerged that one of the Russians, Egor Titov, had failed a drugs test before the second leg. It turned out to be false hope. "In reviewing the case," Uefa said, "the Uefa Control and Disciplinary Body made reference to the FAW's failure to provide evidence that the player was under the influence of a prohibited substance in the second-leg match. In addition, and according to Uefa regulations in the case of a doping offence, the punishment anyway only applies to the player himself and not to the team."

So that was it. My best chance of playing in a major tournament was gone. I tried to put it behind me and concentrate on rescuing my career. I flew to Colorado after the defeat to Serbia and had an operation on my left knee and a course of heavy friction on my right knee. They said I'd be out for four months.

In some ways, it was a blow. In others, it was relief. I had been in so much pain, I had been trying to satisfy so many people, that it had worn me down. I was trying to do my duty for my country and respect the people who paid my wages but in the end I wasn't doing anybody any favours. Not Wales and certainly not Newcastle. All I'd done, actually, was make myself look like an idiot.

15

Change At The Top

Before I had even left America after the knee operations, I got a message saying that Freddy Shepherd wanted to see me as soon as I got back. I knew it was going to be interesting. I went into his office on crutches. He barely looked at me. He barked 'sit there' at me. I didn't know what to do with my crutches. I didn't want to lay them on his oak table so I left them on the floor.

He didn't mince his words. He said everyone on the board wanted me out of the club and so did he. They had run out of patience with me, he said.

"I know what you did," he said. "But did Wales pay for you to go to America for your knee operation? Did Wales pay the surgeon's fees? No, of course they didn't. So you better make sure you work your arse off to come back as good as you were before because if you don't, we will get rid of you as fast as we can. And I don't care how much we get for you or who buys you."

For once, I didn't have a lot to say. I knew I wasn't in a position to have a go back at him so I just sat there and took it.

"Get out of my office," he said, and I picked up my crutches and left as fast as I could.

I was in a bit of a daze. I was so down and depressed that I had no fight left in me. I was 24 years old and I'd had four knee operations. Because my ambitions were ridiculously high, I put too much pressure on myself to try to fulfil them and if I didn't, I saw myself as a failure at everything. It's a difficult way to go about your life.

I withdrew from everyone. I never went out with the rest of the players any more. I knocked all that on the head because drink was the last thing my tendons needed. I just felt isolated. I wasn't socialising with anyone any more. I would come in to the training ground and hardly speak. And if I did speak, I didn't have anything nice to say because I was feeling so bitter.

During my rehab, I made a conscious decision that I would come in later in the day when all the other lads had left training. And that's what I did. I didn't see anyone. I just knuckled down. I had my two boys, I had Claire, we had a lovely new house over near Morpeth and I focused on them and stuck my head in rehab.

I just wanted to come back strong and playing properly again. I wanted to play without constant pain. I heard horror stories about what had happened to the careers of players who had troubles with patella tendons. The Brazilian Ronaldo's was the worst. They blighted his career. Those stories, and the idea that I might never be the player I once was, tormented me.

Christmas was just a blur. God knows how Claire put up with me. I wouldn't go anywhere because I didn't want to bump into anyone. I was afraid I was cracking up because of what the injuries had done to me. But after a couple of months, I began to feel a little more optimistic. I started to jog and it felt different. My right knee felt good because of the friction I had done on it. That treatment numbs your nerve endings and stops the pain. Actually, I started to feel great. I was just praying it lasted.

For once, I was waking up in the mornings without being crippled by pain. Until then, I'd been waking up in the middle of the night and my knees had felt like they were on fire. But now they felt normal again. I played one reserve game and it went well. I felt like I could be a good player again.

I played my first match for Newcastle for nearly four months on the last day of January 2004, against Birmingham City at St Andrew's. I came on for the last 15 minutes and it felt like the beginning of a second chance. I came on for the last 11 minutes of the game against Leicester City at St James' Park the following weekend and that was emotional, too.

Then I got my first start against Blackburn Rovers at Ewood Park and scored a volley in a 1-1 draw. I was absolutely flying by then. I was just so grateful to be back. Lucas Neill tackled me hard just before half-time and I was worried for a little while and disappeared for some treatment in the changing rooms.

I don't think people expected me to come back on after half-time but I actually felt encouraged by the fact that my knee had stood up to the challenge and seven minutes into the second half, I put us ahead after a mistake by Brad Friedel. I celebrated that goal like a madman. It was my first in the Premier League for 11 months.

While I had been gone, the team had recovered from our dreadful start and that draw at Blackburn moved us into fifth place in the table, level on points with fourth-placed Liverpool in the race for the final Champions League spot. Arsenal were in their Invincibles season and they, Manchester United and Chelsea were out of sight but we were confident we could finish above Liverpool.

I was thrilled to be back but then there was another setback. Quite soon after my return, I was involved in an argument with the club doctor and he went straight to Freddy. I was summoned to his office again. He said it was obvious I had not listened to a word he had said during our last meeting and that he had enough. But I wasn't going to sit there and take it this time. This time, I was ready for him.

"You talk all this talk about how you'll get rid of me," I told him, "but as long as I am at this football club, the manager will play me. I bet you any money. If I don't play and I am sat on the bench, the crowd will sing my name. And I will tell them why I am not coming on, because you are not allowing it. And you answer to them. Otherwise, bring my value down and let me go to a club I want to go to."

I thought he was going to come back at me all guns blazing. I was expecting a full-on argument. I was relishing it. I was thinking 'don't threaten me, fucking act'. But he took me by surprise.

"That's exactly the response I would have given," he said, beaming. "That's the player I want. Now you're fighting. That's the player we bought."

I was stunned. It was obvious Freddy considered the meeting over so I went to shake his hand as I was leaving.

He stopped me. "No," he said, waving away my hand. "Hug."

So I gave him a hug and as I was hugging him I was thinking 'is he for fucking real?'

I scored four goals in my first seven games back and we were neck and neck with Liverpool for fourth place. But the mood at the club had changed while I had been injured. There was a lot more talk about how Sir Bobby had lost the dressing room and the fans seemed discontented with the fact that we were not challenging for the title.

The rumours about Sir Bobby losing the dressing room simply weren't true but circumstances around us had changed. Roman Abramovich had taken over at Chelsea and was pumping money into the club. Liverpool had staged a recovery and were stiff competition again. Arsenal were better than ever. Manchester United would continue to be out of our reach.

So the top four was the limit of our ambition as far as the Premier League went and after the previous two seasons, the Newcastle fans struggled to adapt to that. Freddy Shepherd was scathing about the players, too. He said we had Rolls Royce facilities but we were playing like Minis. Despite the fact that we were among the top sides, there was a lot of dissatisfaction among the supporters.

We made the semi-finals of the Uefa Cup that season, too, but lost to Marseille 2-0 on aggregate after two goals in the second leg from Didier Drogba. I missed that game. In fact, I'd pulled a hamstring against Aston Villa in the middle of April and missed all but the final league game of the season against Liverpool. They were four points ahead of us by then so we could not catch them for fourth. We drew 1-1, finished fifth and qualified for the Uefa Cup.

Fifth wasn't good enough for a lot of people at the club. We had finished fourth and third in the previous two seasons so now the suggestion was that we were going the wrong way. Sir Bobby started getting a lot of the heat, which I found hard to take. He might not have won the title but when you consider where that club was when he took over and how quickly he turned an average team into being one of the top teams in Britain, it was remarkable.

I felt the manager was being undermined. Things started to happen I didn't like at all. Like when Hugo Viana came up to me one day and told me he was going back to Portugal because he hadn't been able to settle in England. We shook hands and then he put his finger to his lips. "You must keep it quiet," he said, "because the manager doesn't know yet."

Other things happened that summer. Early in pre-season, Sir Bobby pulled me and Shola Ameobi to one side and said he wanted to talk to us about the rumours that were circulating that Patrick Kluivert would be joining the club from Barcelona. He said he realised that as strikers, we might both be unsettled by the speculation.

He said that Kluivert would not be joining the club. He said his sources in Barcelona told him Kluivert's knee was not right and he was not living the right life. He said he had been a great player at one time and that he still admired him but he didn't want to buy him. He told us not to worry. A week later, Kluivert signed.

I don't think Kluivert was his signing. I felt he was signed by the board in a misguided attempt to appease the fans because we had not qualified for the Champions League. It worried me because I felt that it lessened Sir Bobby's authority and that he found it hard to take. You could feel that he had less power. I started to wonder how much time he had left as manager of the club and I know I wasn't the only one.

Sir Bobby was openly critical of the decision to sell Jonathan Woodgate to Real Madrid, too. He did an interview in one of the local papers about it which gave an interesting insight into the way his relationship with Freddy Shepherd worked.

"I only heard about this offer at 4.30pm on Wednesday," Sir Bobby told them. "The chairman called me and asked to see me to discuss a private matter. I had no idea what. He then informed me that a bid had come in for Jonathan. I said to him: 'You are aware that I don't want to lose him, aren't you?'

"Then I told him: 'You are aware that we would be losing the finest centre half in this country?

"He replied: 'I realise that.'

"I always wanted to fight and keep him but when Madrid came in, I knew it would be hard. But quite simply, if it had been my choice I would have kept him. Of course I would. We've just lost a great player and just how much of a blow that is depends on who we can get to replace him. Finding a replacement will be very difficult. Why should we pay £12m for a player who isn't as good as Woodgate when we've sold him for £15m?"

There was a feeling of intrigue at the club. The chairman had spoken during the season about how finishing fourth should be the 'bare minimum' achievement and that there would be changes from top to bottom. The feeling at St James' Park had changed. There was a restlessness there now that had not existed before.

All the talk after Kluivert's signing was that he and Shearer were the new dream team in attack. That didn't make me feel particularly great. Even Sir Bobby had told the press Kluivert's arrival was as significant a moment for the club as when Alan had signed. I think he was saying what he had to say.

Shepherd talked about them being the dream team in a television interview, too. 'We'll see about that,' I thought. It wasn't that I had anything against Kluivert, by the way. How could you not be impressed by a player like him coming to your club? He was a lovely guy as well. He oozed class. He could caress the ball. He was another level from most of us in terms of his quality.

But his knee would blow up whatever he did. Even after training, it would swell. I felt for him because I knew what he must be going through. He was also in the midst of a divorce so he did a reasonable amount of partying. I knew if I got my knee right, I would be the main striker, and nailing down that place became my sole focus during pre-season.

We played a friendly against Rangers at St James' Park at the end of July and I started up front alongside Alan. Darren Ambrose got injured early on and Sir Bobby asked me to play on the left but I said I'd rather stay up front. I didn't want my versatility to be used as an excuse to accommodate Patrick although he wasn't involved that day. Later in the game, I moved to the left as I was asked. It wasn't a big deal. It was something that Sir Bobby and I discussed and reached an agreement about. He understood where I was coming from.

The biggest problem Sir Bobby had was that he lost Gary Speed that summer, too. Bolton Wanderers were willing to pay £750,000 for him and the chairman thought it was good business. He wanted to get Nicky Butt in from Manchester United and so Speedo went to Bolton. It was only when he had gone that most people realised what a huge gap he had left.

Speedo was the law in the changing room. When he spoke, he spoke. When he had a go, nobody spoke back to him. We were all in fear of him. He was the strict hard-liner. He would have a laugh and he would have fun but you made sure you worked when he was around and you knew how to work hard. Robson lost that influence when Speedo went and his dressing room changed. Sir Bobby lost his most important lieutenant among the players. If you want to know the moment when Sir Bobby really lost his job, it was the day when Speedo was sold.

With everything that was going on and the lingering sense of disappointment over the fifth-placed finish the previous season, we desperately needed to get off to a good start that season. We knew Sir Bobby was vulnerable but people had left and a lot of new players like Nicky Butt, James Milner and Kluivert had arrived and we were all manoeuvring for position.

The first game of the season was against Middlesbrough at the Riverside but the trouble had started before we kicked off. Sir Bobby asked Kieron to play wide right because he wanted to start Jermaine Jenas and Butt in the centre of midfield.

Kieron said he didn't want to. He knew he was at his best in the middle and he had seen me protest successfully about being played out of position at Rangers and thought he was entitled to do the same.

Things got out of hand this time, though. Sir Bobby refused to budge and dropped Kieron to the bench. Jenas and Butt started and Milner played on the right. I scored early on and Kieron came on for Milner 20 minutes from the end but Jimmy Floyd Hasselbaink grabbed a last-minute equaliser for Middlesbrough that robbed us of the win we needed.

The issue with Kieron wouldn't go away. Sir Bobby tried to cover for him but the news leaked out that Kieron had refused to play on the right and when he played for England in a match against Ukraine at St James' Park the following Wednesday, he was booed every time he touched the ball. A couple of days later he apologised publicly to Sir Bobby.

It wasn't a happy episode but the idea that Kieron was somehow to blame for Sir Bobby's departure was totally false. And the notion that took hold that Kieron was the ringleader of a group who mocked Sir Bobby could not have been further from the truth, either. Kieron idolised him. If anything, as I've said, they were too close. They felt they could be totally honest with each other and when that honesty was expressed in public, others misinterpreted it.

Sir Bobby had a real soft spot for Kieron. Maybe it began as a shared history with Ipswich but they got on great. If Alan wasn't playing or if he was substituted, Sir Bobby would always give the captain's armband to Kieron. So, again, this idea that Sir Bobby had lost the dressing room and there was some kind of players' rebellion led by Kieron was just a joke.

I know Kieron felt guilty about what happened but he wasn't the reason Sir Bobby got sacked. Some people may have used what happened around the Middlesbrough game as a stick to beat Sir Bobby with but there were far deeper reasons behind his exit than that. Everyone was fighting for power. The club was a huge institution in the region and there were people there who wanted praise for the club and where it was. They wanted to pat themselves on the back and they didn't like seeing the manager get all the plaudits.

The weekend after the draw with Middlesbrough, we lost 1-0

at home to Spurs. Then we drew 2-2 at home with Norwich. I scored again in that game against my old team but that was three games without a win and we could all feel the pressure mounting on the manager. The next game was Aston Villa away.

Sir Bobby left Alan on the bench and started with Kluivert alongside me instead. That was a brave move because Alan was like a god on Tyneside. Sir Bobby had accepted a bid from Liverpool for him once but Shepherd had put the block on it. Shearer knew about it but he told us Robson didn't know he knew. Alan wasn't working against him or anything like that but it never felt comfortable between them. They were both idols to the north-east public and the unspoken rivalry between them always seemed to be there.

We played well at Villa and goals from Kluivert and Andy O'Brien put us 2-1 up at half-time. A couple of wins were all we would have needed to take the pressure off. We had been slow starters under Robson before and we would have turned it round again. But Villa fought back and overwhelmed us with a rush of goals from Carlton Cole, Gareth Barry and Juan Pablo Angel. We lost 4-2. We had two points from our opening four games. The knives were out.

I knew things were going to get rough in Newcastle. Sir Bobby had been getting a lot of stick from the fans. People conveniently forget about that now but he was booed and jeered towards the end. The fans wanted him out, too. A lot of them will deny that now but it's the truth. The place went into lockdown. The Sky cameras were outside St James' Park, interviewing people about their club being in crisis. It was only going one way.

The announcement came on the Monday morning after the

Away the lad: My first start in a Newcastle shirt, against Lokeren in the Intertoto Cup in July, 2001. I set up the first two goals in a 4-0 win

Good fellas, good times: Celebrating a goal with Speedo and my close mate Kieron Dyer. There was a good buzz in the Newcastle dressing room

New star: Scoring against the local rivals always makes you popular with the fans. I scored the equaliser at St James' Park against Sunderland in August, 2001, shooting past Thomas Sorensen

Rising star: A piece of silverware at the end of my first season at St James' Park – the PFA Young Player of the Year. Ruud van Nistelrooy was Player of the Year that season

Time out: I enjoyed getting involved with various community projects at Newcastle. Those experiences helped me to grow up

Local hero: Alan Shearer was an incredible talent and we struck up a great partnership on the pitch, even if we were different characters off it

Genius: Bobby Robson keeps a close eye on us during a training session. Sir Bobby knew exactly how to handle players. He was the best manager I have ever worked with

Tyne of my life: The goals kept coming for me as we climbed the Premiership table

Double Dutch: An unforgettable night against Feyenoord. We had one eye on securing a Uefa Cup place but I scored two to help us march on in the Champions League

Controversy: The fans stand up for me after things turn sour behind the scenes

Italian job: Sir Bobby consoles me after I was sent off against Inter Milan following a clash with Marco Materazzi

Iron man: Graeme Souness brought a very different style of management to St James' Park. On one occasion, a comment I made after he brought me off sparked a massive row

Pride of Wales: Celebrating as my goal (above) helped us beat Italy 2-1 on a memorable night at the Millennium Stadium in 2002. Sadly, despite our best efforts, qualification wasn't to be

Reunion: Pulling on a Celtic shirt in 2005 and teaming up with John Hartson again

Dream goal: Celebrating with Chris Sutton after scoring the winner in a 2-1 victory over Rangers at Ibrox – a great feeling

Agony and ecstasy: Being consoled after a late goal saw us lose at Motherwell and hand the Scottish Premier League title to Rangers on the last day. Lifting the Scottish Cup after a 1-0 victory over Dundee United was some consolation

Rover time: Mark Hughes made me believe in myself again. Goals like this one (right) against Portsmouth helped me become Blackburn's Player of the Year

Honour: With Ryan Giggs missing, I captained Wales for the first time in 2006. Ryan's a truly inspirational player who has the qualities to make a great manager one day

Tying the knot
Marrying Claire in 2006

defeat to Villa. I had driven down to Cardiff for a Wales game and I was upstairs at my mum and dad's house when my dad shouted that the television was reporting that Sir Bobby had been sacked. The club had released a statement.

"The directors wish to thank Sir Bobby for the way in which he has worked tirelessly over the past five years to try to bring success to the club," the club statement said. "The club agreed early in 2003 to extend Sir Bobby's contract by one further season. However after careful consideration the club decided it was in the best interest of all concerned to revisit that decision. The club will no doubt continue to benefit from the knowledge and experience he has given during his time here."

I knew it had been coming but I was still distraught. He was such a clever man. The best for man-management I ever came across. His whole aim was to get you playing well on a Saturday and he would do whatever it took to achieve that. All the bother I had at Newcastle, I never once felt I was the one to blame. He made me feel like it was everyone else. And that made me want to do well for him even more than I had before. I felt the same warmth towards him I would feel towards a grandfather.

I still felt I had let him down, though, whatever he might have said to me. I knew some of the things I'd done. Even that season, I looked at myself and thought 'could I have done anything different?' We were 2-0 up against Norwich and I hit the bar. If I'd scored then, we would have won that game instead of sliding to a 2-2 draw. But I think by then, the decision to get rid of him had effectively been made.

After the Wales game, I went back up to Newcastle. John Carver was going to be in charge of the home game against Blackburn that weekend but by then, we all knew that Graeme

Souness was going to replace Sir Bobby. Souness had quit as Blackburn manager and it had been agreed he would take over after his old side played his new one.

I was at the training ground on Thursday when I saw Sir Bobby leaving. I found it uncomfortable going to speak to him but I knew I had to. I didn't feel I had let him down behaviourally but I did know that I owed him a great debt of gratitude. The guy signed me and he created the conditions for me to play some of the best football of my career. I loved playing for him and the older I get, the more I realise just what a clever individual he was.

When I was saying goodbye to him, it hit me I was never going to get the chance to play for him again and I felt sad for that because I had enjoyed it immensely. I thanked him for bringing me to the club and for making me the player I was. I told him he was the man most responsible for turning me into that player.

"They think the world of you here, son," he said. "You're a cracking player. Go and have a good career."

Part of me wanted to hug him but I just shook his hand. I began to feel bitter about what had happened to him. He was 71 years old. He was one of the greatest football managers this country had ever produced.

He had been in charge at Newcastle for five years. And yet now, even as he was leaving, there was already another guy waiting to walk into the building.

16

Man In The Mask

Graeme Souness was the new boss. He was like this iron fist. Bang. Straight down. Everybody said he'd been brought in to deal with the trouble-makers and sort out the lack of discipline at the club. He was the hard man who was coming in to sort out the spoilt little rich kids. That's what they said. He was a good manager but it felt like he came in to Newcastle with the wrong mindset. He came in wanting a fight. He wanted to make an example of somebody. I was bitter about what happened to Sir Bobby and I appreciate now that my feelings affected the way I treated the new boss. That was a bit unfair on Souness. It wasn't his fault.

Souness had been offered a great opportunity to manage a big club. He had done well at Blackburn. He was one of the most immense players there has ever been. He deserved his shot at Newcastle, but that didn't alter the fact that I struggled to deal with the change.

Training was different. We had a great sports scientist and he was sidelined. Souness didn't use him. John Carver was sent straight back to the Academy, too. I felt those guys deserved better. But I suppose that was none of my business. I wasn't the boss. It wasn't my decision. As a player, you have to adapt to a new manager because if you don't, you're gone. And I didn't adapt.

I wouldn't say I was actively resentful towards Souness. But I wasn't engaged. I wasn't very approachable when he was around. We would snap at each other at times over the silliest things. Like a decision in training, a foul he might give against me in a five-a-side, something innocuous like that. He tried to wind me up, messing about like it was fun. But I wasn't getting involved in any of his attempts at jollity and he could sense it.

I felt my time at the club was over. I felt I needed to improve as a player and I didn't think Newcastle offered me that any more. My restlessness was kicking in. It wasn't just losing Robson, I had lost Speedo as well and I still felt a bit bitter about that. Speedo was like a yardstick for me. He was an authority figure who gave me unstinting support. It was different without him and not in a good way.

I needed to do something different. I started to feel disgusted with myself. I didn't like how my life had become at Newcastle. I didn't like the person I had become. When you play well for Newcastle, it is an incredible city and it offers you incredible opportunities. Off the pitch opportunities, I mean.

Imagine being a young kid doing really well, playing at the

top of your game in a city that worships its football team. I was going out once or twice a week and you can't do that if you want to keep playing at the top level. My body started to remind me of that. I began picking up more and more niggling injuries.

But I had also started to believe a bit of the hype that now surrounded me. People kept coming up to me and telling me how great I was and I had begun to believe it. All my old self-doubt, all the worries about my deficiencies that used to torture me, floated away on a tide of flattery. I allowed myself to start thinking I was an incredible player.

I didn't like the individual I became then. I became arrogant. I hated the way I was behaving off the pitch. All the temptations that were thrown at me, I didn't turn my back on them. I began to hate myself and I began to push the people close to me even further away.

I have always been a little bit of a hermit. I have always kept myself at arm's length from everyone. It's nothing personal. It's just how I deal with situations. If I've got a problem, I won't come and talk to you about it. I keep a lot of things to myself. Because I was full of self-loathing, that got worse.

If I did have a problem with my knee, it would send me into a spiral of depression. There would be weeks, sometimes months, when I couldn't get myself out of it. I didn't want to speak to anyone. I didn't want to socialise. Claire often couldn't get two words out of me. I feel for the kids because I should have been more approachable but I didn't know any other way to deal with it.

I suppose that was one of the indicators of my self-loathing. There were others. There were no pictures of me in the house where we lived in Newcastle. I couldn't walk along a corridor and see myself in a picture. I couldn't look at myself in the mirror. I didn't like what I saw. I looked into that face and saw a man I really didn't like.

I knew my life needed to change. I knew I needed a different avenue. I didn't like some of the things I did off the pitch. I didn't like some of the decisions I made. I have never touched drugs since my boy was born, I am not a gambler, booze can come or go. I can go months without it. But I like other things as well. There have always been women and I didn't like that. I hated that weakness in myself.

I felt I was not being honest, not just with the people closest to me but with myself too. The realisation of that was difficult for me to grasp. I was cutting corners and I hate cutting corners and it was leading into my personal life and eating into me.

The adulation of the fans seeped into every part of me. My wife was ready to leave me. She was aware of what was going on. This wasn't the father I wanted to be. It wasn't the individual I wanted to be. I wanted a future with my children. I wanted my children in my life constantly but I was behaving in a way that was jeopardising that.

I wanted to leave. It wasn't to do with Souness or the club. I just didn't like who I had become and the strain it put on my partner and my children. I needed to get out of Newcastle. I could feel myself losing my own discipline. If I wanted to be the best I could be, I knew I had to take another step. I knew the nights out and the womanising had to stop and I had to take a proper look at myself. It wasn't the path I wanted to go down.

I hate it when I look back on it because it seems boastful and boorish but you want to know how it could sometimes feel living the life of a footballer at that time? It felt like this. It felt like the scene in GoodFellas where Henry Hill takes his new girlfriend into the Copacabana Club. The soundtrack has The Crystals singing 'And Then He Kissed Me'. Henry Hill leaves his car with a valet. Then he walks across the road, skirts a long queue of people waiting to get into the club and walks in through a side door.

"I like going in this way," he says to his girlfriend, "it's better than waiting in line."

Then they go down a flight of stairs and doors swing open as if by magic. And he presses some money into a guy's hand and walks through some more doors and everybody's smiling at him and joking with him and they walk through the kitchens and out into the club. The maître d' stops talking to the guests he's with and comes straight over. A waiter appears carrying a table with a clean white tablecloth already laid out on it. And the table is carried to the front of the stage.

Henry Hill and his girlfriend sit down. Everybody's still smiling at him. Guests at other tables get up to greet him. Then somebody sends over a bottle of champagne. His girlfriend smiles this kind of smile of wonder. She can't help but be impressed. It feels like he's some sort of royalty in here. And then a comedian called the King of the One Liners comes on.

And that was what it could be like for me in Newcastle when I got carried away with it. An anglicised version of the Copacabana Club. I knew it was wrong and I'm not saying I behaved like that all the time. But it was easy to get caught up in it.

English football was still in the midst of its post-Taylor Report explosion. Football was king. It felt like we could do what we liked, go where we liked. Not queue for anything, ever. Not play by the rules normal people played by. It was intoxicating. But it was also corrosive.

Reality has to check in at one time or another, though, and then you're probably going to be in trouble. I'd got the balance of my life totally wrong. I didn't trust anyone. I had good friends but I hadn't seen them for ages. I have always dealt with my issues on my own, probably because I moved away from home at such a young age. I had no one else around me. I didn't address any of the issues that were eating me up behind all the false smiles and the laughter.

I should have spoken to someone. My partner, perhaps. Or rung my parents up. I didn't do any of that. Psychologists would say I internalised everything. I didn't share anything. Ever. I was thinking 'because I am not bringing football home with me, I am a good man'. But I did nothing but bring it home. I might not have talked about it but it was eating me up.

If something had happened in training that I thought should not have happened, I wouldn't sleep. I thought that was what gave me the edge or made me a better player because I had that self-criticism. I was trying to suppress the fear that one day, someone was going to find me out. They're going to point and say 'actually, he's not very good'.

In Newcastle, for the first time, I felt I had been found out. I had been found out as an individual and as a player. I wasn't nearly as good as I thought I was and I wasn't the man I thought I was. Nowhere near. I didn't have Robson to give me the confidence any more, I didn't have Speedo who could check me in discipline-wise. I thought 'shit, I'm done'.

I thought I was being transported back to the player I was in my year at Coventry. I began to think that was the real me, the real player. I worked hard there but I didn't make much of an impact. So maybe the last couple of years at Newcastle, the good years, were just a fluke. I thought my mask had slipped and that people would start to see that my excellence was just an illusion.

My love for Newcastle ebbed away. I didn't like the chairman. I had lost Robson, who I thought was the best manager in the world. I had lost Speedo. My professionalism had come from him. I had watched him, trained with him, enjoyed trying to copy him. I just stopped enjoying it. I felt I was adrift.

Souness did things differently to Robson. Of course he did. Again, that wasn't his fault. But it added to my sense of dislocation. He was actually a lot less strict than Robson had been in many ways. He was relaxed about a lot of things off the pitch. He had a great aura about him, too. Sometimes he could be a little bit too derogatory about the opposition and to you as well. He could put you down and question you as an individual.

It must have been difficult for someone like him to coach players like me because he was such a good footballer himself. He didn't join in training with us, which was probably a good thing as far as my physical safety was concerned. I think he stopped that after he had a disagreement with Dwight Yorke during a five-a-side at Blackburn and left him with a badly gashed shin.

He was accused of threatening to break Yorke's leg. I can believe that. If he'd still been playing, I think I would have got the full treatment in training. He would have had a lot of fun with me. If he could have caught me. Generally, we were at loggerheads but I played my part in us not getting on. And if I met him now, I'd shake his hand.

He played me on the wing at Newcastle. He made it clear to

me he didn't see me as a striker. He called me in and said his idea of a striker was Didier Drogba, big and strong. He wanted Kluivert and Shearer as his two forwards. He asked me to play wide. He was trying to fit me in until an opportunity came for me to try and take it.

In the middle of October, we played Charlton at The Valley in a live Sky Sunday game and he gave me a chance to play up front with Alan because Kluivert had got injured. Charlton has always been a good ground for me and I scored six minutes before half-time to put us ahead. Then, midway through the second half, Souness made a substitution and I saw my number come up.

I was furious. I just didn't expect to be coming off. They had equalised by then but the game was open and I thought we could win it. The Newcastle fans weren't happy when they saw I was being taken off. Shola Ameobi came on for me and when I got to the touchline, Souness was staring out at the pitch. I looked over at him and muttered 'fucking prick' in his direction. I didn't exactly say it to him. Not really loud enough for him to hear anyway. But the cameras caught me doing it. I had no right to say it. It was stupid.

Souness didn't see it or hear it but when he spoke to the journalists from the daily papers after the game, they told him about it. He looked surprised at first, apparently, and then he began to look angry. I don't blame him, really. I would have been angry, too.

Nothing was said on the journey back to Newcastle but when we went back into training on Tuesday, there was a team meeting. Dean Saunders, who was one of Souness's backroom staff, told me that if Souness had a go at me in the meeting, I should take it on the chin. I didn't like Saunders but it was probably good advice. I didn't take it.

Sure enough, at the meeting Souness started yelling at me. He mentioned a few of the trophies he had won, for a start. And he listed a few of the clubs he had played for.

"And then someone like you calls me 'a fucking prick'," he said. "I'll fucking knock you out."

He was absolutely raging. He came over to where I was sitting and tried to grab me. I pushed his hand away and he lost his balance slightly and stumbled. That made a couple of the other boys laugh which made Souness even more furious than he was anyway.

"In the gym now," he said. "Me and you."

I couldn't believe what was happening. He was going nuts.

"What are you on about?" I said. "I'm not going to go in the gym to fight you."

He didn't say anything else. He just stormed out.

I apologised later for what I'd said to him at Charlton. I meant it, too. I was out of order. He told the press he had taken me off because I had played two games for Wales the previous week and he wanted to save my legs. He said he wanted to persevere with me. He said I was 'a cracking little player'. It was good to hear but we flew to Greece the afternoon after our row in the team meeting for a Uefa Cup match against Panionios and we never really spoke properly again.

I just wanted to get to January so that I could move away and begin my career afresh somewhere else. I knew Souness wanted me out and I wanted to go. It was a shame. I do have a lot of respect for him as a manager. He has given a lot to the game and I still think he has a lot to give even now.

Freddy Shepherd consistently said I was not for sale and I wasn't going anywhere on loan.

But I got a different impression from the manager. January came around and one day I was sitting in the canteen at the training ground reading the newspapers before training. There was a big piece in one of them claiming Newcastle would listen to offers for me during what remained of the transfer window. It was confirmation I could leave, as far I was concerned. I knew who the journalist was and who he was friends with. It was a well-sourced story, put it that way.

Even though I wanted to go, I felt I was being badly treated. I was playing out of position and I was being cast as the villain. I was bewildered but I was angry, too. I said as much to some of the players in the canteen. I went out training but I was a shadow. My head was gone. I felt betrayed. I had my own issues as well at that time, as I've said. I felt worthless. I tried to train. Shay Given went to throw me a ball and I sort of turned my back on him.

I have never done that. I just said 'sorry, mate' and walked off. I told the coach my hamstring was killing me. I went in and Souness passed me on the way out. I saw the physio. I told him I wasn't injured. I said I just needed to get off the training pitch because I had a chance of getting an injury because I wasn't mentally right to train.

When training finished, Souness came to find me.

"Me and you," he said, "we are going to see the chairman right now."

So we went to his office at St James' Park. He sat on one side of his desk. Souness and I sat on the other.

"Did you walk off the pitch with an injury?" Freddy asked me.

"Yes."

"Are you injured?" he said.

"No."

There was a pile of newspapers on Shepherd's desk. I told him to get the Daily Mirror out and look at the article that claimed the club would listen to offers for me.

"I know it's come from someone in this room," I said.

"It's nothing to do with me," Souness said.

"I don't even know this journalist," Shepherd said, looking at the byline. "I'll ring him now. But don't believe what it says. You've got a lot of years left here."

Souness butted in.

"Only on my terms," he said.

We all agreed to agree on that. I shook their hands, apologised for walking off the training pitch and walked out.

That Sunday, we were playing Arsenal at Highbury. Souness named the team before we left and I wasn't in it. He was making a point. I was fine with that. It was right that the other players should see that I had been dropped for walking off the training pitch. On Saturday, I travelled down to London with the rest of the squad.

When we got to Highbury on Sunday, Souness came over to me in the changing rooms.

"You're not getting changed today," he said.

He hadn't even put me on the bench. There was always one player who was brought along and would be surplus to requirements unless somebody pulled out right at the last minute. This Sunday, he had decided it would be me. So he had made me travel all the way down to London for a high-profile match that was live on television and I wasn't even on the bench.

People were surprised. A couple of the Sky reporters came up to me and asked if I was injured. I told them I wasn't. Sky started reporting that I had refused to play. I was astonished. I began to feel like this was some sort of stitch-up. Why would I travel if I had refused to play? Highbury was a tight little ground. There was nowhere for me to get away from the spotlight and the questions. I felt exposed.

We lost the game 1-0 to a Dennis Bergkamp goal. It meant we had only won three of our last 10 matches. I got on the coach outside the ground and waited for the rest of the lads. The radio was on. They were reporting that Souness had implied I had refused to play. Actually, I think he was probably dropping hints about me walking off the training pitch but the message got lost in translation. Anyway, I was fuming. I wasn't ready to accept that. I had a decent rapport with the Newcastle fans and I didn't want them to think I had refused to play.

When we got back to Newcastle, I went out and drank like you wouldn't believe. My head had gone. I ended up in a club somewhere with Patrick Kluivert. I woke up the next morning with a shocking hangover, rang Alan Shearer and had a go at him. That turned into quite a big argument and I said things I shouldn't have said. Then I had the bright idea that I should do a television interview to put my side of the story.

It was one of the most ridiculous things I have ever done. I thought it was me against the world, which was rubbish, but I was in a mess by then. I did the interview with Sky and accused Souness of telling 'a downright lie' about me. I said it was part of a plan to hound me out of the club. There was a lot of confusion about exactly what I was being accused of and maybe if I had kept my counsel, it would all have blown over. But the interview put paid to that.

Freddy Shepherd was livid. He made a statement to the media then, in which he accused me of breaking a promise to apologise to the rest of the players for walking off the training pitch. "In my book," Shepherd said, "this is cheating on the club, the supporters, the manager and the player's own team-mates. Craig Bellamy is paid extremely well by Newcastle United and I consider his behaviour to be totally unacceptable and totally unprofessional. The player will now face internal discipline by the club."

I was fined two weeks' wages, £80,000, but I was not put on the transfer list. Shepherd phoned me and said I had to go and apologise to Souness. Only if I did that could I play for the club again, he said. I couldn't do it. It was too far gone anyway. It was done. There was no way back.

So when I went into training the next day, I wasn't allowed to go outside with the other players. I was told to stay in the gym and forbidden from mingling with the rest of the lads. People I thought I knew at the club, people I thought were my friends, wouldn't be seen anywhere near me. They were worried that might be construed as taking my side. I did a few weights and then went home.

Birmingham City offered £6m for me and Newcastle accepted it but I didn't feel ready for a permanent move. I wanted to see out the season on loan somewhere, repair my reputation a bit and then see what happened in the summer. I knew people would be looking at me as damaged goods after what had happened with Souness and I didn't feel good about myself either. I was deep in self-loathing. I was low.

Then John Hartson rang me up. He had moved to Celtic after

we had gone our separate ways at Coventry and he said Martin O'Neill wanted to take me to Scotland. I loved the idea. I fancied the chance of chasing the league and trying to win a cup. I knew all about Celtic and their terrific support. I thought it would be a good experience.

Things began to get a bit frantic. Celtic approached Newcastle about loaning me but Newcastle turned them down. It came to the last day of the transfer window and things didn't seem to have moved on. I went in to training at Newcastle. I wanted to show I was committed and willing to play. I didn't want any more stories about me refusing to play.

I had only been there two minutes when I got a phone call saying the loan deal to Celtic had been agreed. I drove north straight away.

17

Cursed

I was looking forward to playing for Martin O'Neill. I didn't really have any contact with him when he was the manager at Norwich because I was still an apprentice then but I knew there was an aura about him and something that made players want to play for him. I knew his assistants, John Robertson and Steve Walford, too. I met Steve as soon as I arrived in Glasgow. He hadn't changed. He didn't seem to give a shit whether I signed for Celtic or not. I signed anyway.

That was the way Steve operated. He had that rare talent of being able to make people like him despite being rude to everyone he met. Not caring was what he did. Some of the boys who played for Martin at Leicester told me that Walford was the same there. He used to stand on the touchline at training, telling the boys to hurry up and finish because he wanted to get down the pub. He was a very difficult guy to impress but if he's not slagging you off, you know you've done all right.

While I was driving to Glasgow, John Hartson had called me. He warned me that the media up there was different to anything I would have experienced before. He said they were a law unto themselves and that they did whatever they wanted. I laughed at the idea it could be any worse than what I had been through at Newcastle.

There was a little silence at the other end of the line. "It's worse," Harts said.

He said they would be out to get me. He said that the poison had already been laid down for me and that some people from my time in England had already been on the phone to some of the press lads telling them to give me stick. And the first few weeks I was there, I was followed relentlessly. Everywhere I went, everything I did, there were photographers and reporters not far behind.

I was looking forward to making a fresh start but it was the first time I had moved clubs in the middle of the season and it was difficult. It didn't sit easily with me that I had effectively abandoned Claire and the boys in Newcastle. It wasn't easy for them. They were like the survivors of a shipwreck, clinging to what was left. And there wasn't a lot left.

Claire felt shunned by some of the other wives. My departure hadn't exactly been a model of good grace. And Ellis got a bit of stick at school from other kids. Children can be nasty sometimes so he was teased. He still had to finish his school year off. Terry McDermott did an interview in the one of the local papers that slagged me off. Claire and the kids got more grief.

There was no point in them coming up to Scotland with me for a few months but they had a rough time.

I was okay. At least I had football to keep me occupied. I was lucky, too, in that I was surrounded by a great bunch of lads. Chris Sutton, Neil Lennon and Alan Thompson really welcomed me into the group and made sure they looked after me. I couldn't have been with a better bunch of boys. Lennie put his arm round me and said 'you'll be okay here kid'. He took it upon himself to make sure I ate with him every night and that I wasn't on my own. If Lennie was busy, he got his mate Marty to keep me company. I've never forgotten that kindness.

The spotlight was intense. About a week after I arrived, I made my debut in an Old Firm match. I'd heard all about the atmosphere in those Glasgow derbies and the build-up and the atmosphere in the ground. I thought I'd take it in my stride. I was used to big games, I had played in other derbies. But everything people had told me was true. The atmosphere got to me.

I felt like I couldn't breathe. I was being watched everywhere. Glasgow was a tough city. You were adored and you were hated. Even I realised I had to tread carefully. In the papers, I was the favourite to score, the favourite to be the first to be sent off.

The night before the game, people from a neighbouring building rigged up some contraption that allowed them to fire water bombs across on to the balcony of the apartment I was renting. I wasn't there. I was with the team at a hotel but my family was staying there. It was ingenious but it gave them a hell of a shock.

We had a small lead over Rangers in the SPL when I arrived and when I looked at the Celtic side, I wasn't surprised.

We had Sutton and Hartson up front, Aiden McGeady and Alan Thompson on the wings, Lennon in midfield. But after everything that had gone on at Newcastle, I didn't really feel ready to play in that first match against Rangers at Celtic Park. I was still a bit frazzled. We lost 2-0.

Then there was a period of almost three weeks when we didn't play because bad weather wiped the fixtures out. We went up to Inverness to play against Inverness Caledonian Thistle and the game was called off the next morning. The night we were in Inverness, someone staggered into a police station in Glasgow and said they had just been assaulted by Craig Bellamy. Inverness is about 200 miles from Glasgow. Funnily enough, they didn't press charges.

When the weather improved towards the end of February and football resumed, I was ready. I played well. I made a decent contribution. The first game back, we played Clyde away and won 5-0. I got the fifth. I scored again against Hibs a week later and I got a hat-trick against Dundee United at Tannadice in a 3-2 victory. I was desperate to win the league up there. I thought it would be some form of validation for my career so far. Everything seemed set fair.

I loved playing for O'Neill. It's very basic. There is no miracle to what he does. There was no secret, for instance, to why we were so dangerous at set-pieces. Just get someone with Alan Thompson's quality who can deliver the ball where he wants to and go and attack it. He would go and buy big defenders who could attack the ball. It was that simple. He had uncomplicated instructions. Make sure you are first to the ball in our box and in theirs. Let the good players play.

Usually, he turned up on the Thursday or Friday before a

weekend game, much as Brian Clough used to do when he was at Nottingham Forest. He had great charisma. He was so polite and well-educated, too, way too well-educated for us in football. It was best not to forget he was in charge, though. Sure, he was nice but if you weren't doing your job properly, he would be scathing. If you ever answered back, he would never forget it. He gave some of the biggest rollickings I had ever seen.

But when you played well for him, you felt brilliant because he told you how good you were. And he told you in front of everyone so that everyone else could hear. He made you feel like you were the best player in the world. And the spirit he fostered at the club was the best I've ever seen. Not just among the players but among the entire staff.

If you got fined for being late, you didn't put it in a kitty. You had to go and give the laundry woman £500 or give it to the cook. That made you feel great then, even though the gaffer had told you to do it. It turned you from feeling you were being punished to feeling that you were doing something good and worthwhile and generous.

Because my family was still in Newcastle and I didn't want to spend my days in an empty flat, I would stick around at the training ground in the afternoons. I would do my weights and then play pool with Robbo and Stevie Walford even though they spent all day and every day chain-smoking, which wasn't great for my asthma.

When they weren't playing pool, they watched the History Channel. They were obsessed with crimes. More accurately, they were obsessed with criminals. They loved mass murderers. They were totally fascinated by them.

Now and again, they'd get into big arguments about how

many people one of the murderers had killed or what method he had used.

They shared that hobby with Martin. Martin used to go to court to watch cases unfold sometimes. He was fascinated by the JFK assassination and the story of the A6 murderer James Hanratty. I enjoyed being in his company. He was such a good bloke. The other two could be rude and unpleasant but they were fun. Martin was different. He never looked you in the eye but his manners were outstanding.

We beat Livingston 4-0 away in the middle of April and even though I didn't score, I had a good game. Harts got a hat-trick and I set a couple of them up for him. I was given the man of the match award but the next week, one of my ex-teammates at Newcastle rang me and said Shearer had been laughing about me.

"What about your mate," he'd said. "Celtic batter someone 4-0 and he can't even get on the scoresheet."

That was Alan all over. If you didn't score, it didn't matter how well you played or how much work you did for the team.

The following weekend, we beat Aberdeen 3-2 and I got the winner late on. After the game, we flew to Ireland for a bit of a break. We had a good night out in Donegal that night and the following day, Chris Sutton, Neil Lennon and I went out to a bar to watch the FA Cup semi-final between Newcastle and Manchester United. Manchester United won comfortably. I felt bad for Newcastle. They lost 4-1 and they were never really in it.

Afterwards, Alan did a television interview. He mentioned shortcomings in defence, which made me laugh. Alan needed to look at himself a bit more. He wasn't the player he had been and now he was trying to pass the buck.

When a player's time comes, it comes. Alan had become determined to break Newcastle's all-time club scoring record, which had been held for nearly 50 years by Jackie Milburn but his goals were drying up and I didn't think he was offering the team enough in general play to justify his place. He was becoming an obstacle to the club's progress. It was sad because I had so much admiration for him as a player and I learned so much from him. But time had caught up with him.

As I watched him giving his interview, some of the bitterness I felt towards him over Bobby Robson's departure welled up inside me. I had seen the semi-final. I had seen how poorly he performed personally. I thought it was wrong for him to do an interview afterwards in those circumstances. If I don't perform anywhere near my level, I'm certainly not going to talk about what we didn't do as a team. So I got my phone out and texted him.

"Fucking typical of you," I texted. "Looking at everyone else yet again. You need to look at yourself instead. Your legs are fucking shot. Concentrate on yourself and let the team take care of itself."

I got one back from him straight away.

"If I ever see you in Newcastle again," he wrote, "I'll knock you out."

"I'm back in Newcastle next week," I texted back. "Pop round and say hello."

I certainly wasn't scared of him. I've seen his bite. His big, hard Al act wasn't for me. I have seen younger men than me stand up to him on the team coach. I watched him digging out Lomana LuaLua once and when LuaLua told him to go to the back of the coach and say it to his face, Al didn't really respond to that. He didn't move an inch.

The texts soon got out, which helped Newcastle. Their season wasn't going well under Souness. They were lower mid-table and there was still a little bit of rumbling about why I was with Celtic when I should be with them. There were still a number of Newcastle fans who were agitating for me to be back at the club the following season. But the fall out with the golden boy meant there would be no return. I wasn't going back anyway. My days at Newcastle were over.

I was enjoying myself in Scotland. I loved it at Celtic. The standard of football was nowhere near the Premier League but everyone knows that. I would say it is probably below the Championship. But when you talk about clubs of stature and tradition, you have two of the greatest clubs in the world playing in that league and that makes it special.

When I went into my second Old Firm game, I was ready for it. This one was at Ibrox, which is a fantastic ground, but I wasn't intimidated by it. I knew what to expect. We went 1-0 up through Stiliyan Petrov and then I got the second, which turned out to be the winner in a 2-1 victory. That was a great moment. To score the winner in an Old Firm game was one of the dreams I'd had when I'd made the move.

It felt as though that victory had secured us the league title. We were five points clear with four games to play. Celtic just don't lose that kind of lead in that time frame. Not in a league where the Old Firm is so dominant.

I was forced to come off towards the end of the match with a hamstring strain and I knew I'd be out for two or three weeks. But I thought the job was done. I thought the league was over.

I thought I had done the job I set out to do when I moved to Scotland.

But in the first game after the victory over Rangers at Ibrox, we lost 3-1 to Hibs at Celtic Park. We beat Aberdeen and Hearts in the next two games which meant we went into our final game away at Motherwell with a two-point lead. Rangers, who were away at Hibs, had a better goal difference than us so we knew a draw might not be enough.

Still, we only needed to win at Fir Park and the title was ours. It was going to be a 'Helicopter Sunday'. The league trophy would be airborne until its destination was decided one way or the other and only then would the helicopter deliver it to the champions.

I had come back from injury in the win over Hearts and I was confident we'd beat Motherwell. We were a good side in a poor league. It was still in our hands. And when Chris Sutton put us a goal ahead after 20 minutes, we were cruising. There was only one team in it. As long as it stayed like that, there was nothing Rangers could do.

But the problem was that it did stay like that. We couldn't get another goal. We missed chance after chance after chance. And then as the end of the game drew nearer, we started to get nervous because we knew that one mistake or one fluke or one tremendous shot from them would be enough for us to lose the title.

Motherwell weren't going to give up, either. In some ways, they had nothing to play for but they were managed by Terry Butcher, who was a Rangers hero and who hated everything about Celtic.

There were two minutes left when it happened.

A mishit shot bounced into our area and Scott McDonald cushioned it on his chest and then hooked it over our goal-keeper, Rab Douglas, into the net.

It was a superb goal but we knew what it meant. Rangers were winning 1-0 at Easter Road. A sense of panic swept over us. We had to score again. We threw everybody forward.

We desperately tried to rescue things. We laid siege to the Motherwell goal. But then they broke forward and McDonald scored again with a shot that looped over Douglas via a deflection from one of our defenders.

And then the final whistle blew. We had lost 2-1.

Rangers won at Hibs and that was it. We had lost the league by a point. I was vaguely aware that the noise of a helicopter buzzing overhead had disappeared. It was carrying the SPL trophy with it. It had flown away from Fir Park. It was heading to Easter Road.

It was a desperate, desperate feeling. We went into the changing rooms and there was just silence. I have heard Neil Lennon say in the years that have elapsed since then that it was the most sickening blow of his career. Martin didn't attempt to disguise his disappointment, either.

We still had the Scottish Cup Final to prepare for the following weekend but nobody wanted to think about that. Martin just muttered something about seeing us on Wednesday or Thursday. That was it.

I was in shock. I went back to my apartment where Claire and the kids were waiting. But I needed to be by myself. I left them at the apartment, went straight to the airport and got a flight to Cardiff. I didn't sleep for two days.

I felt tormented.

I thought I was cursed, I thought I was destined never to win anything.

That was typical of the rubbish that used to go through my head in those days. I tortured myself for not passing at a certain moment, or not taking a chance I should have taken.

I stayed at my mum and dad's house and drank. I wallowed in self-pity for a while. I didn't think about Claire and the kids being by themselves in Glasgow.

Eventually, I snapped out of it and told myself I had to get ready for the final. I still felt distraught about what had happened at Fir Park. I still couldn't believe it. But I knew there was a chance to salvage something.

There was extra emotion attached to the game because it was Martin O'Neill's last game as manager. He was going to take some time off so that he could help care for his wife, who was suffering from cancer, and nobody really thought he would be back.

We were up against Dundee United. It was another match we were expected to win but after what happened against Motherwell, no one was taking anything for granted.

We went ahead early. Alan Thompson scored in the 11th minute and we never really felt threatened after that. We couldn't get a second goal and Chris Sutton missed a penalty but we were not punished for it this time.

I felt a sense of elation when the final whistle blew. Martin went up to lift the trophy himself. He was very popular with the players and everyone was keen to make the gesture because they knew it was the end of an era.

It was the end for me, too, at Celtic.

They made noises about wanting to keep me but Newcastle

weren't willing to extend my loan and I knew it was not realistic to think that Celtic would be able to afford either the transfer fee Newcastle would ask or my wages.

I had loved my time up there but I have never been able to shake the regret about the way we lost the league.

I had finally won a trophy but I did not feel liberated by it.

I felt like a failure. I felt like the process of rebuilding my career had only just begun.

18

Destiny Calls

The summer after I lost the league with Celtic, I took a month's holiday in Majorca with my family. I didn't know where I was going to be playing at the start of the following season. I knew I wasn't going back to Newcastle and it was clear to me that even though Celtic would have liked me to stay, they couldn't afford me.

A couple of days before I went away, I met David Moyes at the Celtic Manor hotel just outside Newport. I really enjoyed talking to him. I had always liked the way Everton played under Moyes. I loved their work ethic and their attitude.

The fans are right on top of you at Goodison Park, too. It is a difficult place to go and play when you are in the opposing team.

Moyes was very persuasive. I felt a bid odd about the prospect of joining them because I had been a committed Liverpool fan since I was a young kid. But a lot of Evertonians end up playing for Liverpool and I thought it would be typical if I ended up doing it the other way round.

I spoke to David O'Leary at Aston Villa a couple of times and there was interest from Benfica and Fiorentina but Moyes had sold me on Everton.

The more I thought about it while I was in Majorca, the more I liked the idea of going to Goodison. I agreed terms with them and when I got back from holiday I went up to meet Moyes at his house near Preston. I took my suitcase with me so I could move into a hotel that night and start pre-season training the next day. I was excited about it.

But when I got to his house, I could tell straight away that something had changed. It was like talking to a different bloke. He seemed tense and hostile.

He presented me with a list of rules. They were very detailed and exact. They tried to imagine certain scenarios and dictate how I would react. "If I ask you to move to the right in the 60th minute, I don't want you shaking your head" or "If you have got something to say, do not speak to anyone else about it, come and see me."

They went on and on. I thought 'where are we going with this?' It was a completely different individual to the guy I was speaking to a month ago. It was as if he had spoken to someone who had changed his mind about me. He seemed to have got cold feet. It felt like he was looking for a way out. It was bizarre. If we hadn't had a second meeting, I would have signed anyway. Now I couldn't.

It was awkward. Bill Kenwright, the Everton chairman, was on the phone saying that all the arrangements were in place for the medical once the formalities had been completed with Moyes. My representative didn't go into details. He just told Mr Kenwright I had had a change of heart. It was a real blow to me. I had to get in my car and drive back to Cardiff.

A few weeks later, Moyes rang my representative and apologised. I don't hold a grudge about it. I've got a lot of time for him and he tried to sign me a couple of times subsequently. I don't blame him, really. My guess is that someone had told him I would be trouble and he panicked a bit. It did leave me in limbo, though. Newcastle had begun pre-season training but even though I was still their player, that chapter was over. They told me to stay away.

A few days after the Everton deal broke down, my representative rang to say he had spoken to John Williams, the Blackburn chairman. Mark Hughes had left the Wales job in September 2004 to take over at Ewood Park, which was a big plus in my thinking. But even though they had reached the FA Cup semi-final in his first season, they had flirted with relegation and finished 15th. I wanted more than that. I said 'no'.

I thought it was going to be another tough year for them and my confidence was low. I thought they needed someone better than me. I didn't think I would be good enough to give them the lift they needed and to make them a top half team. After what had happened at Newcastle and the disappointment of missing out on the Scottish title, I felt worthless again.

My representative urged me to go and meet Mark Hughes anyway. At least hear what he had to say. He kept stressing that Sparky was the manager who knew me best and valued me the most. He would look after me. He would breathe life back into my career. He would get my confidence up again. I was still reluctant but I agreed to meet him at the Vale of Glamorgan hotel just outside Cardiff. I owed him that.

After about 10 minutes in his company, I was ready to sign. He said all the right things. He played to my vanity. He said he knew that in the normal course of events, a player of my ability would be beyond Blackburn's reach. He said he realised I was too good for Blackburn really but that they would give me a platform to show what a player I could be and then I could move on to one of the top clubs.

Sparky said I had been made to look a troublemaker and that I needed to repair my reputation. He reminded me he had known me since I was 15. He knew how I worked. He knew what I needed. He said he would put me on a pedestal and before I knew it, there would be a whole queue of clubs after me. It was a clever pitch. The next day, I went up to Blackburn for the medical.

I was impressed by everything at the club. It was only 10 years since they won the Premier League and the place was still full of class. John Williams was great, the staff were lovely and warm and welcoming and the training facilities were unbelievably good. I realised that this was actually going to be a great opportunity for me. I began to feel more confident even before I had kicked a ball.

I wanted to find out who I was as a player. I was at a crossroads. Was I the player who had struggled to step up a level at Coventry or was I the player who had excelled at Newcastle? Was I capable of moving upwards from here and becoming a genuinely top player?

The same kind of themes were whirring round my mind about my personal life. I knew that Claire had reached the stage where she wanted us to get married and if we didn't, she was going to leave. That was fair enough. She wanted commitment and I wanted to try to put the way I had behaved in Newcastle behind me. I wanted to try to prove to myself that I could become a decent husband and a better father.

I didn't want her to leave. Partly, I suppose, that was because I was desperate not to spend any more time away from my kids than I was already spending. I wanted the kids to have the same surname as their mum, too. I needed to become a man for the first time in my life. So on my 26th birthday, July 13th, 2005, I proposed to Claire at The Lowry hotel in Manchester and she accepted.

We bought a house in the countryside just outside Cardiff and decided that this would be our base. No more moving the family around from city to city, trailing around after me when I moved. We wanted the kids to have a settled school life. The plan was for me to come home as often as I could. We knew it would be difficult but we thought it was the best option.

Things didn't start well at Blackburn. I played in the first game of the season, a 3-1 defeat at West Ham, but then I picked up a thigh injury and missed the next four games. Inevitably, my first game back, in the middle of September, was against Newcastle at Ewood Park. We lost 3-0. Shearer scored. The result left us in the bottom three.

I got plenty of stick from the travelling Newcastle fans at that game. That was fine. I had to suck it all up. I felt some of the Newcastle players were gloating at the end of the game, rubbing the result in for my benefit. Souness came out on to the pitch, applauding the fans and milking it. I went out of my way to make sure I shook his hand. I wanted to show there were no hard feelings.

And there weren't. Sure, we fell out at Newcastle. He bore some of the responsibility for that. But I accept that it was my fault, too. And I have never lost sight of the fact that the man is one of the best footballers the English game has ever seen. He is a legend, someone who was at the core of the great Liverpool teams. I remember that about him more than anything else.

I didn't feel too downhearted at the end of the game. It was my first match back after injury. I knew I was going to play a lot better before long. And even though we were heavily beaten, I felt even then that we would have climbed above Newcastle at the end of the season. I knew that we had a better work ethic than them and players who were more hungry for success.

I was right about that. Newcastle's season quickly went downhill and by the time we played them at St James' Park at the end of January, Souness was under a lot of pressure. I missed that game with a hamstring injury but we won 1-0 and the crowd was chanting for him to be sacked. A few days later, after a defeat to Manchester City, Freddy Shepherd fired him.

If Newcastle declined after that September victory over us at Ewood Park, we went in the opposite direction. We began to turn things around. The next match was against Manchester United at Old Trafford, with Cristiano Ronaldo, Wayne Rooney, Ruud Van Nistelrooy and Paul Scholes pitted against us. We won 2-1 with a couple of goals from Morten Gamst Pedersen and that result was the springboard for our season. We won the next game against West Brom, too, and climbed the table steadily.

We had a decent team. We were hard-working and there was a lot of talent in the side, too. Tugay was a magnificent player and David Bentley is a lad who should have achieved more in his career. We had Lucas Neill at the back and Brad Friedel in goal and I played with a variety of players up front. Paul Dickov, Shefki Kuqi and Florent Sinama-Pongolle all played a number of games but, just as Mark Hughes had promised, the team was focused around me.

We had characters, too. Robbie Savage was at the heart of the team. He was not a particularly talented player but he was honest and he would work himself into the ground for the team. I admired that in him. He was still the insecure lad I knew from the Wales set-up and he could be very loud. He tested my patience at times but I liked him. How he never got battered by some of the other boys, I'll never know. But I had a lot of time for him. Andy Todd was a good lad, too. He has got a bit of a fearsome reputation after a couple of bust-ups he has had with people. I heard that he gave Dean Kiely a good hiding once when they were teammates at Charlton. He was one of the hardest players I have ever played with and you certainly wouldn't want to get on the wrong side of him but I always thought he was a lovely man. I guess we all have a switch.

By mid-season, I was in great form and scoring plenty of goals. Between mid-December and the beginning of March, we won seven times in 10 games, including another victory over Manchester United and a win against Arsenal. We were playing so well that the win over Arsene Wenger's side moved us above them into fifth place in the table, three points off a Champions League spot with 11 games to go.

We had got to the semi-finals of the Carling Cup, too, losing narrowly to Manchester United over two legs but we kept our league form going. We won our last three games of the season, away to Charlton and at home to the champions, Chelsea, and Manchester City. It wasn't quite enough to catch Arsenal, who had recovered after we beat them. Arsene Wenger's team finished fourth.

But we had ended the season only four points off a Champions League place. Spurs were fifth and we finished sixth, in the final Uefa Cup spot. It felt like a great achievement considering where the club had finished the previous season and I felt as though I had rebuilt my reputation. I scored 13 league goals that season and 17 in all competitions. It was a delight playing for Mark Hughes. He helped me believe in myself again.

I felt open-minded about what might happen in the summer. I loved it at Blackburn and I knew I was on to a good thing. They loved me, too. I was voted the club's Player of the Year and Sparky had plans to make me captain the following season. But I had a get-out clause in my contract that meant if a club bid £6m for me within a certain time period before the start of July, then Blackburn would have to release me. They soon opened negotiations with me about buying that get-out clause out of my contract and extending and improving my current deal. They were willing to pay £2m just for me to void the clause.

But then everything changed. My representative phoned to say that Liverpool were interested in buying me. Djibril Cisse had broken his leg playing for France in a warm-up game before the 2006 World Cup and he was going to be out for a long time. They needed a replacement and Rafa Benitez had identified me as the main target.

I loved Liverpool. I'd loved them since I was a kid. They were big in South Wales and they were still the top team when I was growing up in the 1980s but that wasn't the only reason I supported them. I loved the kit for one thing, that brilliant crispy, shiny red kit that always looked so beautiful against the green of the turf with its big Liver Bird emblem. The first kit I owned was the yellow away kit they wore for the 1985-86 season.

My dad was a Cardiff City fan and I love Cardiff because it's the club I went to watch as a kid. I don't care who you are, wherever you are born, you have an affiliation with that club like no other because that's your club and it represents you and the community you grew up in. That can never change.

But you were on a bit of a hiding to nothing being a Cardiff City fan in the 1980s. They were a Fourth Division club. You couldn't even buy their kit in the local sports shops. None of my mates supported them. Being a Cardiff fan wasn't going to give you any bragging rights in the playground.

And there was something about Liverpool that caught my imagination. All their success helped, obviously. But even as a kid, I loved the history. I read all about Bill Shankly and Bob Paisley. I looked at all the stats and the old players. I devoured everything about the history of the club and I stayed true to it.

I am a Liverpool fan and will always remain one. I have lived in Liverpool. I know what it means to come from there. It can be a hard, hard place and it breeds tough, resourceful people. I've always been proud to be a supporter. A few years ago, I had 'You'll Never Walk Alone' tattooed on my side.

The way things worked out, it felt as if I was meant to follow them.

The first game I ever saw at Anfield was the match against Arsenal on May 26, 1989, when Liverpool lost the league title to that late goal from Michael Thomas just a few weeks after the Hillsborough Disaster.

On the day of Hillsborough, I was watching my dad play football for his team, Fairoak, like I did every Saturday. He was a sluggish right-back who played for the seconds but I loved those afternoons at Pontcanna. The pitches seemed to go on for as far as the eye could see and you'd hear cheers go up every so often whenever anybody scored a goal.

I was running round the pitches on April 15 that year, asking if anyone knew the score from the Liverpool-Nottingham Forest FA Cup semi-final. People kept shaking their heads. They said there was a delay of some sort. There were rumours of riots. All the early propaganda about crowd trouble had begun. I didn't find out what had really happened until I got home. I couldn't really understand it.

But I understood it when we arrived at Anfield for that game against Arsenal. There were signs asking for help, there were scarves and wreaths, tributes and poems written to those who had been lost. I was only a nine-year-old kid but even I could grasp the enormity of the horror that had happened. There was so much emotion around. And you know what, the main thing that stayed with me from that day was nothing to do with Michael Thomas scoring, even though it was at the Anfield Road End where we were standing. My memory is of the emotion and staring in wonder at the Kop, seeing it moving and swaying like a living thing.

So when I found out Liverpool were interested in signing me, it was bound to turn my head. The easy thing would have been to stay at Blackburn. Mark Hughes had restored me as a player and I knew that if I stayed, I would become the focal point of the club even more. I would have been comfortable. It was a really good club with really good people. But the prospect of playing for Liverpool was something I knew would be hard to resist if they maintained their interest.

I got married that summer. We went on honeymoon to the Seychelles. While we were there, I got a call from my representative who said that Liverpool had made a bid big enough to trigger the release clause in my contract. Blackburn couldn't stand in my way. My representative asked me what I wanted to do. I said I'd think about it for a week. It was my honeymoon. I didn't want to abandon that for the sake of football.

But inevitably, thoughts about what might lie ahead started rushing around my head. Liverpool had finished the previous season like a train. They had won each of their last nine games, including a victory over us at Ewood Park. They had players like Steven Gerrard, Jamie Carragher and Xabi Alonso who I had always admired. They looked like a side that was really going places.

They were in the Champions League, too, of course. They had won it in 2005 and with a manager as clever as Benitez in charge, I thought there was no reason why they could not win it again. I knew it would be tough to break into the first team, that I would have to win people over again at the age of 27, but that didn't concern me too much. My confidence was back.

The main consideration was simple though. I knew that if I didn't go to Liverpool, I'd regret it for the rest of my life. How can you support a club and then turn them down? It went against everything I believed in as a player. I knew it was going to happen. I knew I had to do it. I didn't even think about where I was going to fit in.

I was sad about leaving Blackburn. I saw Mark Hughes before I went to Liverpool to do my medical.

"I don't think you're going to play as much as you need to play," he said. "I know the type of person you are and you need to play. I hope I'm wrong but I don't think you're going to enjoy it."

I thought that was just him trying to keep me at Blackburn. I respected him immensely and I was straight with him. I told him I had to do it. I asked him to imagine what would have happened if the club he had supported as a kid had wanted to sign him when he was a player. He said he still believed Blackburn would be better for me.

But when I went to speak to Liverpool, he knew I was already gone – and I did too.

19

The Rafa Way

When I walked into Melwood, the Liverpool training ground, I felt as though everything in my career had been leading to this moment. It was the first time I had ever been there and it was like being in a dream. This was where Bill Shankly had worked. This was the turf that Bob Paisley had walked on. This was where Kenny Dalglish, Ian Rush and Robbie Fowler had trained. The facilities might have been new and state-of-the-art but the place reeked of glorious history.

A lot of things went through my mind. It was only a year ago that my name was mud and everybody had been branding me a troublemaker and saying I was untouchable.

I had undergone four operations on my patella tendons and two on my cruciates. I had suffered from episodes of depression.

I even thought of sitting in my garage in Norwich on Christmas Eve, doing my leg presses. This is why I did it. To get here. To get to Melwood. To sign for Liverpool.

I did my medical stuff and then I went upstairs to see Rafa Benitez in his office. I sat down. He was business-like. He produced a cutting from a newspaper. The page was dominated by a picture of me with a snarl on my face. Most of the time back then I'd have a snarl on my face. It was nothing unusual.

"Why are you looking like this?" he said.

I told him I couldn't remember.

"You can't play like this," he said. "This kind of aggression is not what you need as a player."

I told him I understood. The memory of the game where the incident had happened started to come back to me. It was a match against Sunderland the previous season. Sunderland's goalkeeper, Kelvin Davis, had shoved me in the back. I had a bad back anyway at that time. I didn't take too kindly to being shoved in it.

I didn't mention any of that to Rafa. I could sense it probably wasn't the right time.

Then he got a board out and started quizzing me about footballing systems. What did I think about this formation or that formation, the positives, the negatives, the benefits of playing between the lines. Where would I run if a teammate had the ball in a certain position. He asked me about every scenario under the sun. And every answer I gave, even if it was correct, was twisted into another answer.

"When you play up top," he said, "if this player has it, where would you go?"

It was like a multiple choice test.

"I'd run to the left," I said.

"Yeah, but run right first, then go left," he said.

The other players told me later that was just typical Rafa.

We had a good chat for about half an hour in his office. Rafa disappeared after a while and left me talking with the club's chief scout. My solicitor was somewhere else, going through the fine points of the deal. Suddenly, Rafa came back in to the room looking angry.

"Do you want to play for this club?" he said.

I was startled.

"Of course I do," I said. "I would have thought the fact that I'm here tells you that."

"Well, tell your solicitor to stop messing about then," Rafa said.

"That's what he's here for," I told him. "I could get much more money if I stayed at Blackburn. I'm taking a wage cut to play for this club, so of course I want to play here."

I was a bit taken aback by his attitude. It was like being in the presence of an unsmiling headmaster. The atmosphere at the club seemed strange, too. It was a place of business and a place of work. There weren't very many people smiling. There wasn't a lot of laughter around the place. Even the physios were on edge when they were doing the medical. Everyone seemed uncomfortable and wary.

I felt unsettled. The way Rafa was talking, it was worse than the experience I'd had with David Moyes. It was Liverpool, sure, it was the Champions League, it was everything I'd ever wanted. But it was the first time I'd met Rafa and he wasn't quite what I'd been expecting. 'This is going to be interesting,' I thought.

The next day, I met Pako Ayestaran, Rafa's assistant and the fitness coach. The fitness routines were not that imaginative. It was army style, really. Long, plodding runs mainly. It was very professional with heart monitors and fitness belts but there was no camaraderie while they took place. It was all double sessions, tactical work, standing in position, walk-throughs of tactical play. Rafa oversaw it all.

A lot of Rafa's tactical work was very, very good. He was impressively astute and I learned a lot from him in that area. But he could not come to terms with the idea that some players need an element of freedom and that we express ourselves on the pitch in different ways. He was very rigid. He worked on specific moves over and over again. It was a bit like American Football in that respect.

Rafa wanted people running designated routes when the ball was in a certain place, just as he had been explaining the first time I spoke to him in his office. The winger comes inside, the full-back overlaps, the forward has to run near post every time. There was no allowance for the fact that your marker might have worked out what you are doing after a few attempts. You had to keep doing it because it might make space for someone else. I felt like a decoy runner half the time.

But I did learn a lot. Defensively, Rafa was exceptional. He was very good on the opposition and how to nullify their threat and stifle their forward players. He would use video analysis to go through the opposition's strengths and weaknesses. Our preparation for games was extremely thorough. Nothing was left to chance. He was the first foreign manager I worked under and I learned quite a bit.

But there was no scope for spontaneity. None. He distrusted

that. Of all the managers I have worked with, he trusted his players the least. That's just how he was. There was not much enjoyment. There were no small-sided games or anything like that. Everything was tactical with timed drills and routines.

It was a bit like Groundhog Day. You came in and did the same stuff over and over again. Sometimes strikers like to do finishing at the end of a session but once the whistle was blown at the end of training, Rafa would personally collect the balls and put them in the bag and no one was allowed to do any extra work. He was a total control-freak. He's not alone in that, of course. I think Fabio Capello used to work the same way with England.

I actually felt my fitness went backwards during that pre-season. I am a fast-twitch fibre player and I was plodding around the perimeter of the training complex on the track that had been marked out around the outside of the pitches at Melwood. There were pole markers here and there to indicate how many metres we'd run. I felt like I was being trained to get a decent time in a marathon, not to sprint away from a central defender.

Pako said my speed was very good but my endurance wasn't. I knew my endurance was fine but Pako said they wanted to take some of my speed off and bring my endurance up. I knew if they did that, they would lose me as a player. The effect it had on me was that I never felt more unfit in my life. I felt slow, I didn't feel I could drop the shoulder and go.

Pako just looked at the data but he didn't seem to be able to understand they were taking my strengths away from me. I spoke to them about it and they wouldn't have it. They were set in their ways. On a Friday before a game, we would be doing heavy lifting squats and that took a lot out of my legs.

I was actually being detrained. I wasn't built for that. By the time the season started, I was nowhere near the player I had been. That was the price I paid to play for Liverpool.

I enjoyed elements of it, too. There were big compensations. One of them was playing day-in, day-out with Steven Gerrard. Gerrard was everything I expected and more. He was a cut above anyone I've ever played with. He had so much in his locker. His passing even from five yards away was just crisp and clean. He was on another level to everyone.

The club asked a lot of him. He is captain and a cult hero at one of the biggest clubs in the world and there were times he had to carry the team. As a Liverpool supporter, I'm glad he didn't go anywhere else but he should have won titles whether it was at Real Madrid or, dare I say it, Manchester United. For me, he was one of the best players in Europe for a good three or four years.

But he's a Liverpool fan. So it's easy for me to say he should have played here or he should have played there. Playing for Liverpool was always his dream, so maybe he didn't want to play anywhere else. He won the Champions League with the club, which only a select few can say. He became a club legend. I just feel he has so much ability that it feels wrong he did not win more.

In terms of temperament, there were some similarities between the two of us. He would be in a good mood one day and then the next his head would be down and he wouldn't talk much. I could be like that too. Some days, I would come in and didn't want to look at anyone.

Some days, I was very bright and in a good mood but people knew when I wasn't. People stayed away from me on those days. But Stevie wouldn't have a go at anyone. He would just be quiet. He was a great guy.

He is an immense player but because he was streaks ahead of everyone – even someone like Alonso – he put too much onus on himself to do everything. The club relied on him. There were days we knew that if we were going to win, Stevie was going to have to be at his best. He knew that, too, and that is a lot of pressure to carry around on your shoulders.

What makes him so good? Well, there is nothing he can't do. He is clever. He sees the game quicker than anyone else. He sees the picture. He can play the ball first time round corners that aren't even there. He has got intelligence. He has got physical attributes. He can bomb past people. He is quick. He is a powerful, proper athlete. Give him a header, he will score. He can play in behind the front man. He can get the ball off the back four and control the game from the quarterback position. He is just an immense all-round footballer. I have never seen anyone put it all together like him, never seen someone with so many qualities. I have been very fortunate to play with a lot of talented players but he was better than any of them.

It mystified me that Rafa didn't seem to trust him to play centre midfield. Stevie was sacrificed to Rafa's tactical plan. Rafa was ahead of his time in that he liked playing with two sitting midfielders in front of the back four. He usually played Alonso and Momo Sissoko there in the first spell I was there and, later, Javier Mascherano. He didn't want Stevie in there, bombing forward. He wanted discipline, discipline, discipline.

Stevie would play on the right and he played well there. But why would you want one of the greatest central midfielders of the last 10 years playing on the right? I think Stevie created a problem for Rafa. It was obvious that the best player in the team has got to play but because Stevie didn't fit his idea of one of the two sitting midfielders, he couldn't play him at the heart of the team. Maybe Stevie was a victim of the fact that he could play anywhere. Look, he could have played centre-back and he would have run the game from there as well.

The other colossus in the team was Jamie Carragher. He was an incredible player, too, a true warrior. He prepared for games and played them at a very high intensity. He was so caught up in it, so determined to do well. There was a lot more to his game than people appreciated. He was a very clever footballer, someone who read the game extremely well. And his knowledge of the game is encyclopaedic. More than anything, he was a joy to be around, a real down-to-earth genuine individual. He is a credit to his club and his family.

Gerrard and Carragher joined pre-season training late due to the fact they had been given some time off after the 2006 World Cup but they both played in the Champions League third round qualifying tie against Maccabi Haifa at Anfield at the beginning of August, 2006, that marked my debut for the club I had always supported.

I should have felt elated when I pulled on the famous red shirt to make my first competitive start but I didn't. It was a special moment, sure, but I was preoccupied. My body didn't feel great. I didn't feel quick. I didn't feel right and that worried me. I was worried I wouldn't be able to show the levels I needed to get the best out of myself. I was worried I wouldn't be able to do myself justice at the stadium I considered the greatest stage of all.

I did okay against Maccabi Haifa. We went a goal down

midway through the first half but I equalised almost straight away and we went on to win the game 2-1. It was nice to score straight away and take that pressure off. I only got five minutes at the end of the second leg, which was played in Kiev because of unrest in the Middle East. Rafa went with Peter Crouch as his main forward and we drew 1-1 and scraped through to the Champions League group phase.

Rotation was something else I had to get used to under Rafa. One week you would play, the next you wouldn't. We played Everton in the third league match of the season and I went to check the teamsheet when it was pinned up at the training ground the day before the match. My name wasn't on it. I wasn't even in the squad.

Rafa had said before the start of the season that some players would be in the squad some weeks and some wouldn't. But this was a Merseyside derby at Goodison. Not only was I not going to start, I was not even going to be on the bench and I was not even travelling. I found myself training with the kids that Friday afternoon. I felt demoralised.

Maybe some people are temperamentally equipped to deal with rotation. I'm not. It unsettled me. And the reaction of the media to the fact that I wasn't involved unsettled me, too. I watched the Everton game at home in Mossley Hill, a suburb of the city where I lived, and I heard everyone on the television expressing surprise that I wasn't involved. It was a massive game, expectations were high and people were saying "where's Craig Bellamy, he's not injured, he must have done something." The same theme was revisited again and again. "Something's obviously gone on there," one pundit or another would say.

But rotation was something I had to get used to. None of the players would ever know until an hour before kick-off who was going to start. I found that hard to adjust to. I found everything about it difficult. I prepared as if I was going to start because I felt that was the professional thing to do. But I need to get myself into a certain frame of mind when I play. I cut myself off from everybody around me on the day of the game. I get intense about it. In those circumstances, it is very difficult if you are then told an hour before the match that you're on the bench.

By preparing as though I was going to play, I was also ensuring that the disappointment would be even greater when I didn't play. So then I started telling myself I had to change tack. I stopped building myself up too much so that it would be easier to deal with the disappointment of not being selected. But then when I did start, it almost came as a shock to me. I had an hour to get prepared. That was it.

Rafa said he would not release the starting eleven until an hour before kick-off because he didn't want to give the opposition an advantage. What he meant was that he didn't want anyone to leak the team early and he didn't trust players to keep it secret. He didn't trust the players on the pitch so he certainly wasn't going to trust them off it.

Crouchie and I made a joke of trying to guess what combination Rafa would pick up front. He and I never started together because Dirk Kuyt, who had been signed from Feyenoord for £9m in the summer, usually got the nod ahead of both of us. So it was one from two. If the opposition had a quick defence, I knew Crouchie was going to play. If they were poor in the air, Crouchie would play. If they were vulnerable to pace, I would get the nod.

Like I say, I thought Rafa over-complicated things. He liked the idea of turning a match into an intellectual contest. He was obsessed with trying to second-guess the opposition line-up, too. Then, if he thought he knew what they were planning, he'd spring a different formation to try to unsettle the team he thought the other manager had picked.

It felt as though it always had to be about him. Maybe this was a striker's paranoia but I noticed a couple of times that he substituted players when they had scored two goals. It was as if he didn't want that player to go on and get a hat-trick because if he got a hat-trick, all the headlines would be about the player, not what a tactical genius Rafa was. It was always about Rafa. It was so important to him to be the one everyone was talking about. It was like he always had something to prove.

A few months into the season, I went up to Blackburn to see Mark Hughes and some of the lads at the training ground. He could see it in my face. "You're not enjoying it, are you?" he asked. He said he wasn't going to say 'I told you'. In fact, he told me to stick at it and I might be surprised how things turned out. He also mentioned I'd be welcome back at Blackburn any time.

After the way Liverpool had finished the previous season, we thought we might have a real shot at the Premier League title. Players like Fernando Morientes, Didi Hamann and Djimi Traore had left the club but they had been replaced by quality signings like Kuyt, Alvaro Arbeloa, Fabio Aurelio and Jermaine Pennant. I thought I could add something, too.

But we started the season slowly. We only won one of our opening four games. We drew on the opening day at Sheffield United and then lost heavily in the Merseyside derby at

Goodison. We had also been beaten at Chelsea, Bolton, Manchester United and Arsenal, too, by the middle of November. When we drew at Middlesbrough on November 18, we were in ninth place, already 16 points behind United, who were top.

That November was a difficult month for me. When I signed for Liverpool, I was facing charges that I had tried to strangle a woman in the No 10 nightclub in Cardiff the previous February, when I was playing for Blackburn. The woman's friend had also accused me of grabbing her wrist and pushing her against a wall so I was up on two charges of common assault.

Liverpool asked about the case when I was signing for them. They wanted to know what the worst-case scenario was. They were told it was unlikely I would go to jail, even if I were found guilty. I knew that I hadn't done anything wrong. I hadn't touched either of them but I also knew that if Liverpool were worried about the publicity the case might generate, it could have derailed my move.

That didn't happen but my trial was set for the end of November and, obviously, the closer it got, the more it worried me. The papers brought it up every time my name was mentioned and I struggled to deal with it. I was at Cardiff Magistrates' Court for five days, listening to the account of how I was supposed to have grabbed one woman by the throat.

But the prosecution case was described in court as 'a shambles' and I was cleared by the district judge who said there were 'serious discrepancies' in the case against me. I understand that accusations have to be answered. I understand that my reputation probably went before me but I also felt bitter that the case had ever been allowed to go to court.

It was a great relief when it was over. My play began to

improve. The first game after the end of the trial was Wigan away and I got the first two goals in a 4-0 win. I scored again in victories against Charlton and Watford and just before Christmas, Rafa called me into his office. I thought maybe he was going to say how pleased he was with my form.

That was naïve. Rafa turned the video on and started showing me clips of matches that had happened earlier in the season and which illustrated what I had been doing wrong then. I told him this was all very helpful but that I was actually playing quite well now.

"Yes," Rafa said, "but I have got to show you what you were doing a few months ago to keep you improving."

I wanted to tell him it would be nice if he gave me just a little bit of praise. He always talked about the negatives. He said he was trying to improve you but sometimes showing you what you are doing well can improve you as well.

It was pointless wanting him to change, though. I know it wasn't anything personal. It wasn't just me that he treated like that. It was just Rafa's way.

20

Spanish Golf

We might have started slowly in the Premier League but we were flying in Europe. We drew away at PSV Eindhoven in our first Champions League group game but then we reeled off successive wins against Galatasaray and Bordeaux (home and away) before securing qualification to the knock-out phase with a game to spare courtesy of a victory against PSV at Anfield.

The draw for the last 16 paired us with Barcelona. That got my pulse racing. I had never played at the Nou Camp before. What a prospect that was.

Every player wants to test himself against the best, too, and this was a chance to play on the same pitch as stars like Lionel Messi, Xavi, Andres Iniesta and Carles Puyol. If I was selected, of course.

A fortnight before the game, I played for Wales against Northern Ireland at Windsor Park and all I could think about was avoiding injury. Rafa's favourite word was 'focus' and I was focusing everything on that game at the Nou Camp. The Windsor Park pitch was hard with frost and there were a few lively challenges flying around. My spell at Celtic seemed to have made me a marked man with the crowd and some of the Northern Ireland players took up the cudgel too. The match was a rather dull 0-0 draw but I was just relieved to get out of there unscathed.

At the beginning of the following week, Rafa took us away to the Algarve in Portugal for a camp to prepare in earnest for the first leg of the Barcelona tie. It was made very clear that this was all about work. No going out. None of that. We were going to be allowed one game of golf and that was it. We knew we were going to have to be at our very best to have a chance against Barcelona. They were the holders, after all, so it was going to be tough. But Rafa had the golden touch in Europe and that inspired confidence in everyone. We worked hard in Portugal. We did a lot of defensive work. By the time the trip drew to a close, we felt thoroughly prepared.

The camaraderie within the squad was okay. The Spanish lads stuck to each other and then there was me Crouchie, Carragher and Steve Finnan in another group. It was just cultural. You could try and have a laugh with the Spanish lads but our mentalities were different. The training regime was all about being focused and the Spanish lads were very intense. Focus was Rafa's favourite word but it drove me nuts. How can you not be focused when you're playing for Liverpool?

Anyway, the last night before we flew back to England, we

were allowed out for something to eat at one of the restaurants at the Vale do Lobo resort where we were staying. The whole squad went out. We were supposed to be back by 11pm but after a couple of drinks, we made a collective decision that we would ignore that deadline.

The evening started to get lively. There was some singing. There was a tradition at Liverpool, as there is at many clubs, that new signings have to get up and sing a song in front of the rest of the squad. I'd done mine at the Christmas party at John Aldridge's bar in Liverpool (I sang 'You're Gorgeous' to one of the reserve keepers who was a great lad but whose looks were, let's say, rather rugged) and now it was the turn of a couple of others.

Javier Mascherano had only joined the club a couple of days earlier but he got up and sang some Spanish song. Then a few of the lads decided that John Arne Riise ought to sing, too.

Riise, who was known as Ginge, had ducked out of the Christmas do because he said he had some sort of family commitment in Norway. But someone discovered he had never actually gone to Norway. The lads set up this mock court where evidence was presented against him and in the end he admitted that he hadn't gone to Norway at all. He had to pay the bar bill for the Christmas do as a fine and he agreed he'd do some karaoke the next time we had a party.

Ginge was a nice enough lad. He was a bit of a child. He was insanely competitive about challenges that might be set. Like if there was a competition to see who could ping a shot against the crossbar, he was always mad keen to win it. People used to make a joke of it and say 'I bet Ginge could do that'.

That night at Vale do Lobo, I was sitting with Steve Finnan, who was my roommate, Sami Hyypia and Ginge. I told Ginge he had to sing a song. I might have said it a couple of times. He said he didn't want to do it. I mentioned it again and he snapped. He got shitty about it. He got up and started shouting.

"Listen," he yelled, "I'm not singing and I've had enough of you banging on about it."

Sami told me to ignore him and Ginge left fairly soon afterwards. But as the evening wore on and I had more to drink, it started eating away at me. At that time, the way I was, I didn't know how to control my emotions if someone disrespected me in front of the rest of the players. I wasn't going to let it go, especially after a drink. I am one of the worst people on drink. It doesn't agree with me. I used to put myself in situations I shouldn't be in.

After a while, I told Steve Finnan we were going. I told him I wanted to sort it out with Ginge.

"I'm not having that," I said to Finny.

"What are you on about?" he said.

"That ginger fucking prick, he ain't speaking to me like that," I said.

Finny told me to ignore him. He told me to forget it and go to bed.

"I'm not ignoring him," I said. "I'm going to go to his room."

Finny told me to calm down. He said I couldn't go to his room.

"I'm going to his room," I said again.

"No, let's go to our room," he said. He was trying to humour me, like a warder with a madman.

We did go back to our room but I still couldn't let it go. We had a shared lounge with bedrooms that were upstairs. Our golf clubs were in the lounge. I'd got one out as I was stewing over what Ginge had done. It was an eight iron. I started taking a few practice swings with it.

"Let's go and see him now," I said.

Finnan tried to stop me again but I was determined. I had got to the point where I wouldn't be stopped.

I knew Ginge was sharing with Daniel Agger so I texted him to ask what room he was in. Daniel was still at the party but he texted me the room number. I marched off to find it. Finny came with me. He had given up trying to stop me by then.

"I've got to see this," he said.

I just wanted to wind Ginge up a bit. He had tried it on with me once or twice in training. He had given me a little nudge in the back, you know the kind of thing. I'd just look at him and think 'fuck off, Ginge'.

So we got round to the room and I knocked on the door. There was no answer. I knocked again and still no answer. I texted Daniel again and made sure it was the right room. He said it was. So I tried the door and it was open. I let myself in and turned the light on. Ginge was in bed.

He was facing away from me and covering his eyes with his hands because the lights had been switched on. I just whacked him across the backside with the club. You couldn't really call it a swing. It was just a thwack really. If I'd taken a proper swing, I would have hit the ceiling with my backlift. Finny, by the way, was hiding behind the door at that point.

Ginge panicked. He curled up in a ball with a blanket.

"You ever speak to me like that in front of people again," I told him, "I will wrap this round your head.

"Listen, I didn't mean it like that," he said.

"Yes you fucking did," I barked at him.

"No, no, I didn't," he insisted.

"Yes, you did," I told him again. "That's a couple of times you've pulled that fucking stunt on me and it won't be happening any more."

I was warming to my theme now, like people who have had too much to drink usually do. I threatened him a few times.

"And if you've got a problem with any of this, come and see me in my room tomorrow," I told him. "Don't go moaning about it."

I look back at what I did now and I cringe. It was pathetic. It was stupidity of the highest level. It was drunken, bullying behaviour.

Eventually, I left. As Finny and I were going back to our room, the coach pulled up outside and all the players poured off it. They bumped into us in the corridor and, not knowing anything of what had just gone on, piled into our lounge. It had been a big night. Nobody even noticed the golf club in my hand. If they did, they didn't mention it.

So the night out continued in our room. The room got wrecked basically. Sofas were turned upside down, lampshades got knocked off lamps, somebody even chucked a plate at one stage and it split someone's head open. By the time I went to bed, that lounge was not a pretty sight.

The next thing I knew, Finnan was knocking on my door.

"The Gaffer and Pako are downstairs," he said.

'Oh, shit,' I thought. 'There are a whole number of reasons why they might be here.'

I went downstairs. It was not a pretty picture. Rafa and Pako were sitting on a sofa that they must have had to pull upright themselves. Rafa, the most ordered, controlling man I knew, surrounded by utter chaos, by a scene that screamed out loss of control. There were plates and lampshades everywhere. Rafa looked at me and told me to put some shoes on before I cut my feet on some debris.

"John Arne Riise has just come to my room to say you attacked him with a golf club," Rafa said.

"I wouldn't say I attacked him, exactly," I said. I gave him my version.

They weren't quite as angry as I thought they would be. They told me I had been stupid, of course. I was already full of remorse. I told them I would apologise.

Rafa looked bemused. It turned out he had had quite a night himself. He said he had been woken at 4am by a phone call telling him that Jerzy Dudek, who was our reserve keeper by then, was being held at a local police station.

Finny and I went down to breakfast. A little while later, Dudek appeared with grazes down the side of his face.

"What the fuck happened to Jerzy?" I asked.

After I had left the previous night, things had got out of hand, apparently. Jerzy had refused to leave the bar and the police were called and he had ended up in the cells. Rafa had to go and bail him out.

I actually felt relieved. 'That's miles worse than my one,' I thought as I stared over at Jerzy. 'That might save me.'

Most of the lads were talking about Jerzy, not me and Ginge. And me and Ginge were fine. I apologised to him straight away and he said he hadn't meant to offend me. We were even talking about it while we were warming up for training that morning. I was still worried the media might find out about it but I thought I'd be okay. 'Jerzy's the story,' I thought.

That delusion didn't last long. When we got back to England, I got a call saying the News of the World had got the story about me and Ginge. I rang Kieron Dyer and spoke to him about it. He said he'd get hold of a copy of the first edition and let me know what it was like. I knew I'd be asleep by then so I told him to text me how bad it was on a scale of 1 to 10. One would mean it had hardly broken the waves, 10 would mean all hell had broken loose.

I woke up, got in the car and went to training. I switched the radio on and listened to the sports news and there was nothing about it. Not one word. I thought maybe they hadn't run it. Then, I remembered about Kieron's message. Just as I was about to walk into Melwood, I turned my phone on and the message waiting icon flashed up. It was from Kieron.

'10,' it said.

21

Nou Dawn

When I got inside Melwood, I saw a copy of The Sun. The headline was 'Nutter with a Putter' and they had mocked up a picture of Ginge with so many bandages wrapped round his head that he looked like an Egyptian mummy. All the other lads knew what had happened already but it didn't stop me getting plenty of stick about it.

When we went outside for training, there were cameras poking out everywhere over the low walls that surround Melwood. It was obvious what picture they wanted. We did a couple of warm-up exercises that involved pairing up. Everybody knew the photographers would be desperate to get me and Ginge together but we didn't play along. In the end, Pako lost his patience.

"When I next say 'twos'," he said, "can John Arne Riise and Craig Bellamy get together. Then everyone gets their picture and we can get on with training." That was the picture that was in the papers the next day and the row between us was the issue that dominated the build-up to the Barcelona game. The court case in Cardiff got dragged up a lot again and a lot of people were saying this episode would be the last straw for Rafa.

If we lost to Barcelona, everyone said, that would be me finished at Liverpool. We were too far behind to have a chance in the league by then and we had been knocked out of both cups. There was an awful lot riding on that game in the Nou Camp. A lot of people expected Rafa to leave me out. It would have been the easy thing to do in many ways. But Rafa often ignored the easy option. When the teamsheet went up, I was in the starting eleven.

Training at the Nou Camp the day before the game was brilliant. I looked up at the steepling stands all around me and the giant Mes Que Un Club logo written into the seats and I knew this was the big league. We were up against the reigning champions, up against Ronaldinho, Messi, Deco. I didn't feel nervous. I just felt an overwhelming sense of anticipation.

I just made my mind up I was going to enjoy it. It was everything I had worked for. I knew I might not get the opportunity to play on a stage like that again. To add to it, my elder son, Ellis, was 10 on the day of the game and I flew him out for a birthday treat. Crouchie said to me that if he played, he would do a golf swing celebration if he scored. I said the same. I didn't know if I was playing at that stage and, to be honest, I wasn't thinking about goal celebrations. I was just hoping I'd get an opportunity to get on the pitch.

The odds were stacked against us. Not many people gave us a chance because Barcelona were such a fantastic team. We were struggling in the Premier League, too, and a lot of the media presented it as almost a formality that we were going to lose. The only doubt in people's minds was that Rafa had over-achieved in Europe before.

In the first 20 minutes, Barcelona were brilliant. Actually, they were breathtaking. We couldn't get near them. The term 'chasing shadows' was invented for spells of football like the one we endured at the start of that game and Deco put them ahead with a bullet header after 14 minutes when he ran on to a cross from Gianluca Zambrotta.

But we did not fold. I missed a decent chance with a back post header that I could only nod into the side-netting and then two minutes before half-time, I put us level. I peeled away at the back post again and when Steve Finnan's cross came to me, I was unmarked.

I put as much power as I could into it and the Barcelona keeper, Victor Valdes, seemed to lose track of where the goal line was. He seemed caught in two minds about whether to try to catch the ball or to parry it and by the time he made up his mind, he was behind the line and so was the ball.

Dirk Kuyt slotted in the rebound when Valdes belatedly pushed the ball away but it was my goal. In the elation of the moment, I forgot all about the celebration for about 20 seconds but eventually I remembered and aimed an imaginary eight iron down the ground. Some people were upset by that. They said it showed a lack of contrition. That wasn't true. It was just an expression of happiness, mixed with a little mischief and a signal that there was more to me than bouts of bad behaviour.

It was a proud moment looking up at the Nou Camp scoreboard and seeing my name on it. I knew that my son would be looking at it, too, which meant more to me than anything. Because of the impact his birth had had on me, because of my determination to create a good life for him, he was one of the main reasons why I was playing at this level in the first place.

We hung on a little bit in the second half but 16 minutes from time, Dirk found himself one on one with Valdes. Valdes smothered his shot and the ball ballooned into the air. Rafa Marquez tried to clear the ball with a back header but it came straight to me. I cushioned it on my chest and let it drop. In the split second that it was falling, I thought about shooting but I was aware of Ginge standing to my left and I squared the ball to him on the half-volley.

It came to him on his right foot and he swung at it first time. I didn't know he could even kick with his right foot but he hit it as sweetly as some of his left-foot pile-drivers and it flew into the top corner of the net. I looked up at the scoreboard again and there were our names in lights, Bellamy and Riise. Football is stranger than fiction sometimes. After everything that had happened the week before, after all the focus on us in the days leading up to the match, events had brought us together again.

There were a few scares in the last quarter of an hour but we saw it out and preserved our precious lead. When the whistle blew, I was overcome. Football: what an amazing game. I felt lucky, too. I'd had plenty of lows in my career but I understood in that moment that not many players get to experience something like that.

It was my favourite moment in football. Whatever might happen to me in the years to come, I thought, nobody could change a moment like that. I saw Ellis afterwards and felt thankful again that he had been there to witness it. I didn't know where my life was going to go, who I was going to be sharing it with, inside or outside the game, but I did know that if football ended for me tomorrow, I'd have that moment. Sometimes, that's worth more than anything.

We flew back to England and everyone was revelling in the story of me and Ginge and marvelling at our win. We knew we had a real chance of confounding expectations and getting through to the quarter-finals now. And I thought maybe this would be the catalyst for me at the club, that I would be a more central figure now as the season headed towards its climax.

Wrong again. The first game after we got back from Spain was against Sheffield United at Anfield. When the teamsheet went up on the Friday, I looked at it with a degree of confidence for the first time. My name wasn't on it. Nowhere on it. Not even among the subs. 'What the fuck is this about?' I thought.

I should have been rolling into Anfield that Saturday on a real high and I wasn't even in the squad. I couldn't even stand to be in England when the game was on. I had to get far away. I went to Dublin to watch Ireland play England in the Six Nations instead. Being left out of that game broke me a bit. It dented me. I thought 'I don't think I can do this again next year, being on the bench, not knowing when you're starting, not knowing if you're in the squad'. It didn't motivate me. It deflated me.

I'm not really criticising Rafa for it. It was the way he worked. And I started the game against Manchester United the following weekend, which we lost to two late goals. I started the second leg against Barcelona, too, which was played in a fantastic atmosphere at Anfield. We hung on a little bit and things got twitchy when Eidur Gudjohnsen put them 1-0 up on the night with 15 minutes left, but we kept them out and went through to the last eight on the away goals rule.

My relationship with Rafa was unaffected by what happened in Portugal. If would have been uncharacteristic if he had let emotion seep into anything. Things stayed the same. I don't know if the Spanish players were close to him but I never had any proper conversations with him. We were there to work and that was it. The longer it went on, the more draining it became. It wasn't enjoyment. It was just hard, hard work. After every day of training, I left feeling unfulfilled and flat.

I clung on to the consolations. The main one was that we were in the quarter-finals of the Champions League. Then there was playing with Gerrard and Carragher. And training with Robbie Fowler. His finishing was still in a different league. He could dink it over the keeper, he could move the ball, he could whip it. And he was a lovely bloke, too.

By the time I got to play with him, his legs had gone. He had suffered a bad knee injury and it had robbed him of his acceleration. I didn't feel sorry for him because he had been a better player than I could ever be and had enjoyed a great career. I just enjoyed watching him and learning from his finishing ability. He is still God. He always will be.

He and I didn't play together that often but we did both start a League Cup fourth round tie against Birmingham City at St Andrew's at the start of November. Rafa liked to nominate a penalty-taker for each game and it was Robbie that night.

But when we were awarded one, I decided that I wanted to take it. Robbie and I had a brief argument but he couldn't be bothered to continue it. He stepped aside. I took it.

The Birmingham keeper, Maik Taylor, saved it. We still won the game but it wasn't my finest hour.

The next day, Rafa called me in. He asked me why I took the penalty. I said I felt confident and I wanted to score.

"But you weren't on penalties," he said. "I have to fine you."

"Really?" I said.

"Yes," Rafa said. "I pick the penalty taker. Not you."

I don't know how much the fine was. I didn't dare think about it because it would have driven me mad.

But at the end of it all, Rafa was successful. I could question his methods as much as I wanted but we were in the quarter-finals of the Champions League and we had just drawn PSV so we had every chance of making the semis. When I thought about the way Rafa worked, I started to wonder if this was how you had to be to win stuff.

We didn't have any problems against PSV. I had a rib injury so I was left on the bench. The first leg was at Anfield and we beat them even more comfortably than we had in the group phase. Gerrard, Riise and Crouch scored the goals in a 3-0 win which put the tie out of PSV's reach. Stevie's goal took him beyond Ian Rush to establish him as the leading scorer in Europe in Liverpool's history. We won the return leg in Eindhoven as well to finish with a 4-0 aggregate victory. When the draw was made for the last four, we got Chelsea.

Two years earlier, Liverpool and Chelsea had been involved in one of the most titanic semi-final clashes in the short history of the Champions League.

On a thunderous night at Anfield, the tie had been settled by what the Chelsea boss Jose Mourinho famously described as 'a ghost goal' by Luis Garcia. Liverpool went on to beat AC

Milan in the final in what became known as the 'Miracle of Istanbul'. Not many teams had a psychological advantage over Mourinho's Chelsea but that victory gave us one. And Rafa was one of the only bosses I've ever seen who managed to get under Mourinho's skin. Usually, Mourinho was the one who sent the opposition manager into a rage but Rafa had the ability to do that to Mourinho.

We were up against the usual suspects at Chelsea. Mourinho was still the boss. This time, there was no Barcelona in his way and he was desperate to win the Champions League with Chelsea. The players that he had won the league with twice – Lampard, Drogba, Terry – were probably at their peak that year. It looked like it would be their best chance to win it.

The first leg was at Stamford Bridge on a Wednesday night. We stayed in Mayfair the night before the game and after we'd trained, we went back to the hotel and watched Manchester United against AC Milan in the other semi-final. United won 3-2 but the abiding memory was of Kaka scoring twice and picking United apart. Milan were the favourites to go through.

That suited us. Everyone at the club was concerned about the idea of playing United in the final. In many ways, Europe was still our refuge. We had won five European Cups and United had only won two. They couldn't get close to our history. They didn't have any bragging rights over us and I think, subconsciously, we were nervous about the thought of losing that sanctuary if we had to face them in a final.

We knew Chelsea would be tough. They were a very good side with top, top players and a brilliant manager. I started the first leg at the Bridge but I didn't make much of an impact and I was substituted six minutes into the second half when Rafa brought Crouchie on. We were trailing to a Joe Cole goal by then and Pepe Reina had to make a couple of outstanding saves to stop the gap widening. They deserved their win and we went back to Anfield feeling grateful we were still in the tie.

I have never witnessed an atmosphere like the one that greeted us in the stadium that night. I was on the bench but even when I went out for the warm-up, it made the hairs on the back of my neck stand on end. I understood the logic for Rafa's team selection. He had picked me at Stamford Bridge because he wanted to exploit Chelsea's lack of pace at the back. But at Anfield, he thought Chelsea would sit back and not leave as much space behind their defence, so he chose Crouchie to lead the line.

Rafa called it just right. Before the game, we worked and worked on set-pieces. He said he was sure that was how the game would be decided and that was what happened. Midway through the first half, Joe Cole fouled Gerrard on the left and instead of swinging the free-kick into the area, Stevie slid it across the face of the box and Daniel Agger slammed it into the net with his left foot.

That meant we were level on aggregate. Both sides had chances but it went to extra-time. Rafa brought me on for Crouchie with 14 minutes to go and Fowler came on for Mascherano two minutes from the end, ready for the penalty shoot-out.

Psychologically, I still felt we had the edge. They had experienced what it felt like to lose in the semi-final at Anfield before and now that they had failed to beat us, I think they felt it heading their way again.

I wasn't in the first five penalty takers. My heroics against Birmingham City probably didn't work in my favour as far as that went. I didn't mind. I trusted the lads who had been nominated by Rafa. Boudewijn Zenden took the first and scored. Then Reina saved Arjen Robben's kick. Alonso scored for us. Lampard scored for them. Gerrard scored for us. Reina saved from Geremi.

That meant if Dirk scored with the fourth penalty, we were through. I stood in the line of players, my arms linked around the shoulders of Finny on my right and Zenden on my left. I looked over at the touchline where Rafa was sitting cross-legged on the turf. I looked along the line and saw Gerrard with his arm around Fowler, two legends of the club together. Dirk ran up and slotted his penalty low beyond Petr Cech's reach. We were through to the final. Anfield went berserk.

I didn't want to go too mad because I had been a bit-part player. I would have felt more satisfaction if I had been in the thick of it. Still, I thought I had a chance of a Champions League medal and my first thought when the final whistle went was that I had to try to force my way into the team for the final. AC Milan cruised past United at the San Siro the following evening so the final, which was to take place in Athens on May 23, would be a rematch of the Miracle of Istanbul.

Rafa had obviously not been too badly scarred by the events of Vale do Lobo because he took us away again for a week's training. We avoided the Algarve this time and headed to La Manga. Funnily enough, we weren't allowed out for a meal this time. Nothing happened. It was dead. It was just work, which was what everybody wanted anyway. Every day, there was specific training to counter Kaka and Seedorf because Rafa thought they were the biggest influences on Milan.

When we arrived in Athens and trained in the Olympic Stadium the night before the game, I was taken aback by how many journalists there were there. I had played in big games but I had never seen anything like this before. There were journalists from Chile, Serbia, China, Australia, South Korea, France, Turkey. But there was no one from Wales. How many Wales players had ever got to the Champions League final? Apart from Ryan Giggs, obviously. There haven't been many.

I was on edge about the team selection. I thought the game would suit me. There was a lot of talk about Milan's lack of pace and how that was a way we could hurt them. They had great players in their defence like Alessandro Nesta and Paolo Maldini but I thought I might have a decent time against them. They tried to play high, which was quite rare for Italian teams, and they liked to press.

Everyone was fit so I fluctuated from thinking I might start to worrying about whether I would even make the bench. Rafa didn't break with tradition. He didn't name the team until very late. We went ten-pin bowling on the morning of the game. I don't like bowling. And then finally, he named the team. I wasn't in it but I was on the bench. He had gone with Dirk starting by himself up front with Stevie in behind him and Jermaine Pennant and Zenden on the flanks.

That was okay. I was disappointed, obviously, but I could deal with it. That was the way Rafa wanted to go about it and it was up to him. There was no point being down because I could still come on and score the winner and you're not going to do that if you are in a negative frame of mind. I had to accept it and see what happened.

We started reasonably brightly but AC Milan were the better team. It was a tight first half but they scored just before the interval when Filippo Inzaghi deflected a free-kick by Andrea

Pirlo past Reina. The longer the game wore on, the longer they held on to their lead, the less chance I thought there was of me getting on the pitch.

If Milan were leading, they would sit deeper and deeper and Rafa's logic would be that there would be less and less space for me to exploit. That was the way it worked out. He brought Harry Kewell on for Zenden after about an hour and then re-placed Mascherano with Crouchie with 13 minutes left. I knew then that my chance of influencing the game in any way had gone and a few minutes later, Inzaghi put the game beyond us when he ran on to a ball from Kaka, took it round Reina and slid it into the net.

In the dying minutes, Rafa brought Arbeloa on for Finnan. Right-back for right-back. Explain that one to me when we're 2-0 down. Dirk did grab a late goal from a corner but there was to be no miracle this time. The final whistle went and Milan were champions.

I was disappointed for Liverpool and the rest of the players. But it felt like a double disappointment for me because I didn't get the chance to get on. It was heart-wrenching not to play any part at all. It would have been the biggest game of my career. To play in a Champions League final is the pinnacle and, hav-ing got there, I had to sit on the sidelines and watch it. It was a massive anti-climax.

When we were on the coach back to the hotel, a couple of the boys expressed surprise to me that Rafa hadn't brought me on. It was nice of them but it didn't help. It didn't make any differ-ence. It was over. The chance had gone. As a fan of the club, I felt sick about the defeat. As a player denied the chance to play in the biggest game in club football, I just felt empty.

Rafa's decision not to play me also indicated that I wouldn't be there next year. I didn't think I could take another year of continual uncertainty about whether I would be playing or not and I didn't think I had his backing anyway. Rafa didn't say a word to me about it on the night. He didn't say sorry for not bringing me on. He didn't come out with any platitudes to try to soften the blow. He didn't do sympathy. That wasn't his style.

I sat by myself on the plane back to England the next day. Rafa came to sit next to me. At first, I thought maybe he was actually coming to justify his decision to leave me out. I should have known better by then.

"What are your plans for next season?" he said.

I looked at him. We'd just lost the Champions League final. I hadn't got on. I was feeling glum. I wasn't in the mood.

"I haven't really thought about it," I said.

Rafa didn't mince his words.

"We're going to buy another striker," he said. "If you want to go and speak to other clubs, that's fine."

He started to get up to go but I told him to wait for a second.

"I'm still trying to come to terms with the disappointment of what's just happened and now you tell me you want to get rid of me," I said. "Classy timing."

Rafa started stuttering. He did that shrug he does, that merciless kind of shrug that says all emotion is futile and, actually, wholly unwelcome.

"Go and speak to my advisers about it," I said. "Leave me alone."

The plane journey home seemed to last forever. I felt thoroughly dejected. I was obsessing about how I still hadn't won a trophy. If I could have won the Champions League trophy, the biggest one there is, the one that players value above all others, it would have wiped out all my other near misses and semi-final defeats. It would have been a one-stop shop for validating my career in my own mind. So the defeat was hard to take.

And to know you didn't get on as well makes it worse. You are part of it but you aren't. You are part of a team and you have to accept it as part of the team. But you are wondering if it would have been different if you had played. Maybe I wouldn't have made any difference in Athens that night. I'll never know.

I wasn't bitter towards Rafa. Not really. I was just disappointed. I didn't want it to turn into bitterness. I didn't want to resent him. I loved the club and I knew how much happiness he had brought the supporters. I didn't want my relationship with him to deteriorate or for anything to affect my feelings for the place.

The timing of him coming to sit with me on the plane and tell me I was surplus to requirements was a bit hard. He could have let me get over the disappointment of not playing in the final. But Rafa doesn't have any sentiment. He's not interested in social skills. He tries to come across as a warm person but he is as harsh a guy as you will ever come across. I don't mind that really. There probably isn't any good way to tell someone they're not wanted.

Rafa signed Fernando Torres that summer. No one could really argue with that. Not even me. He was a great signing for the club. But I was worried about how I was going to move on. I had been in a team that had a chance of winning the league and which had just reached a Champions League final. Where would I find that again?

As we arrived back at John Lennon Airport, I tried to remind myself how lucky I had been to play for the team I loved. I thought about the very first time I had visited Anfield in the wake of the Hillsborough Disaster, I thought about all the things I loved about the legend of Shankly and the empire he had created and the stories older players had told me about facing the great Liverpool teams of the Seventies.

It was still the most incredible club in the world to me. What it represents as a club is what I represent as a person. I feel like a black sheep but people have to acknowledge me because my play demands it. I'm an outsider but sometimes I play so well that you have to let me in. That's what it's like for me and sometimes it feels as though that's what it's like for Liverpool. They have to fight and fight for everything they get.

I didn't want to leave but I didn't really have much choice. I thought maybe I'd move abroad, make a fresh start. It hadn't ended how I had wanted it to end at Liverpool but at least I was part of their history now. And one way or another, sooner or later, as player or coach or supporter, I knew I'd be back.

22

Giving It Back

Maybe it was because I was worried about how I was going to follow playing for Liverpool. Maybe it was because I felt the need to do something completely different to put some distance between me and the crushing disappointment of the Champions League final. Whatever the reasons, I did something random that summer, something that changed my life. I went to Sierra Leone.

Why? Well, I had a mate who was working out there and he invited me to come and visit. I could have said 'yeah, thanks, but the hotels are a bit nicer in Puerto Banus this time of year' but I didn't. I wanted to see what it was like. I'd always been intrigued by Africa. So I got on a plane and flew to Freetown. It was one of the best decisions I've ever made.

When I say I'd been intrigued by Africa, I suppose I mean I'd been gripped by the stories they told on Comic Relief. I wondered what it was really like. I didn't want to go to somewhere like South Africa or Kenya where there is great poverty but there is great wealth as well. I didn't want to go somewhere where you could take refuge in a rich man's lifestyle.

I knew that in parts of West Africa, there was no rich man's lifestyle. Not really. There was poor and there was poor. I wasn't intimidated about going out there. It didn't cross my mind at all. I was fascinated by the idea of what I would find. I wanted to see how people lived.

It was a culture shock. It was bound to be. I landed at Freetown and found out that the airport is on the other side of the Sierra Leone River from the city. So I either had to get a ferry that took a couple of hours, a taxi that took about four hours on a roundabout route or an old Russian helicopter. They have got a habit of ditching in the river, I found out later, but it seemed like the safest option at the time. I took the helicopter.

Freetown was great. It was chaotic but it was great. An 11-year civil war had only just ended so a lot of the city was a ruin. But the people were wonderful and life was vibrant and vital. I'd been worrying about the Champions League final and what was going to happen to me, whether I'd join this club or that club for £40,000 a week or £50,000 a week. Seeing Freetown woke me up. I thought 'you ain't got no problems'.

The poverty I saw made a huge impact on me. But not the poverty in isolation. It was more the fact that the people who were living in all that poverty were so positive. It amazed me. Maybe I'd become accustomed to moaning about inconsequential things. Maybe I'd lost sight of what mattered. But I looked around there and I saw people who had very, very little and still had such a good outlook on life. For them, being alive is the biggest achievement of all. What they have to go through just to have life is more important than any material things.

Yeah, I was worried about diseases and snakes and all the things Europeans worry about when we think of Africa but when you are there, you just get on with it. There was no electricity in a lot of places. For somebody who's grown used to the comforts of western civilisation, it felt quite challenging. But, of course, there was one thing that linked me with the people I saw: football.

I was shocked by how many people knew me. The day after I arrived, I woke up and thought I'd go into the centre of Freetown. I was interested in the history of the place. I wanted to see the effects of the civil war. I wanted to get a better idea of how people lived. I got a taxi into town and climbed out to have a walk. Within a few minutes, I had to get back into the car. I was mobbed.

I was still technically a Liverpool player then and I wasn't really aware quite how popular the leading Premier League teams were. I soon realised. Armed police had to come and get me out and take me back to my hotel because the roads became blocked with crowds. It took me aback. It wasn't like Wayne Rooney or Steven Gerrard was in town. I'm only Craig Bellamy. But it was probably the first time a Premier League player had ever visited the city.

Soon, it became evident it was going to be impossible for me even to remain at the hotel I'd booked myself into. The lobby was packed with people wanting photos and autographs. There were too many people for the hotel to cope with. So I had to move out. I didn't want to leave but I could tell I was making life difficult for the hotel. The hotel put me in touch with a British security company that had houses for ex-pats out there and they took me to one of those.

A couple of days later, I travelled east. I wanted to see the diamond mines in that part of the country. It was a seven-hour journey by car, although in the UK it would take about half that. I'd brought a load of footballs with me so we stopped off now and again on the way up whenever we saw a group of kids and had a kickabout.

It was funny: when the kids saw four or five white men getting out of a car, they just scarpered. You go back in the history of the place, there's probably a very good reason for that. But eventually, they'd come back in their droves. To see their pleasure in a simple football was enough for me. They were used to playing with a bundle of rolled up newspaper bound with sticky tape.

Again, a lot of them seemed to know me. I thought there was no way that some of the villages we stopped in would have any access to television but the power of the Premier League is far-reaching. One of the main teams in Freetown is even called Mighty Blackpool.

When we arrived in the Kono district where a lot of the diamond mining goes on, I found out the local chief wanted to meet me. Word had spread that I was visiting and when we got close, the crowds got out of control again. There were people as far as I could see who had come to greet me. It was absolutely surreal.

I wanted to see the diamond mines because I wanted to see another side of Sierra Leone. It made me sad, seeing the poor panning in the water. They would get a couple of dollars for what we would pay thousands for. I wasn't averse to a bit of bling in those days but seeing the conditions those people worked in – and a lot of them were kids – put me off. I would never buy a diamond now. I certainly wouldn't wear one.

I can see how some people can come away from a country like that, drained and never wanting to go back. But it had the exact opposite effect on me. I felt inspired and energised by what I saw. I wanted to do something positive. What's the difference between me and them? I was born where I was born and they were born where they were born. None of us are given a choice where we are born in this world or which parents we are born to. That's the only difference.

I made up my mind straight away that I wanted to give something back. I knew by then that West Ham were trying to sign me and they were offering me a lot of money, more money than I had ever earned before. Reports said later that I would be earning around £80,000 a week. They weren't far wrong. However much it was, I felt it was the right thing to give some of it away. I didn't need it all. I don't need that much to live. Lifestyle isn't hugely important to me. As long as my kids are comfortable, that's really all I care about.

I wanted to give something to these people in Sierra Leone. I thought about building a school but it would have to be free education and so you'd have to turn people away because there would be too many. So I thought about building an orphanage but then you are fighting with Christian groups and Muslim groups and things can get very complicated.

So then I thought about a football academy, a place where people could come and live and play for free. It would have to be selective. It would be for kids who were talented footballers but I wanted to make sure that they were also academically up to a level where we could teach them and educate them.

I wanted to give them an opportunity in life, not just in football. I wanted to do something for the country and the society, not just for the game. So if they didn't make it as a footballer, I wanted them to be able to go back into Sierra Leone society very well educated. I wanted them to become the next minister of health, the next president, a doctor or a lawyer. Or go to America on a college scheme.

My dream was that one day, one of the kids who goes to the academy would be able to become a top player and look after his family. And then when that happened, he remembered the opportunity he was given and was able to do the same for other kids in his country. I wanted the academy to start what people call a virtuous circle.

That was in the summer of 2007. We started work in earnest the following year. Building the academy took a while. No one works during rainy season, for a start. It just isn't practical. The government gave me land in a nice village outside Freetown called Tombo. It's a fishing and farming village and the 15-acre site where the academy is based overlooks the Atlantic.

There were teething troubles. There were bound to be. Everyone had told me to be prepared for that. But the local people grasped the idea that this was something that would give kids an opportunity. With the help of Unicef, we set up a youth league, too, because nothing like that existed at the time. It was a pre-requisite that the kids who played in the league had to be going to school. If they weren't at school, they couldn't play in the league, no matter how good they were.

The first group of 15 boys arrived at the academy in August 2010. We gave five-year scholarships to children aged 11-13 who live, study and train at the academy. I was ambitious. I wanted the facilities to be good. The playing surface we have now is generally recognised as the best grass pitch in Sierra Leone.

The league has been a success, too. There are more than 40 teams across the country and Unicef loved it. Teams earn league points not only for match results, but also for school attendance, good behaviour and fair-play, and leading development projects in their communities. One of the teams was even called Young Cambridge because of the kids' commitment to the academic side of things.

There's another called Central Professionals, which has attained brilliant school attendance rates and another called Welding United, which is run by a committed lady called Edna Sowa. I read on our website recently that Edna had named her new son Bellamy.

We have a special group of 12-year-olds at the academy now – our second intake – who have blossomed due to the establishment of the league. The quality is improving all the time. Unicef aren't involved any more because their policy, which I agree with, is to work with a project for a couple of years and then move on.

Finding funding is hard. In some people's eyes, I am the Premier League footballer who has endless amounts of money. Why should anyone give me money when I should be paying it all myself? But realistically, my money won't last forever. I set an initial period of five years which was my West Ham contract to get it up and running.

I want the academy to be self-sufficient. I want it to be run by people in Sierra Leone. I want to see kids from it playing in Belgium or in Norway or in the Premier League because that fits the romantic idea of football for me. I would love to be able to see them playing the greatest game in the world and be able to think that I had played a part in enabling them to do that. But like I say, I would get as much satisfaction if one of my students became a doctor in Sierra Leone, saving people's lives.

In October 2012, one of the lads from the academy, Sahid Conteh, was awarded a scholarship to study at the Dunn School in California, a couple of hours north of Los Angeles. He is playing a lot of football but he is also studying English, Algebra, Conceptual Physics and Ancient World History. Even if it all collapsed tomorrow, I have made a difference to his life.

That's what I wanted to do – give kids an opportunity that we all take for granted but which they have never been able to have because of the poverty and the wars that have gone on. I am hoping that it carries on for years to come and gets bigger and bigger.

I have put about £1.4m of my own money into it. It is not an investment. It is not about making money. Say my academy discovered the next Didier Drogba, if a club wanted him, they would have to cover the academy's costs for the education he had received. But that would be it. It's not about making profit. I hope that one day the national team of Sierra Leone will be drawn from players that grew up in my academy, much like the national team of Ivory Coast is largely populated by players that came up through the famous Académie MimoSifcom.

We have about 30 boys at the Craig Bellamy Foundation Academy now. They wake up at 6am and do their chores. Train at 7am. Finish at 8am. Have breakfast. School at 9am. Finish at 12pm. An hour break. School again at 1pm. Finish at 4pm and then training again at 5pm for an hour. Shower. Homework, reading and bed early. They will do two to three hours a day training. It's a long day but they are progressing well.

There have been difficulties along the way but we have got there in the end. I'm pleased I've done it but I wouldn't necessarily call it unselfish because it's been a huge benefit to me as a human being. I hope my own children will feel proud of it, too. I hope one day they'll be able to go to a place in Sierra Leone to see a school that has provided a lot of young kids with a better start in life than they might otherwise have had. And I hope they will feel proud that their dad has been able to do that.

As far as I'm concerned, what I'm doing in Sierra Leone will be my legacy. Not how many goals I scored or how many medals I won or how many Premier League appearances I made. I'm proud of those things, too, but they don't really matter. I hope I'm remembered more for the work of my foundation than for anything I ever did on the football pitch.

23

Striking Out

By that summer of 2007, the summer that I made my trip to Sierra Leone, my family were living in Cardiff after we had made the decision that Claire and the kids would live there on a permanent basis, rather than trailing around after me from club to club and city to city. We'd realised it was getting too hard on them and too disruptive to the kids' schooling. By then, we also knew that Claire was pregnant with our third child and that it was going to be a girl.

So wherever I moved to, I knew that Claire and the kids would not be with me full-time. I had interest from a number of clubs after it became apparent that Rafa wanted to sell me.

Sam Allardyce had just become manager at Newcastle and he wanted me to go back there in a swap deal with Michael Owen.

Newcastle rang Liverpool and Liverpool said they would not even think about it. It was a non-starter. Everton were interested again. So were Aston Villa, where Martin O'Neill was the boss.

And then there was West Ham. An Icelandic consortium led by Eggert Magnusson had taken over the previous November and the club was throwing money around. Scott Parker, Julien Faubert, my mate Kieron Dyer and Freddie Ljungberg were all arriving on big money. Before I left for Sierra Leone, the West Ham boss, Alan Curbishley, came down to my house to see how I felt about moving to Upton Park.

He outlined his plans and talked about the money the owners wanted to pump in, the players he wanted to sign and the targets they had set. It seemed quite exciting. London intrigued me as well. I had always fancied living there. I liked the idea of West Ham, too. It was proper London. It was a tough environment to play in as an opposition player and I knew they would probably be a tough crowd for me to break if I went there as a new signing.

West Ham offered me a five-year deal and fantastic money. It was an exceptional contract. I was encouraged by the signing of Parker, in particular. I thought it had a good feel about it and that it would be a realistic goal to try to get into the top six. I knew that if I stayed fit and played well, the crowd would really take to me. They loved grafters and scrappers there. I thought we might be made for each other.

I made up my mind about West Ham as soon as I came home from Sierra Leone. I went to London to have my medical and signed. I didn't want a big fuss or a news conference. I was a week behind everyone else because they had started pre-season already. There were a lot of British boys there and the atmosphere was good.

The facilities at the training ground at Chadwell Heath weren't quite what I was used to. There were Portakabins everywhere and the training pitches weren't the best, either. But part of me didn't really care. It was okay. If it was good enough for Bobby Moore, it was good enough for me. A few people made sure they pointed that out to me. "If Bobby Moore could train here, you shouldn't have a problem." I got that a lot.

There was a good group of lads there. The camaraderie was first class. Players like Anton Ferdinand, Carlton Cole, Bobby Zamora, Scott Parker, Lee Bowyer and Mark Noble, they were just a really good group of funny boys. They trained hard and wanted to do well but they had great humour about them as well. There was a good atmosphere about the place.

Dean Ashton was already there and I was looking forward to playing with him. He was an exceptional player. He was intelligent and quick off the mark. He had broken his ankle while he was on England duty in August, 2006, and had been out since but I thought if we could get him fit, he could be a great player to play with and that excited me, too.

All in all, we had the basis of a very good side if our first-choice players were fit. But it was as if we were cursed at West Ham that season. Faubert ruptured his Achilles tendon in a pre-season match and only played eight league games during the whole campaign. Parker was out for a long time with a knee injury. So was Ashton. Kieron suffered an horrific leg break early in the season. It was hard work because the top players who were going to make the difference weren't playing.

I started the season quite well. I scored both goals in a 2-1 away win at Bristol Rovers in the League Cup and got another in the Premier League win at Reading a few days later. But in the game at the Memorial Stadium, I started getting a sharp pain in my groin. I had a fitness test before the game at Reading and played but it was still very sore.

I was really worried about the injury. It wasn't going away. But then events pushed it into the background. My daughter, Lexi, was born and a couple of days later, there was an alarm about her health and she was rushed back into hospital in Cardiff. She was in a special unit for a little while, hooked up to all sorts of tubes and machines. It's a terribly helpless feeling to see your baby like that and Claire and I slept at the hospital for a few nights.

I missed Wales' Euro 2008 qualifying tie against Germany because of it but gradually she began to get better and the concern about her began to ease. She was released from hospital and I flew off with Wales for a match against Slovakia in Trnava. It was just about the best game I ever played in a Wales shirt. I think it was partly that I felt this great wave of relief that Lexi was okay and it took all the pressure off me. I played without a care in the world. Football wasn't as important any more and I just breezed through the game. I scored two and should have had a hat-trick in a 5-2 win. It was quite a night.

I got back to Cardiff after the game and it was hard to set off again for London. I had a new baby and I struggled with the idea of being away from her so much. I started to fall prey to some of the homesickness problems I had experienced at Norwich as a kid. They took me by surprise a little bit and brought back bad memories of some of the miseries I went through when I first left home.

The situation wasn't helped by my injury. There was clearly something wrong with my groin. I started the next West Ham match against Middlesbrough at Upton Park but I had to come off after about 25 minutes. My groin was just too sore. I had injections and tried to come back two weeks later but I was no-where near fit. The club sent me to Germany to have a hernia operation.

I came back quickly and played for Wales in a defeat to Cyprus. I felt okay in that game but the next match was against San Marino and I was in a lot of pain again. It's a condition called arthritis pubis, apparently, and I was starting to worry about its persistence. West Ham just tried to shut me down. They rested me. I did loads of gym work to try to build up my core strength. We went to see loads of different groin experts and every single person proposed different solutions.

West Ham decided I needed to keep doing the strengthening work so I stayed at the gym, which was at Canary Wharf. It was tough, mentally as well as physically. West Ham had put a lot of faith in me, they had paid a lot of money for me and they had given me a handsome contract. I was 28 now. It wasn't the time I wanted to be injured for a long period.

I started to sense the depression that I had suffered at New-castle coming back. I felt so low. I wasn't able to contribute to West Ham. I didn't know if the course of action they had decided upon was going to work. I missed my family. I couldn't see an end to any of it. West Ham advised me not to opt for surgery. I felt beholden to them. I abided by what they said.

I was still out in December. I drank my way through Christ-mas, which wasn't particularly clever. By the end of January, they finally allowed me back outside and on to the pitches. I started to do some running and my groin felt terrible straight away. I couldn't move. Anything involving going side-to-side or challenging for possession just hurt way too much. And don't even think about shooting, because it was agony.

We all tried to pretend I was recovering all the same and I came on against Wigan in a game at the JJB Stadium at the beginning of February. Antonio Valencia squared me up at one point and I was thankful he ran inside because if he had run at me, I think I would have collapsed. I played a reserve game after that and I had to come off. I was in too much pain.

Being on my own wasn't good for me, either. I brooded and sulked and bemoaned my fate as I sat on my own in my flat at Canary Wharf. But then if I had my family around me, I would have dragged them down, too. I didn't want to speak to anyone, didn't want to look at anyone. I always had that tendency to lapse into self-pity and I didn't know how to deal with it.

At that point, my treatment took a slightly macabre twist. West Ham were getting desperate. They suggested that I might be suffering from bone-bruising and they sent me for treatment that was akin to chemotherapy. So I found myself sitting in a ward at London Bridge Hospital, attached to a drip and sur-rounded by people suffering from cancer.

I struggled with that. I was sitting next to a poor woman who was praying that her next set of results were okay so that she could go on one last holiday. I tried to tell myself how stupid I was to be in a dark mood about a football injury when I was being confronted by the sight of people who were dealing with life and death. I knew I was being pathetic but I couldn't get myself out of my dark mood.

And that played on my mind a lot, too. Why am I feeling so

sorry for myself when I have just seen these people suffering with cancer? I felt selfish. I felt worthless. I was supposed to go back for another session at the hospital in the chemotherapy suite. I couldn't do it.

I was reeling. I went to see a physio called John Green who I knew by reputation and whose opinion I trusted. He took me to see a surgeon who said I needed another hernia operation. I agreed to it. I had a nagging issue with my patella tendon, too, so I thought if I was going to be out for a little while, I might as well have that done as well. So I had a knee operation and two days later, I had a hernia operation. Then I started rehab.

I have always worked really hard to get back after injury. Like a demon, actually. Like somebody who cares about nothing else. I'm capable of blocking everything else out. And everybody, too. It becomes an obsession for me, a desire to get back something I've lost, a manic determination not to lose my career before I'm ready to let it go.

Now, at West Ham, it made me unbearable to be around. But I didn't want to end my career like this. It wasn't going to happen. So I threw myself into what felt like a ridiculously hard rehab regime with John Green which was all built around strengthening work for my groins. I had been out for a long time and I was 28 years old, so it was the flip of a coin whether I came back the player I had been before.

If I didn't give it everything, I knew I would return diminished. So my days consisted of spells on the rowing machine and boxing, swimming or spinning classes. Tough cardiovascular stuff. The programme was designed to batter you. I dreaded it but I knew I needed it. I did so much boxing, I actually began to believe I could fight after a while.

Kieron was working with me as well. He had broken his leg and we were pushing each other. He knew I was watching how hard he was working and trying to beat him. He's my best mate in football but I still wanted to be better than him. Better than him at getting better. Once we got outside, we told each other we would be kicking balls again soon. But even on a gentle jog, Kieron pulled up in pain. There were problems with the rod that had been inserted in his leg. It was too long. It took him four operations before his leg was right. His problems dwarfed anything I had suffered.

After a while, I began to enjoy the rehab. I got so, so fit. Running has always been a strong point of mine but even I felt quick. Because of the work I had done in the gym, I pushed the running, too. Towards the end of the season, I was able to train with the boys which was like a dream. I even thought I could have played the last couple of games but they told me not to push my luck.

I trained all through the off-season with John. I went down to the Algarve, where he was spending the summer, so we could keep working together. I took my family down there too as a kind of holiday but they didn't see that much of me. I worked with John in the mornings and the evenings. Football came first for me. I was determined I would be fitter than anyone for pre-season, ready to make up for all the time I had missed.

The first suggestions were beginning to surface that the owners of West Ham might be facing a financial crisis. The collapse of the Icelandic banks was only a couple of months away and the club went on a selling spree.

Bobby Zamora and John Pantsil were sold to Fulham. George McCartney and Anton Ferdinand went to Sunderland. Freddie

Ljungberg and Nolberto Solano were released. I couldn't let any of it deflect me. I had to focus on my own fitness and making a flying start to the new season. Then I pulled my hamstring at Ipswich in a pre-season game.

How on earth was that possible? I felt fitter and stronger than ever. But after what I'd been through, I could cope with a few weeks out with a hamstring pull.

I came back for the third league game of the season against Blackburn Rovers and scored in a comfortable victory but the club was suddenly in turmoil. Alan Curbishley quit a few days later. I don't know why. I wasn't exactly his confidant. He'd hardly set eyes on me the whole time I had been at the club. But there weren't a lot of funds available and a stream of players were leaving. You don't have to be too bright to work out that must have had something to do with it.

I felt sorry for him and I felt guilty that I had never been able to justify the money he had spent on me. Sometimes managers are the victims of bad luck as much as anything else and that certainly applied to Curbishley at West Ham. He got lucky in so far as the club had stacks of cash. But the players he bought were injured most of the time. And then the money ran out.

The people who were making the decisions at West Ham called me in and asked who I thought would be a good manager. I said I'd play for anyone. I was grateful for my contract and I wanted to try to start to justify the money they were paying for me. I told them they could get who they wanted and it wouldn't matter to me.

Ten days later, they appointed Gianfranco Zola as Curbishley's successor. I liked him straight away. He was brilliant. He had a clear vision on how he wanted to play and it very much revolved around keeping the ball on the deck. Almost immediately, we started playing really well under his management but despite our performances, we just couldn't get the results.

Gianfranco just told us to keep playing as we were and that the results would come. That's difficult sometimes when you are losing because confidence can seep away. But his training was first class. He brought in Steve Clarke, who was a top coach and Kevin Keen, who was innovative and clever.

There was one problem player he had to deal with fairly soon: himself. He still trained with us and the problem, basically, was that he was too good. It is difficult to be the manager while you're lobbing your goalkeeper from 30 yards one minute and trying to tell him he's the best in the Premier League the next. He could still have played for us and made a big difference. No question. He was embarrassing some of the players in training, he was that good.

In the end, he made the decision to watch from the sidelines instead. He was a great guy and an outstanding coach. It was no surprise to me when he took over at Watford and did so well. He is a terrific man-manager as well as a clever tactician.

Not long before Curbishley resigned, the agent, Kia Joorabchian, phoned me. He was working closely with Manchester City at that time when Thaksin Shinawatra was the owner. He said that City, who were managed by Mark Hughes, wanted to sign me. I didn't speak to Sparky but City stepped up their interest. They approached West Ham and I was pulled aside at the training ground to talk about it.

The club said they didn't want me to leave. They said they had been waiting for me to get fit and now they were looking forward to seeing me start to flourish in a West Ham shirt. I told them the last thing I was going to do was ask to leave after being out for a year. I wasn't like that. I wanted to get on with playing for West Ham. I wanted to prove myself at West Ham. I had it in my mind to stay there for a long time.

From the beginning of October until Christmas, we only won once in 12 matches. It was a terrible run but after Christmas, things really picked up and we began to get the results our standard of play deserved. I scored two goals in an emphatic victory over Portsmouth at Fratton Park on Boxing Day, then we beat Stoke, Fulham and Hull at Upton Park, squeezing in a draw at Newcastle in between. Those results were a fairer reflection of our ability.

But as January wore on, I became more and more aware that negotiations were going on about my future. My adviser had rung on Christmas Eve to say that Spurs had offered West Ham £6m for me and that West Ham had turned it down flat. That was fine by me. In fact, I was pleased that West Ham still held me in that much esteem after my injury problems.

Then things began to get complicated. Manchester City rang me. They said they had an agreement with Tottenham that Tottenham couldn't sign me. They told me they had had an agreement with Spurs that they would not bid for Jermain Defoe if Spurs would not bid for me. They had kept to their side of the bargain and stayed out of the race for Defoe and now they felt Spurs were reneging on the deal.

Spurs and City started firing in bids to West Ham and arguing with each other. I was called in by the club before the FA Cup third round tie against Barnsley at Upton Park on January 3. "You must be aware of some of what is going on behind the scenes," I was told. "Do you want to play?"

I said of course I did. The point was made to me that I'd be cup-tied. I said I was a West Ham player and I wasn't bothered about being cup-tied. I said I wanted to play. I found it strange that I was even asked about it. I wondered if the club was thinking about whether the fee they might attract for me would be adversely affected if I was cup-tied.

Soon after that, it became clear to me that the club was now encouraging bids from Spurs and City. I asked them what fee they were looking for. I understood that, particularly given the club's financial problems, they needed to get as much as they possibly could for me, but the situation was starting to unsettle me.

West Ham said they didn't want me to go to Tottenham. They said they would like me to sign a new contract with them, which I was open to. I told them that they needed to speak to my adviser about it. Then they asked me who I wanted to join. It was getting bizarre. I said I loved living in London and I would prefer it if they would stop encouraging Man City.

As I was about to leave the office, there was a call from Spurs. I could hear someone from the club on the phone. He said Man City had 'gone to 10'. Then he phoned Man City and said 'Spurs have gone to 10, what are you offering?' I felt exasperated by it. It was draining me. Gianfranco didn't know what was happening either. It was a mess.

I played and scored at Newcastle on January 10 and came off eight minutes from the end. A few minutes after the final whistle, I had a phone call from Man City. "We heard you pulled your hamstring," they said. It was bizarre. I told them I hadn't pulled my hamstring. I had just come off as a precaution because my hamstring felt tight. They sounded reassured.

I went in to training the following Monday to be told that the Tottenham deal was done. They said they had agreed a fee with Spurs but that I had to put in a transfer request. I said I wouldn't do that. I knew they were trying to make it look as though I had been pushing for a move when, all along, I had watched them conducting an auction for me.

I said if they wanted to sell me, they had to tell the fans they wanted to sell me. Otherwise I'd stay. I was happy there. It was obvious they needed the money but they needed the highest fee. I understood that and I didn't resent them for it but they needed to be straight about it. They said again that the deal was done so I went in to the training ground to say goodbye to everyone and went back to my flat in Canary Wharf.

I was sitting in my apartment watching Sky Sports. They started reporting that I had walked out of training. I didn't know what to do. We were at home to Fulham on Sunday but the way West Ham had been talking, I would be sold before that happened. I had City on the phone, too, angry because word had reached them that the deal with Spurs was done.

I decided to go back to Cardiff. If I had to come back on Saturday to be involved in the build-up to the game, that was fine. But West Ham had told me I was going to be a Spurs player. I presumed I wasn't going to be involved in the Fulham match and I was loathe to sit around in an empty flat on my own, fretting about what was going on.

I woke up in Cardiff on Saturday morning. I got a phone call to say that the back page headline on the Daily Mail was 'Bellamy on Strike'. You couldn't get further from the truth if you tried. It got people angry, understandably. A lot of West Ham fans were disgusted with the idea that I'd go on strike after the club had been so patient with me. I didn't blame them.

Again, I didn't know what to do. I couldn't just ring up a jour-nalist and say it wasn't true. I tried not to get involved in that sort of stuff. But I was really angry about it. I knew the news-papers must have been fed the line about me going on strike from someone at West Ham. They were trying to turn me into the bad guy, which, given my history, wasn't the most difficult thing to do.

Gianfranco rang. He said I wasn't right to play. He said West Ham wanted him to put me in the squad but that he had refused. I suppose they wanted to strengthen the picture of me as some sort of contract rebel, a greedy player demanding even more money from a club that had behaved well towards him.

It reflected well on Gianfranco that he wasn't willing to play that game. I imagine they had put him under a fair amount of pressure to play along. I just told Gianfranco I wanted it sorted out. I didn't want to miss any games. I wanted to play. He said he was still hoping they would get me back.

The situation got even more complicated. The Spurs boss, Harry Redknapp, rang and said that they had just made an approach to sign Wilson Palacios from Wigan Athletic and that City were threatening to scupper the deal in revenge for Spurs signing me. City didn't want Palacios, Harry said, but they were saying that they would try to sign every player Spurs targeted over the next two transfer windows if they persisted with their attempts to sign me.

I got a message from him later that day. "Fuck Man City," it said. "We're going to try to sign you anyway."

It got very ugly. It began to appear that West Ham wanted to sell me to Man City because Man City would offer more money. So on the eve of the game against Fulham, I was told that the fee with Man City had been agreed and I had to go up to Manchester to sign the contract. I was on the M56, heading into the city, when I got a phone call saying the deal wasn't done after all.

City had offered £12m but there was an argument about an extra £2m. City said they'd pay it if City won the league but West Ham wanted it if City qualified for the Champions League. City wanted me to stay up in Manchester until it was cleared up but I didn't want to get caught up there if the deal hadn't been done. That would have made me look really clever. I could have been the first Peter Odemwingie, knocking on the gates at Eastlands and being told to go away. So I turned around and drove back down to Cardiff.

It seemed West Ham had just been threatening City with the Spurs deal to drive the price up. They were still doing their best to make me look the bad guy, too, and when the game against Fulham kicked off that Sunday lunchtime, I got a thorough slating even though Gianfranco said publicly it was wrong to suggest I had gone on strike.

I was even more fed-up now. I rang one of the people at West Ham at half-time and told him I wasn't going anywhere. I said I'd sign the new contract he had mentioned to me. I told him to make sure it was on his desk on Monday morning and I'd come in and sign it there and then. I told him I was happy with what I had got at West Ham and that I had never wanted to leave.

He sounded taken aback.

"Leave it with us," he said.

My head was spinning. I didn't really want to go to Manchester City. I knew it was an interesting proposition though.

Sheikh Mansour had taken over from Shinawatra the previous summer and their ambitions, not to mention their cash reserves, seemed limitless. But I was happy in London. I had a lot of friends at West Ham and Spurs. I think I would have found the transition to playing at White Hart Lane easy. My kids loved coming to see me in London because it was an exciting place to visit. I didn't want to move.

I went out for a jog around the lanes near my house for half an hour. When I got back, there was a message on my phone. It was from the club.

"The deal with City is done," it said. "All the best."

24

Sparks Fly

I had made headlines at a lot of the clubs I was at. Sometimes for the right reasons. Often for the wrong ones.

The day I signed for Manchester City, I realised I was playing with the big boys now. But I arrived at the club's winter training camp in Tenerife to find all hell had broken loose. Robinho had walked out.

In some ways, I wasn't complaining. City had paid £14m for me and Mark Hughes had fought tooth and nail to sign me, above the objections of some people at the club who weren't too keen on paying that amount of money for a 29-year-old with a lot of injuries on the clock and a few controversies in his past. If I could settle in quietly while everyone raged about Robinho, that was fine by me.

There wasn't a lot that was quiet about Manchester City at that time, though. The club was like a great big building site with new skyscrapers appearing every day and work going on around the clock. Sheikh Mansour was an owner in a hurry. Robinho had been signed from Real Madrid on the last day of the previous transfer window for £32m. Nigel de Jong arrived from Hamburg for £16m two days after me. Wayne Bridge had been signed from Chelsea for £10m earlier in January. Shay Given was about to arrive from Newcastle.

Oh, yeah, and they were trying to sign Kaka from AC Milan for £91m. That deal broke down on the day I arrived, too. Garry Cook, City's chief executive, said famously that Kaka had 'bottled it'. And Robinho was arrested in connection with an alleged rape. He was soon cleared of any involvement in anything but all this was before I'd even played a game. It was chaos even without any help from me.

I made my City debut against Newcastle – who else – on January 28 and scored the winning goal. The talk was still all about Kaka and Robinho but it was a good way for me to start. The City fans gave me a great reception. They were brilliant with me from the first game to the last. I was delighted to score, not just for them but for Sparky, too. I could see the relief in his face when I scored.

He has believed in me more than any other manager in my career. He has got the best out of me, too. I knew what I could offer him. I felt comfortable with him and with the people around him. I could be honest with him and he could be honest with me. And sometimes, when you are highly rated by someone, that alone can give you the confidence you need to excel.

It made the Man City transition very easy football-wise. But it was difficult finding somewhere to live and it put an extra strain on my family as well because it was further for us to travel to see each other. I have to be honest with myself and say that, when it came to moving from club to club, I never really consulted my family that much. I did what I thought was best for my career and it was my decision.

It was all done for football. My decision was made on the basis of where I could progress the most. I always chased that. If I had to move to another club to get better, then that's what I would do. Sometimes, I wonder how staying at a club for longer would have affected my career. I'll never know. There are positives and negatives to moving on as frequently as I have. The way it's worked out, I have had to try to prove myself all over again every couple of years, which has probably been a good thing.

We had some very good players at City but we were inconsistent. I saw what the problem was straight away. It was Robinho and Elano and a centre-back called Glauber, a centre-back who only played once for City. They had formed a Brazilian clique and as far as I could see, they didn't give a shit. They didn't train with any intensity and if you tackled one of them, it was like you had committed a crime.

The three of them were glued together. Elano was the voice. Robinho was the Sheikh's man. If you had a problem with Robinho, take it up with the Sheikh. Elano would always say that if Robinho wanted something, he got it. That was his boast. If you had words with Elano, he would tell Robinho and then Robinho would tell the Sheikh. That was what Elano said.

Elano didn't appear to have much interest in pulling his finger out. He wanted an easy life. Training was too intense. When they played for Brazil, though, they were transformed. In mid-February, I watched them play for their national team against Italy at the Emirates and they were both magnificent. I mean, really magnificent.

Elano scored the first goal in a 2-0 win. It was like something out of the 1970 World Cup. He backheeled the ball to Robinho, who slid a pass back to him and he lifted it over Buffon as Buffon rushed out to meet him. And then Robinho got the second goal and that was even better. He stole it off Pirlo, turned Zambrotta inside out about three times and then smashed a left foot shot across Buffon and in off the post. It was breathtaking stuff.

The following weekend, we played Portsmouth at Fratton Park. Portsmouth were without a manager and were fighting relegation. We lost 2-0. Robinho and Elano were a disgrace. It was like they only wanted to pass to each other. We weren't good enough that we could carry them but when they lost it, they didn't track back or anything.

We were woeful. I'd only been there a couple of weeks but I'd had enough of them. I came in after the game and I had a real go at both of them. I told Robinho I was his biggest fan and that I thought he was an immense player.

"But do you think how you behaved today was right?" I said.

Robinho pretended he didn't understand. So Elano started to say something.

"You're in no position to pipe up," I said. "You were a fucking disgrace, too. You didn't track your runners, you did what you wanted on the ball, you wasted possession."

They seemed to be shocked that someone was having a go at them. They didn't say anything. So I filled the silence.

"You think we're all here to do your running for you, do you?" I said. "What, you can lose it but I'll go and win it back for you so you can lose it again? I know that you're incredibly talented. There's no two ways about that. You proved that against Italy. But great players don't come to Portsmouth and put in a performance like that."

Sparky had been listening. At that point, he went out and left me to it.

Vincent Kompany backed me up as well. He was an outstanding professional and he had fallen out with the Brazilian clique before I arrived. I had only been there a couple of weeks but I felt so let down and so pissed off about what had happened. I didn't want to be the one saying it. I would have loved to keep my head down. But I couldn't help myself.

When I got to training on Monday, Robinho called me over to a corner of the changing rooms. Elano was standing behind him, just like he always did.

"Why you talk?" Robinho said.

"Do you think I'm out of order then, yeah?" I said. "I gather you do."

He turned to Elano and they exchanged a few words of Portuguese. Elano took over then.

"I play for Brazil," Elano said. "I play in the first team. I come here to Manchester City and I don't play all the time. How do you think I feel? It hurts me. I can play for a great national team and not even play here at Man City.

"That's not my fucking problem," I said. "You had your chance on Saturday. And look how you played."

"You never had a bad game?" Elano said.

"It wasn't that you had a bad game," I told him. "It was just the lack of effort. You weren't interested. That hurts more."

"You always talk," Robinho said. "It should be the manager who talks, not you."

"If I've got something to say, I'll fucking say it," I said. "If you don't think I've put in my shift, then you tell me and I'll take it on the chin. But you have let everyone down."

"Okay," Robinho said, trying to bring the conversation to an end, "don't you talk to me again."

"What are you on about?" I said. "You mean talk to you as in talking to you at all or talk to you after the game?"

"No, no, we are finished," Robinho said.

"Whatever," I said. "I'll lose a lot of sleep over that."

Robinho and Elano walked off. I saw Stephen Ireland sitting nearby. He caught my eye. "Now you see what we've had to put up with," he said.

I scored in the next game against Liverpool at Anfield, although it was put down as an Alvaro Arbeloa own goal, and then it was West Ham at Upton Park. I got hammered by the West Ham fans, which wasn't a problem. It didn't change my high opinion of them. It's their club and they thought I had treated them badly. It wasn't true but they weren't to know that. They're entitled to react how they want.

I played well. I set up a decent chance for Robinho, which he missed. But in the second half, I landed awkwardly and felt the strain on my knee. I had to come off with about 25 minutes to go. The West Ham fans loved that. And I was replaced by Elano.

I made a substitute's appearance in a victory over Sunderland three weeks later and then played 90 minutes in a defeat at Arsenal at the beginning of April. And then the pain in my knee got too much. I didn't play again that season. The surgeon told me that if I didn't rest it, I would need another operation and I didn't want that.

I was upset about missing more time with injury, particularly because I felt like I was letting Sparky down. He had staked a lot on me and I had made a decent impact when I arrived. But now all the people who had warned him against me and said I would just get injured were being proved right. I was eaten up with guilt about it.

After I'd rested my knee and let it recover, I trained all through the summer again. Just like I had the last summer. My family loved me for that. It was an incredibly selfish way to behave but if you want to have a career as a Premier League footballer, you have to be selfish. If you want the rewards, you have to make sacrifices.

This time, I really didn't have much choice. I knew City would go on another spending spree in the summer. If I wasn't raring to go at the start of the season, I'd have no chance of getting in the side. But if I did get in the side, this could be everything I'd ever dreamed of. I could be part of something really big. It could bring me the honours and the medals I had always thought I needed to validate my career. It was my big, big chance.

I knew it was going to be a huge task but that if I succeeded, I was going to have the chance to play with some of the best players in the world. I knew I was good enough. The only problem I was going to have was if I was not fit. If I was in the treatment room, I couldn't show everyone how good I was.

I went in on the first day of pre-season training and saw the fitness coach and the physios and told them that whatever they told me to do, I would do it. No more railing against what they told me. No more going my own way. No more ignoring their instructions. If they told me I had to miss training or do half a session, I would do it. I promised them.

So all pre-season, I was getting pulled out of sessions. There were days I wanted to train and they wouldn't let me and I was chomping at the bit.

They brought in a fitness guy called Raymond Verheijen who I hated with a passion because he was one of the ones pulling me out of sessions. He was opinionated and a little arrogant but he had an annoying habit of being right about fitness issues.

Towards the end of pre-season, I began to feel great. The regime I had followed was paying off.

It was just as well. Before the end of August, City had spent more than £100m on new players. Carlos Tevez arrived from Manchester United. Emmanuel Adebayor was signed. So was Gareth Barry. So was Joleon Lescott and Kolo Toure. It was just a quality group of players. I felt like I was in Wonderland.

I didn't make that much of an impact pre-season but I didn't care about that. You make an impact when that whistle goes for the first game of the Premier League campaign. I made the starting line-up for the opening game away at Blackburn Rovers. That was my first goal achieved. I started up front with Adebayor because Carlos was not quite fully fit, although he did come on midway through the second half. Robinho was in the side, too, at Ewood Park. He started on the left.

Carlos started the next game, against Wolves at Eastlands, and I was on the bench. Then we played Portsmouth away and I started at left wing. I felt really fit. I felt stronger than I ever had.

We beat Blackburn, we beat Wolves and we beat Portsmouth.

Adebayor scored in every game and we were flying. It seemed like the sky was the limit.

Then we played Arsenal at Eastlands. We knew that would be a test of how good we really were. Micah Richards put us ahead but then Robin Van Persie equalised a quarter of an hour into the second half and it was anybody's game. We were the ones who stepped up. I put us 2-1 up and then Adebayor made it 3-1 with 11 minutes to go.

Adebayor had been taking fearful abuse from the Arsenal sup-porters throughout the game. He had also been involved in an incident with Van Persie where he had trodden, deliberately or not, on Van Persie's head, and cut him above the eye. That had just ramped up the hostility towards him even more and made the atmosphere increasingly feverish.

So even though Adebayor scored at the opposite end from the away section, he celebrated by running the entire length of the pitch and throwing himself to the turf in front of them. I'd never seen anything like it. I doubt anybody in the stadium had. I understood why he did it but I also understood there might be consequences. Even I felt a little bit nervous about it and I went over to try to lead him away as a hail of missiles were thrown at him.

That was a crucial moment in our season and in all our careers. We had got off to a great start. We were about to record our fourth straight victory and we were starting to feel invincible. Adebayor was playing brilliantly. He was unstop-pable. He was looking like the complete forward that so many had predicted he would become. With him playing like that, and with the strength in depth we had acquired, we would be a danger to anybody.

We beat Arsenal 4-2 in the end but the result was overshadowed by the furore that raged around Adebayor.

I was a bit puzzled by the stamping controversy. I saw Van Persie shake Adebayor's hand after the game but then a few minutes later he was accusing him of stamping on his head. If you stamped on my head, I ain't shaking your hand. I certainly ain't going crying to the press and the authorities after it. If somebody did that to me, I would wait until next time around. I wouldn't want the boy banned.

I don't know whether Manu had a big problem with Van Persie (there were rumours afterwards that they had disliked each other when they were teammates at Arsenal) but it all seemed rather strange. I'd had a really good game and the team had played superbly but no one was talking about that. They were talking about Adebayor and how long he was going to be banned for. If the celebration didn't get him, the stamp would.

In the end, he was banned for three matches for violent conduct for the stamp and escaped with a £25,000 fine and a suspended ban for the celebration. But that was enough. It pricked our bubble. It deprived us of him for the next game against Manchester United at Old Trafford and when he came back at the beginning of October, he wasn't the same player. The magic had gone. The momentum had been lost.

The derby against United was an amazing match. We were still confident even without Adebayor but they were gunning for us.

There was extra needle because of Carlos and he got a lot of stick even in the warm-up. Carlos wasn't back to full fitness then but he is a warrior. I've seen heart in a lot of top players but his heart is as big as anyone's. I got on very well with him. He's a great guy. We had the same work ethic and a good understanding.

I enjoyed his attitude. He made me want to be better. Just watching him took me on to another level. Even when things weren't going well for him personally, he still made good decisions and still chased balls that looked like lost causes. When you are watching him at close hand, it inspires you to try to do the same things.

The United players said he wasn't a good trainer but he put so much into games, it took him a long time to recover. His body looked battered after a game. He was tired for a few days afterwards. Everything was about Saturday for him. He didn't let you down on Saturday. I have never seen a guy put their body through as much as him. He does not look like an athlete so imagine the hard work he has to put in to perform like one. I tell you this, you would want to go to war with him every time.

Old Trafford was baying for blood and two minutes into the game, Rooney scored. They were laughing. Same old City, always losing. They were expecting a rout. We all looked at each other. It was the last thing we needed. The last thing Sparky had said was 'don't concede early'. Well, Plan A was straight out of the window.

We dragged our way back into the game. Some hard work by Carlos caused a mistake in the United defence and Gareth Barry equalised.

We went 2-1 down just after half-time but three minutes after they had taken the lead, I equalised. Ji-Sung Park and John O'Shea came out to the edge of the box to try to close me down but I cut inside O'Shea and hit a screamer around Rio Ferdinand, across Ben Foster and into the top corner. It was one

Rafa's team: Completing a dream move to Anfield, along with another arrival in the summer of 2006, Mark Gonzalez

Off the mark: Scoring at Anfield against my old team Blackburn – my first Premier League goal for Liverpool

Double delight: I put my off-the-pitch troubles behind me and hit top form in December, 2006, scoring twice in a 4-0 win at Wigan

Best Bar none: My favourite moment in football, scoring in a 2-1 win over Barcelona at the Nou Camp – complete with a cheeky golf swing celebration. After what happened between us, maybe it was fate that John Arne Riise got the other goal

Final countdown: I was soon told my time at the club was up

All smiles: With some of the young players at my academy in Sierra Leone. Going to Africa the summer after the Champions League final was one of the best decisions I've ever made

On the sidelines: At the West Ham training ground, Chadwell Heath. Injuries meant I didn't play as much as I would have liked

Eastender: Celebrating a goal against Chelsea in December, 2008. The fans didn't realise what really happened during my spell at Upton Park

City revolution: There were some talented players like Robinho but we struggled for consistency

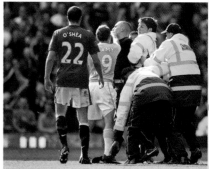

New boss: I didn't always see eye to eye with Manchester City manager Roberto Mancini after he took over from Mark Hughes in 2009

Thriller: I thought my late goal – my second in the game – had rescued a point for us in a dramatic game at Old Trafford in September, 2009. But Michael Owen scored a last-gasp winner to give United a 4-3 win. I also ended up in trouble after I confronted a pitch invader (above, right) following the goal

Home on loan: It was a special feeling to score on my Cardiff City debut against Doncaster Rovers. Sadly our promotion campaign was to end in disappointment in 2010-11

Right man for the job: Gary Speed (right) persuaded me to carry on playing for Wales and started to transform our fortunes when he took over as manager. Above: getting Speedo's support for my foundation in Sierra Leone

Proud dad: Pictured with my two sons Cameron (left) and Ellis

Emotional night: I didn't want to cry but couldn't help it before I returned to action for the first time after Gary's death. I was determined to do well and Chelsea couldn't get near me. We won the Carling Cup quarter-final 2-0 and I set up both goals

Standing together: With Gary's sons Ed and Tommy before a special Wales tribute match against Costa Rica in February, 2012

Winner: I had things in perspective before Liverpool faced my old club Manchester City in the Carling Cup semi-final in January, 2012. This goal in front of the Kop put us through to the final

Follow the leaders: Paying my respects at the Hillsborough service with two true Anfield legends – Steven Gerrard and Jamie Carragher

Derby delight: I came off the bench and crossed the ball for Andy Carroll to score the winner against Everton in the FA Cup semi-final – much to Carra's relief!

Team GB: I never thought I'd make the Olympics! Here I am scoring in our opening game at London 2012 against Senegal

The King: With Kenny after we had won the Carling Cup. He's not only a legendary footballer and a Liverpool hero, he's also a fantastic person

Going up: Finally getting Cardiff City in to the Premier League – an amazing feeling and (above) celebrating with my daughter Lexi, who enjoyed wearing my Championship title medal

of those goals where I knew it was in as soon as it left my boot.

It was a superb end-to-end game. Ten minutes from the end, they went ahead when Darren Fletcher headed in a Giggs free-kick. Set-pieces were City's Achilles heel under Sparky. We couldn't mark and if we did mark, we got it wrong.

But then in the last minute, Rio tried to chip a cheeky pass over Martin Petrov near the halfway line. Petrov fed it to me and suddenly I was one on one with Rio. Down the years, it had been hard to outpace him but I found myself sprinting away from him this time. He was an outstanding player, Rio. He can annoy me but he is one of the best players I have played against.

As I bore down on Foster, he came off his line to try to narrow the angle but I knew he would be anticipating that I would try to curl a shot round him. I think he got a bit disorientated because he left a gap at his near post so I jinked to the left and slid it past his right hand. That was 3-3 with 90 minutes gone and I thought I had saved the day. I thought I was the hero.

But the referee played six minutes of injury time and in the last of them, Giggs played a beautifully weighted pass through our defence. It went to a red shirt. I thought 'who's that?' and then realised it was Michael Owen. I didn't even know he was on the pitch. 'When did he come on?' I thought as he controlled the ball. He'd come on 12 minutes from time for Dimitar Berbatov but he'd hardly had a touch. Still, that was Michael Owen. He didn't need many touches to score. He controlled Giggs' pass with his first touch and, with his second, he slid the ball past Shay Given.

It was 4-3 to them. It was obvious time was almost up. But

the game had been such a thriller I thought anything might still happen. Then I saw a United fan running on the pitch. Some stewards had grabbed him and wrestled him to the floor but he was delaying the restart. I marched over to where he was standing. I was thinking about getting my hat-trick.

"Get the fuck off the pitch," I yelled at him.

"Fuck off," he said.

So I pushed him in the face. I didn't punch him, like some people said. I just couldn't be bothered with him. I didn't even get asked to see the FA. A few people tried to make it a problem but the police didn't want to speak to me.

Then the final whistle went. I couldn't believe we had lost. It was a great game. A joy to be a part of but we had lost. United and their fans were exultant. Maybe it was a bit early in the season for it to be a turning point but we struggled to recover from it. We beat West Ham at home in our next match but then we went on a run of seven successive draws.

I was playing well. I was creating goals and scoring them. I was getting plenty of playing time. But as a team, we just kept conceding daft, daft goals. We outplayed teams and took the lead but we made a habit of allowing the opposition to come back at us. We got panicky. If we hadn't made so many errors, we could have been top of the league but we had slipped out of the Champions League places and below the notorious line on Garry Cook's graph.

I got on well with Garry. I was playing well so I was everyone's mate. If you're playing well, everyone's saying what a great signing you have been and what an asset to the club you are. I liked Garry's passion. Whether he was talking bullshit or not, I still liked his passion. People ridiculed him and he did make one or two gaffes but he did an awful lot to establish City among football's elite.

The run of seven draws left us in sixth place. We were only three points behind Arsenal, who were fourth, but the owners were desperate to qualify for the Champions League the following season and I think they were getting nervous about our prospects of achieving that. In the last of the draws, I was sent off for two bookable offences at Bolton. That meant I missed the next game at Spurs.

We played badly at White Hart Lane. Robinho was particularly poor. I had actually grown to like Robbie. He was a lot more approachable when Elano wasn't around but I don't think he ever really settled properly in Manchester. We lost 3-0 that night in mid-December and the loss dropped us to eighth. There was a lot of speculation that Sparky's job could be in danger.

The following Saturday, we were playing Sunderland at Eastlands. I got up that morning and saw I had a couple of missed calls from Kieron on my mobile phone. I didn't return them. No one can get hold of me the morning before a game. It won't happen. But before I got to the ground, I turned the radio on and found out why Kieron had been ringing.

The Sun had printed a back page story saying Sparky would be sacked whatever the result against Sunderland. I didn't think much of it. How could they have decided that already and let it leak out without telling the manager? It wasn't possible, surely. I think that if we lost against Sunderland, that would be the end for him but I didn't think we were going to lose.

I could see the strain in Sparky before we went out to play but nobody mentioned anything about The Sun story. We went 2-0 up quickly but then allowed them back into the game and they drew level. I put us 3-2 up and I was determined to get Sparky out of the mess it seemed he was in. Sunderland got it back to 3-3 but Roque Santa Cruz scored the winner for us 20 minutes from time.

After the game, we were all sitting in the dressing room and Sparky came in and made a speech. He thanked everyone for what they had done. He said he didn't know what was going to happen to him or his staff. He said he did not know anything but that he was aware there appeared to be some uncertainty about his position.

"If this is it," he said, "I would like to thank you all. We have started something here and no one will be prouder if you go on and win stuff. I would like to wish you all good luck."

I looked at Shay Given. "What the fuck's going on here?" I asked. Shay just shook his head.

A couple of minutes later, I'd climbed into one of the ice baths when someone came down from upstairs and asked Shay and Kolo Toure to go up to the boardroom. They came back down after 15 minutes and said Sparky had been sacked and that Roberto Mancini would be replacing him. We were told we shouldn't say anything to the press and that our Christmas party had been cancelled. Like I felt like going on it now anyway.

It was reported the next day that I had flown into a rage when I heard the news. Well, I hate to damage my image but I was too tired to fly into a rage. I was more sad than angry. I went to see Sparky in his office. He was there with his staff. Everyone seemed a bit stunned. I didn't know what to say. Part of me thought that he had brought me to the club and if he was leaving, maybe I ought to leave, too.

I had a quick chat with him. I said how sorry I was about what had happened and that I hadn't been able to do more to get the results he needed. I asked him what he thought I should do now, whether I should leave, too. He told me to stay and to fight for my place and build on everything I'd already achieved. I felt angry towards Garry for the way it had all been handled. I felt Sparky had been humiliated. Everyone had known about this apart from him.

Sparky's wife came into the room next and she was trying hard not to cry. Then his old man came in as well and he was tearful. And then I looked at Sparky and saw that he was welling up.

I knew it was time for me to leave. This was his big opportunity and now it was gone. It sunk in then what had really happened. I got out of there and drove back to Cardiff. There was still a Christmas do, which some of the boys went on. Life goes on. It's football. That's the game.

25

Lost In Translation

The following Monday, Roberto Mancini spoke to us all in a group. He spoke well. He said he felt sorry for Mark Hughes but that he had won championships at Inter Milan and been sacked. He was right about that. It happens. It wasn't his fault that Sparky had been fired. Mancini had been given an opportunity. He had to take it. I didn't feel any bitterness towards him.

I went to see him in his office later. I told him I had been close to Sparky and that I found the way he had been forced out hard to deal with. But I also told him I would give as much effort for him as I had for the last manager. I told him I believed in what the club was trying to do and would do everything I could to help it reach its goal.

It was quite a speech but he looked a little bit blank when I'd finished. His English wasn't great then. I'm not sure if he understood any of what I'd been saying.

Then Garry Cook and Brian Marwood, who was the club's Football Administrator (whatever that meant) called me in and told me that they were going to let Robinho leave. They said that was a measure of how much they valued me. They were going to let the club's record signing go because they recognised that I was keeping him out of the team and I deserved to be keeping him out of the team.

Roberto's first game was against Stoke at Eastlands. He asked me whether I wanted to start that game or the match the following midweek at Wolves. I told him the tougher game would be Wolves away and that Robinho probably wouldn't do so well in the away match. I said that, for that reason, it would probably make sense to start me against Wolves.

So that's what he did. I was pleased he'd consulted me, to be honest. Of course, when I was named on the bench for the Stoke match, the papers said I'd paid the price for my loyalty to Mark Hughes and that Roberto had dropped me. That suited their narrative but it wasn't true.

Roberto brought me on for the last 20 minutes for the Stoke game anyway. I replaced Robinho, who had had another difficult game. I felt for him a little bit when he came off. I got a massive cheer when I was coming on and it must have been a little bit difficult for him. I had come to like the guy but I didn't worry about it too much. I felt proud of how far I'd come at a great club like City.

Roberto changed a lot of stuff straight away. I saw some good people who had helped me a lot at City lose their jobs. They got rid of Raymond, for a start. It was obvious they would do that because he was so outspoken. Every couple of weeks, someone else was gone. I felt guilty. These people had done so much for me. I kept convincing myself this was football, this was just how it was. I asked myself if it was acceptable that I was just standing by while they were getting fired. In the end, I just got on with it.

It didn't take long for a little friction to build between me and Roberto. He couldn't understand why I didn't train every day. He said I had to train every day. I told him I couldn't because of my injury history. He said I had to do double sessions – training morning and afternoon – and I told him I couldn't do double sessions. If I do two sessions, I put too much stress on my hamstrings. I am an explosive player. He shook his head. He said in Italy, you have to train all the time. It was frustrating. I had been doing so well. I had felt so comfortable with my routine and it had been getting the best out of me. Now Roberto wanted to change it.

In mid-January, we played United in the semi-finals of the Carling Cup. There was a lot of hype around it and a lot of talk about how this was the gateway to City winning their first trophy since 1976. We won the first leg 2-1 at Eastlands but I didn't hang around celebrating on the pitch for too long afterwards. I shook hands with the United players and got down the tunnel as fast as I could. I knew we still had to go to Old Trafford for the second leg and if we milked it, they would make us pay.

We didn't milk it but Garry Cook did. Garry was a brilliant talker. I loved listening to him. He was very entertaining and could talk you into anything.

But sometimes, by his own admission, he didn't know when to

stop. In the build-up to the second leg, he was filmed telling City supporters in New York's Mad Hatter Saloon that City would get to Wembley "not if, but when, we beat United again."

That played straight into United's hands. There were other things I was worried about, too. Roberto was still learning the ropes. Some things that he introduced were beneficial. We went zonal at the back and that sorted us out defensively. It suited us. But sometimes, his lack of experience in the Premier League was a problem. Sometimes, the ProZone guy was taking the team talk because Roberto didn't know enough about the opposition. Roberto was listening in like he was a player. I didn't have time for him to feel his way into the job. I needed to win things now.

The atmosphere at the club quickly became tense under Roberto. The mood changed. He was not worried about whether players liked him or not. It was of no interest to him. You could walk past him and he would not even say hello. Brian Kidd was brought in to be the good cop. But he didn't really have much of a line in to Roberto. He had no say whatsoever, from what I could see.

The Carling Cup was important to us that season. People made fun of the competition but it would have been the perfect stepping stone for us. Clever managers can use a victory even in a lesser competition as a catalyst for greater achievements. Jose Mourinho won the League Cup at Chelsea in 2005 on the way to winning the Premier League. The League Cup was his first trophy.

I'm sure United realised how important it was to try to stop us making that psychological step, too. Sir Alex Ferguson had been talking about us being 'noisy neighbours' and they were desperate to silence us. They went some of the way to doing that at Old Trafford in the second leg when Paul Scholes put them ahead on the night.

Michael Carrick put them 2-0 up but then 15 minutes from the end, I swung over a cross and Carlos darted ahead of Rio Ferdinand, stuck out his right leg and flicked the ball past Edwin van der Sar to bring the scores level on aggregate. It looked then as though the tie was heading to extra-time. If that happened, having interrupted their momentum, I fancied our chances.

The last few minutes were mayhem. I'd already been hit by a coin when I went over to take a corner earlier in the game and the atmosphere got more and more intense. Then, two minutes into injury time, Giggs swung a cross over and Rooney, who was in the form of his life that season, rose unchallenged in our box and headed it past Shay Given to take United to the final.

When we got back to our changing room, we could hear the United boys celebrating next door. I was devastated. We'd got what we deserved. We'd been naïve in the build-up and we had fed them motivation. I knew that, in time, we would go on and win the league and the Champions League but I wondered if my time was running out to win something with the club.

I found it increasingly difficult with Roberto. I felt that faith in me was slipping. When I played that season, I had been staying on until the end of matches because I had been playing well and had been regarded as a constant threat. But during a defeat to Hull at the beginning of February, Roberto substituted me. It was a bad sign.

I went out in Manchester that evening with Wayne Bridge and Shaun Wright-Phillips and at the end of the night, I allowed myself to get into a scrape with a United fan. It was a bit of pushing and shoving. There was a group of United fans waiting for me as I went to get into my car. They were taunting me and because I was in a bad frame of mind, I got involved. It was nothing serious but it was serious enough that I aggravated my knee injury during the fracas.

I was out for two weeks because of that. I came back to training and I did some running. Roberto said I would be running the next day, too. I said I couldn't do two days solid in a row. He said I had been off for two weeks so I had to. I told him I couldn't. I had to stick to my programme. He called me into his office for a meeting with him, his fitness coach and the club doctor. He was confrontational from the start.

"Is it okay for you to be out for two weeks and think you can decide what you are doing?" he said.

"I am sticking to my programme, that's all," I said. "It has kept me fit all season and I don't want to risk being injured now."

"Okay, then, you have been away for two weeks," he said. "Now you can go home for the rest of the season. Go on."

"What are you on about?" I said.

"Well, you don't want to train," he said.

"It's not that I don't want to train," I told him. "I know my knee. I know it will react tomorrow if I train again and if it doesn't, my hamstrings will.

"No, no, no," he yelled.

So I went home. I told Brian Marwood and Garry Cook what had happened. Garry came round to my house to talk about it. He said something had been lost in translation. I went in the next day and trained but Roberto and I didn't speak after that.

That was a cut-off. That was him done with me, really. Rafa was harsh. Roberto wasn't far behind.

He didn't freeze me out. I still played and I still put in some good performances. But it became common knowledge that we'd had a big disagreement and the tension between us grew.

At the end of March, we lost to Everton at Eastlands and David Moyes and Mancini had a bout of handbags on the touchline. At the end of the match, Moyes came up to me and we had a bit of a chat. We'd had contact before when he'd tried to sign me for Everton and I had a great deal of respect for him.

"What about you two, pushing and shoving," I said. "Why don't you just have a fight?"

We had a bit of a laugh about it and that was it. The next thing I know, there were rumours that I was being investigated by the club because I had told Moyes he should have battered Mancini. Or something like that. It was bizarre but it did worry me a bit. I didn't want Roberto to turn against me completely.

Roberto kept playing me. I scored twice in a 4-2 win over Chelsea at Stamford Bridge and I got another in the 6-1 win over Burnley at the beginning of April when we went 3-0 up inside the first seven minutes.

By then, we were neck and neck with Spurs for the fourth and final Champions League place. With three games to go, they were one point ahead of us. We beat Aston Villa 3-1 in the next game and I got the last goal. Roberto started me in the next game, the showdown with Tottenham at Eastlands that would decide who finished fourth.

The Spurs defender, Younes Kaboul went right through me with a bad tackle after about 20 minutes and caught me with his knee in the small of my back. I was having back spasms for the rest of the game. The more the game went on, the more I struggled to run. Eight minutes from time, Kaboul went past me to the byline and cut a cross back. Our keeper, Marton Fulop, pushed it out and Peter Crouch headed it in for the winner.

So we finished fifth. The whole point of replacing Sparky was supposed to be that Roberto would get us into the top four but it didn't work. Although I wasn't terribly fond of Mancini, I was upset for the club. The fans had been tremendous to me from start to finish and I only wanted the best for them. I didn't feel too bad for them. I knew the good times were just around the corner.

I had got a fairly clear idea of the way things were going as far as my future was concerned about a month before the end of the season. I'd been accused of getting into a scuffle with a charity worker in Sierra Leone and I sued The Sun over it because it had never happened. It got complicated and in the end I dropped the case but by then it had cost me about £400,000 in legal fees. I asked City if they would pay it off for me and take it out of my wages month by month the following season.

"We don't know if you're going to be here next season," Brian Marwood said.

I was annoyed. I told him he was taking the piss. But I suppose I should have seen it coming really. Things were moving on and Roberto had no particular loyalty to me. It wasn't personal. These things aren't usually. It was just about one man's vision for the club and whether you fit into it or not.

So the game against Spurs was the last time I ever pulled on a City shirt. Mancini took me off six minutes from the final whistle and that was the end of my City career. I wasn't selected for the last game of the season against West Ham at Upton Park and, during the summer, rumours started to circulate that City were offering me around to other clubs.

I knew that Liverpool were trying to get me back. Roy Hodgson had taken over and they wanted me on loan but City said they weren't interested in a loan. Then Tottenham were pushing and pushing but City told them they wanted £10m. Spurs are never going to pay that for a 31-year-old. Daniel Levy is too cute for that.

Steve Walford rang to say that Martin O'Neill wanted to take me to Villa. He said City were offering me in part-exchange for James Milner. Steve McClaren rang me, too. He was manager of Wolfsburg at the time and he said my name had been mentioned as a makeweight for City's attempts to sign Edin Dzeko. I didn't like that. I didn't want to be a makeweight for any deal. I wanted to decide where I would go but it was obvious City were getting increasingly keen to offload me.

I suppose I'd known it was coming but it still hurt. I had begun to come to terms with the idea that I wasn't going to play any further part in the great revolution that was sweeping over the club but I was also acutely aware of what I was going to miss out on. I did feel some regret about leaving City because I could see what was coming and what they were going to achieve.

But I knew I would be a bit-part player and I didn't want that. I had been through all that at Liverpool and I didn't want to do it again. It wasn't enough for me. I wanted to be playing, not watching and wondering whether I was going to see my name on a teamsheet or not. At some point, City named a Uefa squad and my name wasn't among the 25. I got told by the media about that. It could not get any clearer what was happening.

I didn't know what to do. All the transfer talks seemed to have broken down so when pre-season began, I did the only thing I could and went back to train with City. I gave it everything in the first weeks of pre-season. I didn't have much contact with Roberto but I trained hard and tried to make an impression. The first pre-season match was against Valencia. I was on the bench. Mancini used every substitute except me. As messages go, it wasn't very subtle.

Garry Cook rang and said he was unhappy about the situation. He said the way things were was no good to anyone. But he made it clear that Roberto ran the show in terms of making the decisions about who came in and who went out. Garry asked me what I wanted to do and I said I just wanted to play at a good level somewhere. He said I would have to give up on the idea of going to Spurs because they were trying to get me on the cheap. He said Celtic had been on, too. I didn't want to go back up there. It was too far from my family.

"What about Cardiff?" he said.

26

Home And Away

What about Cardiff? The team my dad supported, the scarf my father wore, all that sort of stuff. There was an emotional pull to the idea, of course. I was a Liverpool fan but Cardiff is where I'm from and Cardiff will always be my home. I had always been determined that I would play for them at some point in my career. It was just that I had never been sure when.

When Garry Cook mentioned it, I was sitting in my house on the outskirts of the city. It was a nice, hot day. My garden looked lovely. The kids were playing outside on the lawn. It started to seem like a brilliant idea. I knew I had to get out of City. I thought 'why not?'

Things moved fast. City put the idea to Cardiff, who took it to Dave Jones, who was the manager at the time. City offered to pay a big percentage of my wages and the idea was that I would go on loan for a year. It suited City, too. It got me out of Mancini's hair and ensured that I couldn't come back to Eastlands with one of their rivals and embarrass them.

Soon, the news of the proposed move leaked out. The city went nuts about it. Before I'd even signed, everyone was saying Cardiff were bound to get promoted now. They were rejoicing about the idea that there was going to be a Welsh club in the Premier League for the first time. Everybody began to get a little bit ahead of themselves.

But the deal gained a momentum all of its own and the next thing you know, I'd signed. I was in a bit of a state of shock. I hadn't really intended to be playing in the Championship just yet. I'd just been at one of the richest clubs in the world and now I was playing in the second tier. I had always wanted to play for Cardiff. I just wasn't sure whether now was the right time. Still, I knew I had to get out of City. I knew it would drive me mad playing in the reserves and I knew it was bound to lead to conflicts of one type or another. I kidded myself that I was doing it so I could be closer to my family. The truth was I didn't really have much choice.

I wasn't in a great state physically. I had been trying so hard to prove a point to City in pre-season that I had taken part in every training session and every double training session. I knew it was dangerous for me to do that after all my knee operations and sure enough, it came back to haunt me. I played in a friendly for Wales against Luxembourg at the beginning of August and my knee swelled up after the game. But I knew how much was expected of me. I knew that now was not the time to be trying to rest and recuperate.

Cardiff had finished fourth in the Championship the season before but had missed out on promotion when they lost to Blackpool in the play-off final. There were some concerns that it would be hard to bounce back from that and that it would infect the new season but before I signed we started the 2010-11 campaign with a draw at home to Sheffield United and a win at Derby County.

I felt the pressure as soon as my signing became official the week after the Luxembourg match. There was a huge banner advertisement with my face on it hanging from the ramparts of Cardiff Castle as soon as the news was officially announced. The town was abuzz with it. My debut at the Cardiff City Stadium against Doncaster Rovers on August 21 was sold out.

And that debut was like a dream. My old man had travelled everywhere to watch me play during my career but I knew it would mean something extra special to him to see me running out for the team he had always supported. And it meant something special to me, too. Dave Jones made me captain and so I ran out at the head of my home-town team.

I didn't feel I played particularly well but I helped set up the first goal for Jay Bothroyd. I hit a great pass to free Chris Burke to put us 3-0 up and then I scored a decent goal to round off a 4-0 win. Scoring in front of the Cardiff fans felt immense. The write-ups in the papers the next day called it 'the perfect debut' and, for what it was worth, it left us second in the table.

After the game, though, my knee swelled up again. I had to have it drained of fluid during the week and I needed a pain-killing injection in order to be able to play against Portsmouth at Fratton Park the following Saturday. I was eager to help Wales get off to a good start in our Euro 2012 qualifying campaign and I played the full 90 minutes against Montenegro the next weekend. We lost 1-0. My knee ballooned again.

I knew there was something wrong but I was desperate not to be injured. No one knew what percentage of my wages Cardiff were paying but there was a lot of speculation about it. I knew people would be saying I was taking it easy, that I didn't care and that I was a waste of money. I felt the pressure even more. I had to play and get the team up to the Premier League or I would be a failure.

I knew the recent history of the club. I knew how the supporters had been let down before by big-name signings who never quite reproduced the form of the days that had made them famous. Players like Jimmy Floyd Hasselbaink and Robbie Fowler had come to Cardiff late in their careers and been disappointments. It wasn't their fault but that was Cardiff's curse. They wanted to attract big-name players but the only ones that ever arrived were past their prime.

My knee wasn't getting any better. I saw a surgeon and he said it would get better with rest and that I didn't need another operation. I was out for about five weeks. I came back against Barnsley at Oakwell at the beginning of October and scored in a 2-1 win that kept us second in the table behind the runaway leaders, QPR. My knee swelled up again.

I tried everything. I hired Raymond Verheijen to come and work with me and paid his salary out of my own pocket. But it was a constant struggle to stay fit enough to play. I couldn't train from match to match and I felt like a shadow of the player I had been the season before. Jones substituted me in most matches. I was being nursed along.

My knee felt unstable and I started to spiral into depression. I didn't leave my house except to go to training. I wouldn't take my kids to school because I didn't want to be in the car too long in case my knee stiffened up. I wouldn't go out with the kids because I didn't want to walk around in case my knee reacted. I went out for an easy jog once and it swelled up even after that.

I really feared for my career. I thought 'this is how it is going to end'. I just couldn't get the swelling down no matter what I did. It left me miserable. I felt like I was letting everyone down. I wasn't nice to be around. I didn't speak to anyone. My wife bore the brunt as usual. I never took her anywhere. I locked myself in my own world.

What an irony that was. I was playing for my home-town club so I could spend time with my family and yet I couldn't have been further away. I wasn't there. I was in the house every day but I slept in a different bed to my wife. I even had an altitude chamber built specially for my bed, so I ended up camped out in that a lot because I thought that would help my knee. I was a poor husband and I was a poor father at that time. I thought this was the end of my career and I started trying to prepare myself for that.

I was worried about the reaction in Cardiff. More than anywhere else, I didn't want to let people down in my home town. It was the one place I wanted to be remembered. I didn't want to be a failure here. I always wanted to be a hero here more than anywhere else. It is where I am from. It is where I grew up. It is where so many of my friends are, where my family is, where my kids are.

I wanted to be able to achieve something with the club that no one else had been able to achieve and to be remembered for that. I am not saying I wanted a statue but I wanted the

affection that would come with having been able to do something for my own people.

And the crushing, awful thing was that I just wasn't able to do
that. It pushed me into the destructive cycle of isolating myself
from everyone. I hardly spoke to the other players. My friends
had seen more of me when I lived away. I had enjoyed better
quality time with my wife and kids when I was away. I tortured
myself and I tortured the people who love me most by being so
distant.

Eventually, around Christmas, the misery started to lift a little
bit. The work I had been doing on my knee, the rest it had
been getting between matches, finally began to pay dividends.
It took me a while to get my sharpness back. I still had to get up
to speed, but I started to feel better. My confidence returned. I
started to play to my potential.

By the beginning of February, I felt sharp again. We played
Swansea at the Liberty Stadium, both of us near the top of the
table, both of us vying to be the first Welsh club to make it in
to the Premier League, both of us desperate not to be beaten
to the honour by our most bitter rival. It wasn't a great game
but with five minutes left, Aaron Ramsey, who was on loan to
us from Arsenal, passed me the ball 20 yards out and I curled
it round the Swansea keeper, Dorus de Vries, for the winner.
It was the first time Cardiff had beaten Swansea on their own
patch since 1997 and I knew how much it meant to the fans.
Like I said, I was one of them. That goal, that win, brought me
a lot of happiness.

It also took us above Swansea and into third place in the
table, behind QPR and Nottingham Forest. I felt we had a good
chance of automatic promotion. QPR were away and gone but

I felt it would be between us, Swansea and Norwich for second place. I did realise quite quickly, though, that it was a hell of a difficult division to get out of.

The quality of football is not the same as the Premier League and there are a lot of managers with the same philosophy which basically revolves around playing safe, percentage football. A couple of clubs played differently, like Norwich and Swansea. They played a diamond formation and tried to pass the ball and by and large, they were rewarded for it.

Some managers got success from being brave and some didn't. The ones who didn't were gone pretty quickly and replaced by managers who are more 'Championship'. By that, I mean a switch in play is fairly rare, patience on the ball is rare, keeping hold of possession for more than a couple of passes is rare. Decision making on the ball is not at the same level. That's why we were playing in the Championship.

It wasn't a great dressing room at Cardiff that season. Dave Jones had been at the club since 2005. He had got the club to the play-offs and to the FA Cup final. He had done a great job for Cardiff and that should always be remembered. But by the time I joined the club, training was easy going. It wasn't intense. A couple of times, a player just didn't bother turning up for training and it seemed to go almost unnoticed.

Michael Chopra's problems with gambling are well known now but he was so caught up in his betting that he would be pawing over his phone at half-time in matches to check how his wagers had fared. Once, during the match against Bristol City at Ashton Gate on New Year's Day, one of the coaches hid his phone because they wanted him to concentrate on the half-time team talk. When he came in at the interval and couldn't find it, he went mad. He said he wasn't going out for the second half until he found it. And he meant it. I was looking at this scene unfolding and thinking 'what the fuck is going on here?'

We would be travelling to a game on a Friday and the horse racing would be on the television. Fucking hell. I had to bite my lip a lot. Sometimes it was unbearable but I didn't go crazy about it at first because I was caught up in my own self-pity about my knee. My own insecurities and self-doubt came to the fore more than they ever had.

But as the season approached its climax, the fitter and sharper I got and the more able I felt to start saying what I felt. There had been no point me digging anybody out before that. How could I when I wasn't playing up to the standards I set myself either? But I got to a point in the season when I couldn't accept what I was seeing from some of my teammates.

We played Barnsley at the Cardiff City Stadium in the middle of March and allowed them to come from behind twice. The second time they equalised, in the last minute, was a particularly sloppy goal to concede. The game finished 2-2 and we dropped to fourth in the table. That was it for me then. I went back into the dressing room after the game and let it all go.

"This is bullshit," I started yelling. "We are not training at anywhere near the intensity we need. If someone doesn't track a runner in training, how do we expect them to track a runner in a game? That's what just happened now. That's why we conceded that goal. But it's fine. No one says anything."

I didn't have a direct go at Dave Jones but I had a go at his fitness people, his coaches and one or two players as well. And I felt better.

"We've got nine games left," I told them. "We win all nine

and we are promoted. We win eight and we are promoted. Let's fucking get this together now and save what we have got otherwise we won't even make the play-offs."

I felt fresh by then. I felt fit and I felt ready. I was ready to make an impact and I wanted the rest of them to get on board. I thought we could do it. No one could catch QPR, although there was a suggestion towards the end of the season that they might be docked points for some player irregularities. I'm glad that didn't happen. They deserved to go up.

But we had a chance of second. It was between us and Norwich. With three games left, we beat Preston at Deepdale to send them down. Norwich were playing Derby at Carrow Road and if they got anything other than a win, we would move ahead of them into second place.

Robbie Savage was playing for Derby at the time and I spoke to him the day before their game with Norwich. I told him that if they won, I would give them £30,000 to share between them all. Pay for a night out, have a meal, do whatever you want. I told Sav I'd even give them the money if they got a draw. That's how desperate I was.

And you know what happened? They were drawing 2-2 and we were back in the dressing room at Deepdale after beating Preston. We thought Norwich had blown it and then they fucking won it in the fifth minute of injury time. I looked at our players when that result came in and they were on the floor.

I tried to rally them.

"Good luck to Norwich for doing that," I said, "but fuck it, we'll go and win the next game. There's still everything to play for."

We had a full week then until our final home game of the

season, against Middlesbrough. During that week, there were two Player of the Year parties. It was the worst timing ever. I couldn't believe it. Everyone was patting each other on the back and saying we were going up. We had too many weak characters and after one of the awards ceremonies, four or five players went out on the lash in the city centre.

Training that week was poor. Even in the warm-up before the Middlesbrough game, I kicked the ball away in disgust twice because everything was just so sloppy. I knew what was going to go down. I knew what was happening. We weren't ready. We didn't look like a team with a defiant mentality. We were 3-0 down after 21 minutes and that was the way it stayed. Norwich won 1-0 at Portsmouth and claimed the second automatic promotion spot. We were in the play-offs.

I had another go at the players after the game. I said I knew players had gone out on the lash in the week and now we had all paid for it. We went to Turf Moor to play Burnley in our last game and drew. We didn't even finish third in the end. Swansea finished above us so we were to play Reading in one semi-final and Swansea were to face Forest in the other.

Out of the four sides in the play-offs, Swansea were the best. No two ways about it. If we had had to play Swansea over two legs, Swansea probably would have been too strong for us. But if we got past Reading and they beat Forest, I thought we had a better chance against them in a one-off game at Wembley. In the heat of a South Wales derby and the tension of a final, I thought we might be able to beat them.

Forest and Swansea drew 0-0 at the City Ground in the first leg of their semi-final. We played Reading the next day at the Madejski Stadium.

My hamstrings felt incredibly tight and after about 15 minutes one of them went. I limped around for a couple of minutes and then I had to come off. It was only a strain but I knew it was probably the end of my involvement in the play-offs. We played well enough in the rest of the match and got a 0-0 draw.

Everybody was tipping us as the favourites to go through now. People were making plans for Cardiff-Swansea at Wembley. Security plans were swinging into action. People were talking about service stations on the M4 being closed on the day of the final because they were so worried about fighting between the rival sets of fans.

Swansea kept their side of the bargain when they beat Forest 3-1 at the Liberty in their second leg. But when I got to the Cardiff City Stadium a couple of hours before our second leg against Reading and saw the lads in the changing rooms, I had a bad feeling about it. We had gone mentally. We weren't strong enough. We were scared of it. There was a lot of pressure on us in Cardiff in front of our home fans who had come so close in past seasons. It was a game for characters and for people to take responsibility and we didn't have the mentality to rise to that.

We started well but then we conceded a comedy goal. They say that usually goals are conceded when teams make consecutive errors. Well, this was a quadruple fuck-up. Jlloyd Samuel attempted a long back pass from near the halfway line but it smacked into Kevin McNaughton's head. It ricocheted towards goal and our keeper, Stephen Bywater, came hurtling out to try and clear it from Shane Long.

But Bywater miskicked the attempted clearance and it cannoned into Long. He reacted instinctively and lobbed the ball towards the empty net from the edge of the area. It looped slowly into the goal. There was less than half an hour gone but it was such a ridiculous goal that it left us totally deflated. They scored again just before half-time and finished things off six minutes from the end. We lost 3-0. The dream of winning promotion was over.

I watched the game from my box at the stadium. It was painful. I had to be a man and go down and congratulate the Reading players afterwards and see everyone. Then I went on a two-day drinking binge to try to escape the pain. It doesn't make it better. It never has. But it was the only way I could cope with it. I am not a huge drinker but sometimes it can numb the pain. Then it comes back worse.

The fact that Swansea won the play-off final and were promoted added an edge to the disappointment. I wanted them to go up because they are a Welsh side and I admired their style of play. But I was also aware that it was a bitter blow for Cardiff fans who were still reeling from the manner of our defeat against Reading. We were supposed to be the first Welsh side in the Premier League, not Swansea.

I felt like I had let everyone down. I'd played well towards the end of the season and helped to give us a real chance of automatic promotion. But it wasn't enough. I was out for too long. I came back too late. I tortured myself about whether I should have tried to come back earlier. I analysed everything over and over again and drove myself mad.

I had a miserable summer. I didn't know where I was going to end up. There wasn't really any chance of me staying at Cardiff. They would have had to buy me outright from Manchester City and they didn't have the money either to pay the transfer fee or to pay my wages. Dave Jones was fired and Malky

Mackay, the Watford boss, got the job. I had played with Malky at Norwich City. I liked him and admired him. I thought it was a wise choice.

He came round to my house to see me. We had a frank discussion. I told him I felt the club was nowhere near right in things like sports science, nutrition and professionalism. He needed to get all that right. His year was going to be all about gaining his identity as a manager for the club and improving its professionalism. He knew the best he could hope for that season was the play-offs again. I liked his plans and we agreed to keep in touch but I wanted one more shot at the Premier League.

Spurs were interested and so were Liverpool. But it was only interest. Nothing concrete. So I was left with no option but to go back to City. I wasn't in Mancini's plans, of course, but I made up my mind to train hard and try and make the most of a bad situation. I had to get into good shape so that when a club did come in for me, I would be ready to go.

At the start of pre-season training, I was told to report with the Elite Development Squad, which is like a mix between the youth team and the reserves. It was also a euphemism for a holding pen for a group of outcasts and rejects.

There were a lot of good kids in the squad and there was also me, Adebayor, Nedum Onuoha, Roque Santa Cruz and Wayne Bridge. Part of me felt a little bit embarrassed, a bit demeaned. I would never treat an established player like that if I was a club manager. I have had 70 caps for my country. I had been a good player for City. And, even after the odd difference I had had with Mancini, to be told I was with the kids disappointed me. I expected it, I suppose, and it was obvious my only real option was to suck it up.

So I trained as hard as I could. I didn't take any short cuts. I wanted to set a good example to the kids, not degrade them. I remembered when I was a kid at Norwich, the older players who used to come down to train us now and again were pricks. Their attitude was shite. They moaned at you. They wouldn't try.

I wasn't going to do that. I wanted to conduct myself better than that. Maybe I was at an age where I was starting to think about more than just myself. I was starting to think about my responsibilities to the game a little bit. I moaned, of course, but that's normal for me. It wasn't because I was with the kids.

I played at some of the outposts of football in the north west. I played at Hyde. I played at Altrincham. I played at Stalybridge Celtic. Hardly any fans there. Rubbish changing rooms. Week nights under dim lights. Kids trying to make a name for themselves. I tried my hardest.

I had the option not to play in the games but I wanted to play. I wanted to make sure that whoever was watching, they could see I was showing the right attitude and trying to improve the young players around me. I gained some satisfaction from making the best of a bad situation.

When the season drew a bit closer, some players who had been on tour in the States with the first team filtered back down to us. One of them was the manager's son, Filippo Mancini. That was really the only time when the situation tested me. But I kept my head down and got on with it.

I had one more year left on my contract at City and as the season approached, they began to negotiate a deal to pay me off. Garry Cook was in charge of that and I think he admired the way I had knuckled down and tried to set an example to the kids. Before the season began, we came to an agreement. It was a very fair settlement.

I think they thought I would go to QPR and I did speak to Neil Warnock, who was the manager there at the time. Stoke offered a really good deal, too. But the interest from Liverpool and Spurs was getting stronger.

On transfer deadline day at the end of August, I was training with Wales in Cardiff in preparation for the home game against Montenegro and both Damien Comolli, Liverpool's director of football, and the Spurs boss, Harry Redknapp, were ringing me.

Liverpool took the initiative. They sent a helicopter to Cardiff to pick me up and fly me to Merseyside. As soon as we landed in Liverpool, Harry was on the phone telling me not to sign. I told him I would do my medical and see what happened. I wanted a two-year deal and both Spurs and Liverpool agreed to that. I was still undecided.

There was an element of farce about deadline day, as there often seems to be. I was in Liverpool's MRI scanner at one point when the lady who was operating it turned it off because she said my adviser needed to speak to me.

He said Spurs had matched the deal Liverpool were offering me and had even waived the need for me to do a medical. They had laid on an office and were going to fax the contract to it for me to sign.

It was tough. I thought Tottenham were probably the better team but Liverpool were in my heart. I had unfinished business at Liverpool, too.

It had never really felt right playing under Rafa and I wanted to have better memories of playing for the club I loved.

Kenny Dalglish, one of my great heroes, was in charge now, too. I decided to sign for Liverpool.

As soon as I walked back into Melwood that day, it felt different to the first time. People had a smile on their face. The dictatorship had gone. Everybody was happy to see me. It felt relaxed. It felt right.

27

Speedo

Gary Speed was a strong character. He was a leader. He was probably the person I admired most. He was someone I tried to copy, someone I tried to emulate. Throughout my career, I looked up to him and I always took it as a great compliment that he, in turn, looked out for me and valued me as a player. Long before he died, at the age of 42, he had become one of my best friends.

He was a mentor to me, someone whose advice I sought, someone I listened to. I was a little in awe of him, too, and I certainly knew not to cross him. I knew that he rarely lost his temper but that if he did, it was best to make sure you were nowhere in his vicinity. And I knew that above all other things, he doted on his two boys, Ed and Tommy.

I was delighted when he took the Wales job in December 2010. I was happy mainly because I knew it was a big deal for him. I love my country but he loved it more. I have never seen a Wales player who loved their country more than him, who had that pure passion and real drive for Wales. It was one of the many things about Speedo that I had used as inspiration. He was the example I followed. That was one of the reasons why I always turned up for friendlies. Because he did it.

I spoke to him on the day he got the job. He said he wanted to come and speak to me. I had been beginning to think it might be time for me to retire from international football. I hadn't particularly enjoyed playing for John Toshack, who had taken over from Mark Hughes.

Things had regressed under Toshack. There were a couple of good performances, like the 5-2 victory over Slovakia, but generally things were on the slide. We hadn't even looked like being able to challenge for qualification for a major tournament. The height of Toshack's ambitions appeared to be making sure we didn't get too heavily beaten rather than actually trying to win games. We didn't even try and compete and I found that hard.

But suddenly, we had a great bunch of young players coming through. Really outstanding players like Gareth Bale and Aaron Ramsey and I thought that now a progressive young manager like Speedo had replaced Toshack, maybe it was time for people like me to step away and let him get on with bringing the young players through.

So Speedo and I went out for something to eat in the Canton area of Cardiff. He asked me what my plans were. I told him I was going to retire.

"You talk about Wales," he said, "and you talk about your love for your country but you won't be able to help your country if you don't play."

I had a few objections. We'd already lost our first couple of qualifying games for Euro 2012. We weren't going to qualify for that tournament. I wanted the younger kids to be able to come through and be bedded in ready to have a real go at making it to the 2014 World Cup.

"Don't worry about that," Speedo said. "I'm talking about now."

My objections got weaker. Speedo was insistent.

"I need a player like you here now," he said. "You believe in everything I do. I am going to improve the professionalism, sort out the sports science, get a good staff. Things will get better."

He asked me about Raymond Verheijen. He asked me about other fitness people I had worked with.

I said I didn't want to be captain any more. I didn't want to deal with the media. My knee was giving me so much trouble that I couldn't commit to playing in every game.

"Don't be captain then," he said. "I'll pick another captain."

We both wanted a Welsh-born player to be skipper. That's what we believed in. We wanted someone young and exciting. Someone with a voice who could lead the team for the next decade.

He asked me who I thought and I said Aaron Ramsey. He had a piece of paper with his choice already written down and he passed it to me. It had Rambo's name on it.

"This will be our set-up," he said. "It won't be like it was before. You know how I work. I can't do this without you. I need a player everyone looks up to, believing in what I do. If everyone sees you responding to what I am telling them, we will get there quicker and you will play in a major championship. Don't leave like this."

The argument was over. Speedo had won.

He was incredibly enthusiastic and energised about the task he faced. He started asking me about this physio and that physio and he made it plain he wanted me to have a real influence on how things were going to develop. We sat there for three hours, talking it through, having some wine, dreaming about the future and what might come to pass. I was in. He had talked me into it. I thought 'fuck it, let's go and do this'.

I prepared him for Raymond Verheijen. I told him he was a difficult man but that he was worth it. We got Damian Roden in from Manchester City, who was one of the fitness guys I had admired most there. He was on board. Everything pulled together. I thought we could give it a right good go. The Welsh FA, for the first time, were letting a manager have his way. We thought we had an opportunity to get our country to a major championship at last.

We had a friendly against the Republic of Ireland in Dublin at the beginning of February 2011. I wasn't playing but I went out there to show my face and show that I was buying into it all. We lost 3-0 so I know this might sound daft, but you could see the change in how we played. The mood changed. The staff were professional, too. If the players weren't allowed to drink, the staff didn't drink either. They were small things but it's always the details that are important.

Six weeks later, we played England in a Euro 2012 qualifier at the Millennium Stadium. The build-up felt good. We lost Gareth Bale a couple of days before the match which was a huge blow. We were sure England were going to play 4-4-2 because their manager, Fabio Capello, was renowned for not changing but he played 4-3-3 and it took us completely off guard.

They went 2-0 up inside the first quarter of an hour and by the time we switched things around, it was too late. England were worthy winners but we didn't feel too downhearted. The game finished 2-0. We didn't cave in. We fought back, in fact. There was no sense of optimism being dented.

We played in a mini-tournament in Dublin in the summer. We lost to Scotland and beat Northern Ireland. We played Australia at Cardiff in August and lost. We did not play particularly well and it felt like we had gone backwards a bit. It was the first time I saw Speedo getting a little impatient. He dug me out a couple of times, too. He was harder on me. He had a go about me wearing the wrong t-shirt.

"Listen," he said, "they look up to you. Start leading."

He was a bit deflated by the Australia defeat. It was the first time the Welsh FA got under his skin. They were talking about staff cuts and he lost his rag a little bit.

But he began to turn things around. In September 2011, we beat a good Montenegro side 2-1 in a Euro 2012 qualifier at Cardiff and we played well. I got a yellow card that ruled me out of the tie against England at Wembley four days later. I could only watch but as I watched, I felt very proud. Wales lost 1-0 but we played brilliantly. It was Speedo's team now.

For the first time in all my years with Wales, I felt like we had a proper identity. We had a decent spell with Sparky but this was the future. I could see how proud Speedo was after the game. He was disappointed, sure, but you could tell when Speedo was proud because he would jut out his chest and strut around. He had that spring in his step.

Our training camps had become a joy to be involved in. They were so professional. Before, under Toshack, it had felt more amateur when you joined up with Wales. Now it felt like you were with a Premier League club. The sports science was great, the analysis of the opposition was excellent and the leadership from Speedo knitted it all together.

In October, we beat a good Switzerland team 2-0 at the Liberty Stadium with goals from Ramsey and Bale. That lifted us off the bottom of the group. That felt symbolic of the progress we were making. Then we backed that up by going to Bulgaria and winning 1-0 in Sofia with another Bale goal.

I couldn't wait to play for Wales now. We had become a team. We were not just winning games, we were holding the ball and dominating possession and I could sense Speedo's pride. He was becoming a manager. I told him to stop talking like a player. I told him he was my manager now.

The next game was a friendly against Norway in Cardiff at the beginning of November. Speedo was quiet. I had a coffee with him down at the St David's Bay Hotel and I noticed he had a bit of a beard, which was unusual for him. I was having a bad time in my marriage and we spoke about my situation. We talked about his life, too.

His quietness during that week disconcerted me a little bit but I put it down to the fact he was becoming a manager. I thought maybe it was just that he was putting a bit of distance between himself and the players. Everything was evolving fast. We beat Norway. In fact, we battered them. We won 4-1. Bale got one, I got one and Sam Vokes got a couple late on.

Speedo was normal after the game. He seemed proud of the performance and pleased with the way things were going. I had my own personal issues, so the game was a great relief for me. I wished at that time I could just play constantly and not go back to real life. I had a quick chat and a bit of a laugh with him and then I headed off.

I didn't speak to him for the next couple of weeks. At the end of November, Liverpool had a big game against Manchester City at Anfield. It was the Sky Sunday game. On the Saturday night, I took a sleeping tablet like I do the night before every match to make sure I sleep through. It was a 4pm kick-off so I had a bit of a lie-in. When I got up, I looked at my phone.

I had several missed calls. Two were from Kieron and one was from my adviser. These were people who never called me on the day of a game. Back then, I always wanted to keep my mind entirely focused on the match and they knew that. But my phone kept going off. I began to realise something must be wrong. When Kieron rang for the third or fourth time, I answered.

"Have you heard about Speedo?" he said.

"What?" I said.

"Shay's rung our agent to say Speedo's committed suicide," Kieron said.

"Fuck off," I said. "No chance."

"I've heard he's hung himself," Kieron said.

"Fucking no chance," I said again. "You know what Twitter and the internet are like. It's bullshit."

I got in my car to drive to Anfield. That was the routine on the day of a home match: drive to Anfield, hop on the coach to Melwood, do all the pre-match stuff there.

Then my adviser called me. He was ringing with the same news. He said Speedo had committed suicide. I still didn't believe it. I couldn't see it. Not with Speedo. I still thought it was bullshit. I rang Shay Given.

"It's true, mate," Shay said.

"I don't believe it," I said.

I rang Raymond Verheijen. He didn't know anything.

I rang someone at the Welsh FA. They didn't know anything.

Then I got on the coach at Anfield to go to Melwood. Kevin Keen was sitting at the front.

I asked him if he'd heard anything about Speedo.

"What do you mean?" he said.

I went to the back of the coach and rang Suzanne who worked as a PA for both me and Speedo.

I asked her if she had heard anything.

"No, nothing," she said.

I asked her to find out. I was starting to freak out.

I rang Speedo's phone then. It started ringing.

'He's alive,' I thought. 'He's alive. Thank fuck for that.'

Stupid, wasn't it. A dead man's phone can ring, too.

Suzanne rang back. She was hysterical. She told me it was true.

I was on the phone on the coach and all the players were around me.

I couldn't comprehend it. Speedo was my idol in football. He was everything I tried to become. I spoke to him pretty much once a week for the last 10 years. Then the tears started to fall. I knew it was real then. I just broke down. The other players knew by then. Things get around quickly.

I rang my wife. I told her. She was numb with shock. She was worried about me, too.

I got off the coach at Melwood. Keen told me Kenny Dalglish

wanted to see me in his office. I walked up to Kenny's room. He was with Steve Clarke, his assistant manager.

"Look mate," Kenny said, "I don't know what to say or how to say it but I have been told that Speedo committed suicide. He hung himself this morning."

I started crying. You don't get prepared for that.

My mind was racing. How the fuck has he done that? Why has he done it? Everything was going well. Everything was going so well. Something's happened. What's happened?

"Go home," Kenny said. "Go back to Cardiff. See your kids. You're not playing today."

"I want to play," I said. "I want to play through it."

"You can't play today," he told me. "You're not in a fit state of mind. I'm taking the decision. Not you. I don't care how long you want off or how long it takes. Come back when you're ready."

I didn't want time off. I knew we had Chelsea at Stamford Bridge on the Tuesday in the Carling Cup quarter-final. I needed football to get me through it.

"If I go home now," I said to Kenny, "I will be even worse. I need to train tomorrow."

I was still crying as I said it.

Kenny has dealt with a lot of grief. He has seen too much grief. He knew how to deal with mine.

"Go home, Bellers," he said.

I went back to my apartment in Sefton Park. It was only a few miles. It was the worst journey I've ever taken. It was horrible.

I didn't want anyone else to share in my grief. I wanted to be alone. Despite our troubles, my wife wanted to come up to be with me. I said no. I regret that. It wasn't fair to her. After all the years we had been together, I should have let her in.

I sat down and watched the television. I had it on Sky News. There were pictures of Shay standing in a line of Aston Villa players before their game against Swansea at the Liberty Stadium. He was crying.

I spoke to Speedo's dad, Roger. God knows how he managed to speak to anyone.

I spoke to Shay after his game. I don't know how he played.

I didn't sleep that night. I was thinking about his kids. He adored his kids. I couldn't believe he had left them.

And you know what, I felt angry with him, too. I adored him and looked up to him and had the highest respect for him. And now he was dead and I felt angry with him. I felt angry with him for leaving. I felt angry with him for leaving like this.

It started to scare me a little bit as well. If he is capable of that, what chance have the rest of us got?

Some time later, at the inquest into his death, his widow, Louise, described him as 'a glass half-empty man' and she was right about that. He got down easily. There was always a line with him. He was very cheerful but he could get down and he could get uncontrollably down. When that happened, you stayed away from him. Don't say anything because if you say anything out of turn, he will flip.

There was a side of him which could go. Just go. If you took liberties, or he was worried about something, you could see it in him. You could see the tension. You could see him ready to explode. A lot of players were like that. Not just him.

I was determined to play against Chelsea on Tuesday. I had to play. I needed to play to help with my grief. I needed to do something to try to escape what had happened.

I travelled down to London on Monday. Kieron came to see me. Monday night was another sleepless night. There was a minute's applause for Speedo before the Chelsea game. I stood in the line with the rest of the Liverpool players. I felt okay.

Then the Liverpool fans started singing his name. It was real to me then. That was when I started crying.

I'm a man's man. I'm not supposed to cry. I didn't like Chelsea fans. I didn't want to cry in front of them. But I couldn't help it. The Chelsea supporters didn't sing his name but I don't expect that from them. They're not my cup of tea. They're not the type of fans I'd want to play for.

'I'm going to play fucking well tonight,' I thought.

Jamie Carragher was great. He didn't say anything. He just gave me a little pat. When I wiped the tears away, I thought 'let's go'.

And Chelsea couldn't get near me that night. It was one of the best games I have ever played. We won 2-0 and I set up both goals. The game was easy after the two days I had just had. It was a performance worthy of Speedo's memory.

Kenny brought me off 10 minutes from the end. He gave me the biggest hug when I got to the touchline, which is typical of him.

Then I sat on the bench, put a coat over my head and cried.

28

Winning And Losing

I was happy about signing for Liverpool again in August, 2011, but it also represented a significant moment in my personal life. After a year in Cardiff, I was moving away again. I didn't consult Claire about joining Liverpool. I didn't really give her an option. I don't think she really cared anyway by then. But this was the final straw. When I hit the motorway for the drive north for the beginning of pre-season training in the summer, I knew my marriage was slipping away.

Our prospects of staying together had been hurt by the way I'd acted when I was living at home during my year of playing for Cardiff. It was a difficult season for me on the field and my behaviour at home was often surly and withdrawn. And now it was either Liverpool or my wife. That's how I felt. And I took

Liverpool. The way I saw it, playing for Liverpool was my destiny. This is what I was here for. I was born to play this game and Liverpool was my team.

It was a joy to be back at Melwood. Some of the players from my first spell were still there, of course, Jamie Carragher and Steven Gerrard among them. They were just even bigger legends now than they had been four years earlier. The most significant change, as I say, was that Rafa had gone and Kenny was now in charge.

People talk about Kenny being the greatest Liverpool footballer of all time. He probably is. But you know what, he is the greatest man who has ever played for Liverpool Football Club. There is no shadow of a doubt about that. To be involved with him was just a huge honour. He was brilliant to play for.

He had such a calming influence over everyone at the club. He was just The King. He was a true man. The humility he shows constantly on a daily basis to everyone was overwhelming. When I say 'everyone', I don't just mean the players. I mean all the employees of the club. The impression you get of him on the television, defensive and monosyllabic, is the exact opposite of what he is like when the camera is turned off.

We started the 2011-12 season reasonably well without being outstanding. We were inconsistent. We had a good win at Arsenal but we were heavily beaten by Spurs. We drew matches we should have won. I didn't start that many matches. In fact, my best spell was around Christmas and the New Year when Luis Suarez was banned after he was accused of racially abusing Patrice Evra during the Liverpool-Manchester United match at Anfield on October 15.

I was on the bench for that game against United. I didn't have a clue what had happened. There's no reason why I would. The referee came in after the game and I saw him speaking to Kenny and Luis but I had no way of knowing what had happened. All I knew was that Liverpool often seem to get a raw deal from the authorities and that Manchester United wield an awful lot of power.

I liked Luis. He was an incredible player and a lovely guy. He trained hard and he worked relentlessly during matches. People talk about him diving but he took a hell of a lot of punishment, too. He would take his socks off after a game and his calves and his ankles would be black and blue from where he had been kicked. He was a brilliant professional.

Luis was accused of calling Evra 'negro' during the match against United. I'd heard that used before. The first time was when Nolberto Solano was speaking to Lomana LuaLua at Newcastle.

I pulled him up on it straight away.

"You can't say that," I said to Solano.

Nobby looked surprised.

"Why?" he said. "He's my black friend."

I heard Luis using the same term when he was speaking to Glen Johnson, Liverpool's right-back, too. Johnno certainly didn't take any offence and he speaks fluent Spanish, too. He knows a little bit about the culture. I didn't really see what the difference was between that and what Luis was alleged to have said to Evra.

Some people said it was all about the context. If it was said in an angry way, it took on a different meaning. It all got very complicated.

Liverpool closed ranks. I was 32 and I'll be honest, I didn't want to get involved. I had enough troubles of my own. I liked Luis. I certainly knew he wasn't racist. The other players in that squad knew he wasn't racist. I knew because of the way he interacted with the black players in our squad and the way they interacted with him.

I stayed out of it. Five days before Christmas, Luis was banned for eight games and fined £40,000 by the FA over the Evra incident. The next evening, we played Wigan at the DW Stadium and in the warm-up before the match, we all wore t-shirts with an image of Luis on the front to show our support for him. Kenny got a lot of criticism for that but we all wanted to do it.

I was happy to wear it. I wouldn't have worn one if I thought Luis was a racist but I knew he wasn't. And I thought the ban he had been given was harsh. I thought he'd been set up, actually. I think most of the players felt aggrieved about the way he and the club had been treated. If it was a Manchester United player, I think it would all have turned out very differently.

Luis was banned when we played the first leg of our Carling Cup semi-final against Manchester City at the Etihad Stadium in the middle of January. It was a loaded game for me but even though I wasn't on great terms with Roberto Mancini, I really didn't feel any great desire for personal revenge or anything like that. I had a great deal of respect for the club and especially for the City fans. I certainly didn't harbour any bitterness towards them. I felt a bit calmer about things.

The news about Speedo had hit me incredibly hard at the end of November. Some time after his death, I went home to Cardiff for a couple of days. Those days are just a blur. I can't remember what it was like. I wish I could tell you that I was comforted by my wife or my family but I don't know. Then

I went up to Speedo's house. I knew Ed was a big Liverpool fan and I wondered if taking both the boys into Melwood might give them a tiny bit of relief from what they were going through. They were all smiles about that so I took them and Speedo's dad into training with me.

You know when you take people to Melwood that you are taking them into the greatest club in the world. Moments like that make you realise why. The boys were greeted with open arms by every single person at that club. They had kits and boots lined up for them. Kenny was there waiting for them. That's Liverpool Football Club. I have always been proud to support them but that day was the best.

The days went on and I still found it very difficult to come to terms with what had happened. I was haunted by what I heard people saying about Speedo, about how it was sometimes difficult to get a conversation out of him, about how he didn't have very many close friends, about how he would shut himself off, about how most people didn't really know what he was like. I was haunted by it because it sounded like they were talking about me.

I started to feel afraid. What's going to happen to me in a few years' time? My personal life is gone, my marriage is basically over, I am extremely unhappy. What am I going to do when I stop playing football? Who am I going to be? There were so many questions left unanswered.

While I was in this state of mind, Liverpool's club doctor, Zaf Iqbal, approached me. He told me I needed to see someone. For the first time, my guard was down. I knew he was right. I agreed. He recommended Steve Peters, a psychiatrist who was working with Britain's Olympic cycling team. And when I sat down with him, not one single person in this world has ever made more sense to me than him.

Steve took a lot of the anger out of me. All the bullshit about getting back at people was gone. So I felt like I didn't have anything to prove to anybody at Man City. They knew I was a good player. I got on well with the lads there, too. I had good relationships with Nigel de Jong, Carlos Tevez and Micah Richards. They held me in high esteem and I did the same with them. I wanted to enjoy the matches against them. Over two legs the best team would go through. Whatever would be, would be.

We won the first leg at the Etihad 1-0 with a Steven Gerrard penalty. I felt confident after that. For them to get to the final, they would have to beat us at Anfield on a midweek night in front of a packed house. It was going to take a performance from Man City that would have to be out of this world. And if they were capable of that, then they would deserve to go to the final.

Nigel de Jong put them ahead after half an hour and we equalised with another Gerrard penalty just before half-time. Edin Dzeko put them 2-1 up midway through the second half but then 15 minutes from the end, Glen Johnson and I exchanged passes in front of the Kop end and I darted into the area and slid the ball past Joe Hart into the corner of the net. City couldn't score again. We were through.

And so I had scored the goal that had given this incredible club that I loved so much the opportunity to go back to Wembley for the first time since 1996. Kenny brought me off two minutes from the end and even the Man City fans applauded me. I loved them for that. City were class, actually. The players I'd played with came up to me at the final whistle and hugged me. I shook Mancini's hand and wished him all the best in their bid to win the league title.

I wanted them to win that but I knew I had a chance now to lift a trophy with Liverpool. A trophy with Liverpool with Kenny Dalglish as your manager. That was why I played the game. It was why I wanted to be involved in the game. It was a wonderful night. I also felt calm. I had things in perspective. Speedo's kids were at the game. Stevie G lent me his box and the kids and Gary's father came.

There was something else special about reaching the final. We already knew who we would be playing: Cardiff City. I had never played against Cardiff before and I had never wanted to. I didn't want to upset people at home. I didn't want people to feel I was trying to beat Cardiff. I had never felt comfortable with the idea of putting myself through that. But there was no way around it this time. It was the final.

I spoke to Steve Peters the night before the game. On the morning of the match, I found myself looking at pictures of Speedo as I sat in my hotel room at The Grove. His kids were going to be at Wembley too. I made sure all the people who had been there for me had tickets. People like Andy Williams, the knee surgeon, and Garry Cook, City's former chief executive, who had been forced out of the club by then. I was going to make sure I enjoyed the day. I wanted to win the trophy but I was prepared to lose as well. And if Cardiff won, that would be fine.

Kenny named the team and I wasn't in it. I was surprised but I wasn't down. I would have loved to start because I thought the game would have been made for me and Luis up front but I was happy to be involved. I knew I would be coming on, too.

Before the match, the manager showed us a short film that illustrated what Wembley meant to Liverpool and what it meant to the club being back there. I sat there watching Shankly talking and Kenny scoring that magnificent winner against Bruges in the 1978 European Cup final. And I thought about all my years of growing up and wanting to be part of this club. When the film ended, there were tears in my eyes.

Twenty minutes in, we went a goal down against the run of play. But we dominated the game and Kenny brought me on for Jordan Henderson 13 minutes into the second half. It was nothing to do with me but two minutes later we drew level when Martin Skrtel scored from a corner. The game went to extra-time and Dirk Kuyt put us ahead with 12 minutes left. It looked like it was over because Cardiff were exhausted but in the last few minutes, they pinned us in our own half.

They missed one great chance when Dirk cleared off the line but the ball went for a corner. Peter Whittingham bent a brilliant delivery into the box and Ben Turner scored. Credit to them. There is even a picture of me smiling after they had scored. I admired their refusal to give up.

So it went to penalties. Kevin Keen had asked me if I wanted to take one of our five and I said 'yes'. Then I thought about it. I didn't want to score a pen to win a trophy for Liverpool but cost Cardiff the chance of winning one. But I didn't want to miss a penalty and be responsible for one of Cardiff's greatest moments. For the first time in my life, I asked to be left out of it. I think they put me down for number six or seven.

I wasn't needed. We missed our first two penalties but scored the next three. That meant that Steven Gerrard's cousin, Anthony, had to score Cardiff's fifth penalty to keep their hopes alive. He put it low to Pepe Reina's right but it went wide. The trophy was ours. Most of the lads sprinted over to leap on Pepe. I didn't go with them. I went to see the Cardiff players straight away. I congratulated them and Malky Mackay. It was a good moment for me but I had been playing with those players the previous year and I was proud of the guts they showed that day at Wembley. I had so much respect for them.

Even when we lifted the trophy, I was speaking to the Cardiff owners. If you look, I'm not even in the team celebration photo. I was speaking to the Cardiff physios and players. I was sharing the moment with them. I had got my trophy. This was what I'd chased all my career. I was happy but I was happy before. I just didn't know it.

I had other things to think about as well. I knew that the problems I had been having with my marriage were now beyond repair. When the adrenaline stopped, I went up to see my wife and kids in the area where the families had been watching. This was going to be the last time. My wife was happy for me but I knew there must have been part of her that felt exasperated, too. 'You've chased this your whole career and now you've got it,' I imagined her thinking. I knew my marriage was over by then.

I went back to Cardiff with her after the game and we didn't really talk on the way home. There was nothing more to say. Once you have been 18 years with each other, you separate, then there's an in-between where you can't live with them but you can't live without them, then there's divorce. It was a lot for us both to adjust to. Because of the work I'd done with Steve Peters, I'd suddenly become a nice guy. She didn't want nice. She needed to hate me. So she resented me even more.

The following Wednesday, I captained Wales for the Gary Speed Memorial game against Costa Rica at the Cardiff City Stadium. How do you prepare for a game like that? The last time I prepared for a Wales match, Speedo was in charge. The whole thing was weird in a macabre way. It was Chris Coleman's first match in charge of Wales. It wasn't exactly an upbeat way to begin.

Everybody, players and fans, wanted to pay their tributes to Speedo but no one really knew what to say. Don't forget, this was a group of Wales players who had been given absolutely no support by the Welsh FA in the wake of Speedo's death. No one ever checked on us or asked how we were dealing with things. No one asked any of us how we thought the succession should be dealt with. No one asked us what we thought the most sensitive way to proceed might be.

This was a group of players who had been through a terrible trauma and I found the Welsh FA's insensitivity strange. They didn't seem to understand that a tragedy like that heightens players' loyalty to the regime Speedo had represented. We didn't want all the work he had done to be wasted. We wanted it to be nurtured. I think we probably felt that was a good way of respecting his memory. Most of us wanted Raymond Verheijen and Osian Roberts, Speedo's assistants, to retain senior roles in the set-up.

To his credit, Aaron Ramsey spoke out about it. "We don't want to be taking a backward step again, having a big change and players not wanting to turn up and play for their country," he said. "At the moment everybody wants to play, everybody is reporting for international duty and enjoying themselves. We just want as little change as possible; we had great results in the last few games and the team was playing full of confidence."

Judging by what happened, it seemed that the Welsh FA hunted him over that. At least he had the courage to say what he had to say. I tell you what, Speedo would have been proud of him for that. That's what Speedo would have done, too. He would have said the right thing and he would have said the honest thing.

The truth was it was our first time together as a squad since Speedo's death and we didn't know what to do. We didn't know how to act. We didn't know whether to try to treat it as a celebration of his life or to mourn. His two boys stood with me in the line-up before the game because I was captain for the day in Rambo's absence. They were incredibly brave. They inspired the rest of us.

I didn't want to play. I don't think any player did. The fans wanted to show their respect and we had to be there for them. Part of you feels you have to go and put on a show but it wasn't like that. It was just a sad occasion. We lost 1-0 and then everybody limped home. When I got back to Liverpool, I was emotionally drained. Won my first trophy, played in a memorial game for one of my best mates, marriage over.

The breakdown of my marriage had started to take a heavier and heavier toll on me. I struggled to sleep the night before games. Even with sleeping tablets. I couldn't block it out any more. I spent more and more time talking to Steve Peters. I was using him more than Ronnie O'Sullivan was, which is saying something.

I missed games through injuries that I'm convinced were caused because of the fatigue brought on by my sleeplessness.

But Liverpool still had big games to play that season. We were struggling to make any real impact in the Premier League but we had one trophy under our belt already and now we were going for the FA Cup, too. We beat Stoke at Anfield in the quarter-finals in mid-March and drew Everton in the semis.

Everton were ahead of us in the league by the time the match came around in April and their fans convinced themselves this was the occasion when they were going to get one over on us. There was a lot of talk that there was finally going to be a shift in the balance of power on Merseyside and that Everton were ready to take over the leading role.

What drove me on was not just pride in the club but seeing the nerves that were afflicting Jamie Carragher and Steven Gerrard. I told Carra he was one of my heroes and there was no way I was going to let him lose. We got the train down to London and I sat at the same table as them. They were petrified by the thought of losing to Everton.

I knew we would be all right. I started on the bench again so I was watching when a mix-up between Carra and Daniel Agger let in Nikica Jelavic to put Everton ahead midway through the first half. Poor Carra must have thought all his nightmares were coming true at that point.

But Everton conjured a defensive mistake of their own in the second half when Sylvain Distin left a backpass short and Suarez ran on to it and clipped it past Tim Howard. Kenny brought me on for Stewart Downing with six minutes to go and I could sense Everton had gone. They were out on their feet and before long they had conceded a free-kick on the touchline level with the edge of their area.

I had only been on for three minutes. I bent the free-kick in and Andy Carroll glanced it in. There were a few minutes of injury time but Everton didn't threaten us at all. When the final whistle went, I looked for Carra straight away. I couldn't see him at first. Then I discovered why. He was on his hands and knees on the floor. It was relief that had felled him more than anything, I think. Sheer relief. I ran over to him and gave him a pat on the back. He looked up at me.

"Thank fuck for that," he said.

My wife wasn't there this time. My eldest boy, Ellis, was there. He always has been. But I didn't go back to Cardiff this time. I flew back to Liverpool with the team. I didn't fancy going back to an empty flat on my own and Carra was going straight from Liverpool airport to his local pub in Bootle. He was ready to celebrate. He said if we had lost that day, everything he had achieved in his Liverpool career would have been thrown out of the window. People would always have reminded him of that defeat.

I went with him to the pub. I sat with him and watched as he taunted every Evertonian who came through the door. I could see them glance over at him and roll their eyes at each other, smiling, when they realised he was sitting in the corner. They all knew he wouldn't spare them. He didn't spare them, either. He gave them merciless stick. It was a great night.

The semi against Everton was worth more than the final to me. The first FA Cup final I remember watching was 1986 when I was six years old and Ian Rush scored two against Everton. So that semi let me relive a lot of my childhood memories.

We trailed off in the league and finished eighth. Damien Comolli, the director of football, was sacked in April. There was uncertainty about whether Kenny would stay on. I dearly hoped he would, of course, but by the time the FA Cup final against Chelsea came around, I was in a real mess about my divorce. I didn't sleep the night before it. Like I said, I wasn't sleeping most nights by then.

Perhaps I was getting blasé about playing at Wembley all of a sudden but the cup final didn't quite live up to my expectations. Perhaps it couldn't. I loved all the footage from the old finals at the old stadium, the long walk across the turf from the tunnel, the game played in the bright sunshine of mid-afternoon. This game kicked off at 5.15pm. There was no long walk across the turf. It was the new Wembley.

I was in the starting line-up this time, up front with Luis. I didn't play particularly well and Chelsea were 2-0 up seven minutes into the second half. Andy Carroll came on for Jay Spearing with about 35 minutes to go and dragged us back into the game. He scored one and only a terrific save from Petr Cech denied him an equaliser. They were worthy winners, though, and I took it on the chin. I had bigger things going on in my life. I knew my time at Liverpool had probably come to an end. I needed to be back in Cardiff, to be there for my children.

When Kenny was fired 10 days after the cup final and a few months after bringing Liverpool their first trophy for six years, I knew for sure it was time to go.

For someone like me, you don't get much better than playing for Liverpool under Kenny Dalglish. That was my dream and now I felt that my dream was done.

29

Letting Go

The time I spent with Steve Peters made me look at myself in a different way. A lot of what we talked about, to begin with at least, was about the struggle between the rational side of the brain and the rage that comes from our primitive origins. He has written a book about it called The Chimp Paradox. The chimp is the part of us that rages and lashes out and when I play, I am completely chimp-orientated.

That's why I have never been able to watch a recording of myself playing. Because that's not me. I hate it. I hate watching how I confront the referee. I don't like that side of me. There has always been this Jekyll and Hyde. I have had the chimp fighting me. Do you know how many times I have wasted energy over thinking about a decision and it has prevented me doing something two seconds later because I was still thinking about what just happened?

I have always been told, 'that's who you are and to play well, that's what you've got to be like.' But if you see the top athletes, they are not like that. Do you know why? Because the other part of their brain, the computer, takes over.

Steve made me understand I could fix a lot of the things that were making me so unhappy. Some of them were simple things. I was petrified that I would finish my career without a trophy. Petrified. He told me I had been nothing but a success as a player and that I didn't need trophies to prove to anyone how good I was as a player. He told me I'd already won.

The fear of not winning a trophy, of even losing games, had taken over my life. When you let go of those kinds of things it is amazing how relaxed and calm you become.

I won a trophy with Liverpool a few months after all this partly because I was at peace with the idea that we might lose. Would winning a trophy change me as a person? No. Would it make me a better player? No. So what the hell was I worried about?

I went to New York 10 days after the FA Cup final. The last thing I wanted to do was play football but Wales had a friendly against Mexico at the MetLife Stadium in New Jersey and I had committed to playing in it. They battered us and we lost 2-0. I came home from that flight to nothing.

I found myself living at my mum and dad's in Trowbridge for a couple of days. I didn't have a home any more. I'd agreed to let my wife live in that for the sake of the kids while the details of the divorce were thrashed out. I stayed in my old bedroom, staring out of the front window on to the street where I used to play.

Then I flew to Singapore for the launch of Liverpool's kit for the 2012-13 season. The club had signed a new deal with Warrior and Warrior asked me to be involved at the start.

Brendan Rodgers was named as the new manager the morning I arrived in Singapore. He phoned me a few hours later. He said he wanted to keep me and I would be perfect for the way he wanted to play. I told him I had a few problems at home. I told him things were uncertain. He was brilliant with me. He said I could have all summer to think about it.

I had a busy summer lined up, which was probably a good thing. I didn't particularly want to be playing football but it was better than having time to think. A few months earlier, Stuart Pearce had come to see me to ask how I felt about competing for Great Britain as one of the three overage players in the Olympics.

I hadn't expected to be part of that. I didn't think I fitted the bill, really. I thought there would be pressure for Pearce to go down the David Beckham route. But I was keen. I knew I could offer a lot off the pitch as well. I didn't think he would follow through with it but the idea excited me. I liked Pearce, too. We just sat there talking about football for hours. He impressed me a lot.

In late April, he rang and asked what I was doing in the summer in terms of training. He told me to keep fit because he had finalised his plans and he was definitely going to pick me as one of his overage players. I promised I wouldn't let him down.

I lived at my mum and dad's during much of that summer. I got close to them again for the first time since I had left that house at the age of 15. It was one of the best things that came out of the mess of my divorce. They had lost me for a long time and it was nice for us to be a strong unit again. There were other good things. I trained with Ellis a lot. I went to Malta for a week. I was the youngest person on the island. It's Gary Neville's favourite place, which says it all...

I knew there would be a lot of pressure on me as one of the overage players. The fact that Beckham wasn't involved would increase that pressure because we would have to justify his absence. If it went pear-shaped, everyone would say it was because Beckham had been snubbed. I was also worried about quite how I'd stand up to it all after the problems I'd had in my private life.

But I knew this was a once in a lifetime opportunity. To be involved in the Olympics was amazing. It was my major tournament at last, I suppose. Ryan Giggs was the captain and it was an honour to be in the same set-up as him. Even at a late stage of my career, it was great just to be around a player who has achieved what he has achieved.

He'll be a manager one day soon, I'm sure of it. He'll be successful, too. He has so much to offer. The way he talks and the way he comes across, I'll be shocked if he doesn't make it. He has got a separateness. Even as a player, somehow he manages to keep a distance between him and his teammates. Managers need that. He knows what to say and when to say it. It's difficult not to want to listen to him after everything he's done.

We went to a training camp in Spain. It was like trying to cram a pre-season into a week. I shared with Ryan for a month but the younger players were a good bunch, too. It was a really good group. Stuart Pearce was great, training was enjoyable and the closer the Games came, the more the anticipation built.

We played Brazil at the Riverside in a warm-up match and

they beat us convincingly, partly because they were ahead of us in their preparations. Then we went down to London to stay in the Olympic Village for a night, just so we could get a taste of it before we stayed there during the Games when we played at Wembley.

The first competitive match was against Senegal at Old Trafford the evening before the Opening Ceremony in London. There was a full house and we knew Senegal would be a decent side. I was nervous but I knew I was going to enjoy it. Being round the young players brought the best out of me. I liked being one of the senior pros. I embraced that.

I spoke a lot in the changing room before that first game. Ryan and I were given a lot of responsibility. It was a great experience all around. The crowds were more generous than they are in league football so Senegal got a lot of applause when they came on as well. It wasn't like football, really. It was so refreshing to be involved in.

The opening game went well for me. We got a free-kick after nearly 20 minutes that Ryan swung into the box. Senegal couldn't clear it and it bounced out to me about 10 yards from goal. I hit it first time, down into the ground, and it went into the corner. It was Britain's first goal in an Olympics for 52 years. I had to come off near the end after I took a bang on the knee and Old Trafford rose to give me a standing ovation. That was a novel experience for me. I thought 'I've seen everything now'.

Senegal equalised in the end but it wasn't a bad point and we knew we would get stronger. It was a decent start and most of the reaction was positive. The only thing that seemed to concern people was that the Welsh players had not sung God Save the Queen when it was played before the match.

I'd made a point of grabbing the Welsh players – Neil Taylor and Joe Allen (Aaron Ramsey was on the bench) – before we lined up and making sure we all stood together. I didn't include Ryan in it because he was captain and he had different responsibilities.

But I wasn't going to sing the national anthem and nor was any other Welsh player. It's not our anthem. I sing one anthem and that's that. That's my country's anthem. I'm not being anti-English or anti-British. It was just the way it was.

A lot of people were offended that we didn't sing. I can understand that. It was a difficult situation. But you have to remember that we took some stick in Wales just for playing for Team GB. It was important to strike a balance. If we had sung the anthem, that would have been a step too far. You have to be respectful to the people of your country. The problem is that the British anthem is the English anthem. It was impossible to get around that.

The other point I wanted to make to the Welsh boys was that we were not just representing our country here, we were representing Speedo. He had given us this opportunity. He had given us the platform to play for our country and to excel. So don't just think about how well you're going to play or what the score will be, just remember we are here to honour his memory, too.

The next match, against the United Arab Emirates, was at Wembley. We stayed at the Olympic Village and this time it was packed out. The game was another great experience. Wembley was full and expectant and I set up our opening goal with a cross to the back post that Ryan headed in.

The UAE equalised but goals from Scott Sinclair and Daniel Sturridge gave us our first win. I was substituted again and this time I got an ovation at Wembley. It was almost as good as being applauded at Old Trafford. Then it was to Cardiff for the last group game against Uruguay. I knew we wouldn't lose there. Ryan was on the bench so I was named captain which was an unbelievable honour.

Uruguay had players of the calibre of Luis Suarez and Edison Cavani and we knew we needed a draw or better to go through. In the end, we won the game with another goal from Sturridge on the stroke of half-time.

That meant a quarter-final against South Korea and another game in Cardiff. It was getting exciting. We were feeling stronger and stronger and everyone was talking about the prospect of a semi-final against Brazil and the chance of winning a medal. But South Korea were a good side. They took the lead and then Aaron Ramsey missed a penalty. He made up for that by scoring from the spot later to equalise.

I came off with six minutes of normal time to go. South Korea stayed calm and solid. In extra-time, it looked like they were playing for penalties and when the shoot-out arrived it became clear why. We scored our first four but they scored their first five and they were some of the best penalties I've ever seen. Every single one of them seemed to go in the top corner. They were unstoppable.

That left Sturridge needing to score to keep us in the Olympics and the goalkeeper saved his kick. He got some criticism later because he marched off the pitch and wouldn't accept it when teammates tried to console him. Did people expect him to be happy?

I saw how upset he was and I went to speak to him in the changing rooms. I told him he was going to have a great career.

I told him moments like this would help him in the long run. I told him that as soon as he left the changing rooms, he had to let it go. I wouldn't have said that a year earlier. I probably would have blanked him.

So the adventure was over. It was time for real life to intrude again. I had one last chat with Brendan Rodgers during the Olympics. I liked him immensely and I wished I could have gone back to Liverpool to play for him but I had to come back to Cardiff.

I wasn't coming back for one last shot at saving my marriage. That was gone. It was for my kids. I knew I couldn't be away. I wanted to be here for them because I knew it was going to be a difficult period in their lives. If I just drove off up the road and ignored the situation, I might never be able to heal the wounds.

I wasn't prepared to do that. I wished Brendan good luck and began to prepare myself for another shot at trying to get Cardiff into the Premier League.

30

The Only Way Is Up

My mind was in turmoil at the start of the 2012-13 season. It was probably the worst time of my life. I was still struggling to cope with Speedo's death, I was being confronted with the realities of the break-up with my wife, I had turned my back on Liverpool and I was beginning to wonder whether I even wanted to play football any more. I moved into an apartment in Penarth, a few miles from Cardiff city centre. It looked out over the Bristol Channel and sometimes the sight of the sea brought me a bit of peace.

It was the first time I had put my family in front of my career. I had tried to convince myself I was doing that when I had played for Cardiff a couple of seasons before but I was deluding myself. I was so disillusioned with what was happening at

Manchester City back then that I would have gone and played in Chechnya just to get away.

Now, I really was doing it for my family but I still felt dislocated from my kids. I couldn't live in the house I had bought for me and my family any more and I had been naïve about how much I would be able to see my kids. I thought I'd be able to have them pretty much every day, pick them up from school all the time, look after them in the evenings. But it wasn't like that. My access was strictly limited, like it is for a lot of divorced fathers. I found that very hard. I still do.

I felt overwhelmed by it all. I played in our opening league game against Huddersfield at the Cardiff City Stadium, which we won 1-0 with a late, late goal, but I felt exhausted after the Olympics. I was struggling to come to terms with everything that was going on in my personal life and when I got a minor calf strain, I asked Malky Mackay if I could have some time off.

I told him I needed to adjust to everything that was going on. I couldn't lead the team when I wasn't leading myself. I didn't know when I was going to come back. I didn't know if I wanted to come back. The club was brilliant. Vincent Tan, the owner, and the chairman, Dato Chan Tien Ghee, who everyone knew as TG, told me to take all the time I needed.

I took a couple of weeks off. I played a lot of golf. I got bored shitless. Rumours started to spread that I had retired. Then I thought 'fuck that, I'm a footballer'. And I went back to work.

There was a huge change from when I had been at Cardiff under Dave Jones. I knew I had made a mistake within a week of signing the last time. But now, things were so different. Discipline was better. Nobody turned up late for training. Nobody was allowed to drive silly distances just to get to training every day. Malky was hard line. We all worked. There were no exceptions, no prima donnas, no one excused when it came to tracking back. We were a team. We were all in it together and after they had been so understanding about what I was going through, I felt I owed it to the group of players to become a valuable member of the team.

It took me a while to get back up to speed. Anyone who has been through a divorce knows you are fighting a number of battles. Like I say, I had a lot of sleepless nights. It's a difficult period for anyone. I had to play through that but I needed football to help me through it as well. The players at Cardiff pulled me through it. There was no resentment from them. There was no feeling I was shirking my responsibilities, which there easily could have been.

The manager was open with the rest of the players about what I was going through and they were brilliant with me about it. I was invited out to dinner with them. I was given all the encouragement and all the space I needed. I realised then that this was a group with real character. I owe them more than I will ever be able to repay.

I returned to the side in the middle of September and scored in the victory over Leeds but then a few weeks later, I ruptured my ankle ligaments in a home win over Watford. I was out for almost a month. We lost a couple of games but we won a few tough ones, too, and I started to think it might be our year. From the sidelines, I watched the team closely and I saw how hard they worked. No one in the division worked harder.

This was a group I wanted to be a part of. I loved their attitude. No one slagged each other off. There was no bitchiness. The manager was brilliant. I began to realise I'd never been involved in more of a team than I was now. Even when we weren't playing well, everyone did their bit to try to turn it around. Even the boys on the bench were willing the team on and that's not always the case in football, believe me.

There was one divisive issue at the club around the start of the season, although it was nothing to do with the players. In the face of a lot of opposition from the fans, Vincent Tan had changed Cardiff's home kit from its traditional blue to red. Red is viewed as a strong colour in parts of Asia, including Malaysia where Vincent is from, and he thought the move would help with the marketing of the club for that reason.

I understood the opposition of the fans but I was okay with the change. I was looking at the bigger picture. Vincent was putting a lot of money and commitment into the club. If he wanted to change the kit, it didn't bother me. He owned the football club and I worked for him. The way I saw it, he was giving me the opportunity to have a decent shot at helping Cardiff get into the Premier League and in that context, the colour of the kit wasn't a problem for me.

In an ideal world, you would want your traditional colours but nothing in this world is ideal. You have to be prepared for change and if this is the change it takes for us to be a much more stable and powerful club, we have to be prepared to do that.

I didn't actually give it that much thought. There were more important things to worry about. I knew how hard it was going to be to get to the Premier League.

The Championship is the hardest league in football. The pitches, the referees, the unpredictability: it is difficult for every single team. In that situation, you have to work and work and work. Our Prozone stats showed we worked harder than anyone.

I came back from the ankle injury in the middle of November for a home game against Middlesbrough. We won that and when we beat Barnsley at Oakwell the following Saturday, we went back to the top of the league. I knew then it would take quite a lot to shift us but I also thought that there was a group of other sides that would start to challenge us.

I thought Leicester would be strong and Middlesbrough. I'd been worried about Wolves, too. You are always wary of the teams that were relegated from the Premier League the season before. Look at Blackburn. They spent £8m on Jordan Rhodes. I thought they would be a threat, too. You always know there is going to be a surprise package as well, and this season it was Watford.

When people looked at Cardiff and the players we had, they were surprised that we were in the mix for promotion. Because you look at us and you don't see stars. You see grafters. Malky Mackay was given the option to spend money. In fact, when the January transfer window came around, the club was urging him to spend. He didn't want to.

He had spent the best part of two years building a team that had got where it was because of hard work and he was very wary of upsetting the team spirit by bringing in someone who might not share the same mindset. I understood exactly why he was concerned about that. We are more of a team than any team I have been involved with and that's what you need most of all in the Championship. Because games come thick and fast, you have to be together.

We tried to abide by the old rule of approaching the season

one game at a time. We never looked at other teams. Never looked at Palace or Leicester. Never thought about how many points we would be ahead of someone if we won one game or drew another. No one mentioned promotion. We weren't scared of it. It was just one game at a time.

Before every single game, the manager had a number of team talks and the preparation was fantastic. The last thing he did before we walked out on to the pitch was put up a sign on the board. 'Individuals win games, team work and intelligence wins championships', it said. It was similar to something Michael Jordan once said and the manager left it on the board every time we went out.

And that was us. That was Cardiff City. I never thought of myself as an individual during last season. I thought of myself as someone who was giving everything for the team. We got where we got through sheer hard work and doggedness. If we weren't going to win, the opposition was going to have to play damn well to beat us. We never gave an easy defeat away.

We were still top of the table going into the Christmas period. On December 22, we went to Leicester and won 1-0. Leicester started strongly but we limited their chances and managed to hold them. Then I scored to put us ahead and we locked the door. We saw it out. It felt like a big win.

Then we beat Crystal Palace, Millwall and Birmingham, away, in the space of six days. Each time it was by a single goal. We were grinding games out. We didn't play particularly well in any of those games but we won them all. And at the start of the new year, we were seven points clear of Hull City, who were second. There was distance between us and the rest and no one ever really narrowed the gap.

No one put a run together to exert any pressure on us. The form teams towards the end of the season were the relegation teams. And until a few weeks before the end of the season, no one really talked about us that much. Maybe it was because of our lack of stars and lack of controversy, but we pretty much went under the radar. We played one home game on Sky all season and that was the first match of the season.

We did begin to tie up a little bit when the prize was in sight. We only won one game in March, a month that was bookended by defeats to Middlesbrough and Peterborough. But even then, none of our pursuers took advantage. Hull, Leicester, Crystal Palace and Watford were all dropping points, too. Nottingham Forest came with a bit of a run but they were starting from too far back to be a real danger to us.

By April, we were close. Really close. We drew at Watford, who were third, on a Saturday evening and that was a big step forward. It kept them at arm's length. There was a hiccup when we were leading Barnsley deep, deep into injury time in a mid-week home game only for them to steal a deflected equaliser with the last kick of the match. But a few days later, we battered Forest and Watford lost at Peterborough.

Hull, who were second, could still catch us but now we were 12 points clear of Watford with four games left to play. We only needed a draw at home to Charlton the following Tuesday to be out of reach of Watford and sure of promotion.

The excitement building up to the Charlton game was great. You couldn't get a ticket for love nor money. This was it. This was something the city and the region had been waiting 56 years for, something that we had begun to think would never come.

Now we were one point away from the realisation of the dream.

It was difficult to know how to approach it. The excitement around the ground was all-consuming. I couldn't think. We only needed a point but the idea of playing for a draw is foreign to any player. I did my utmost not to get carried away because I knew that it might not happen that night. But I desperately wanted it to happen. I wanted it to happen here in Cardiff, in front of our own fans, in front of friends and family, in the city where I grew up.

I felt emotionally exhausted before the game even began. I just hoped adrenaline would get me through. Charlton were a useful side and they had come into form but we tore into them in the first half, eager to get the goal to settle our nerves. But the goal never came and in the second half, the mood changed.

Now, we were concentrating on not losing the game. Now we were focused on getting that solitary point.

I made bigger efforts to sprint back to cover than I made to sprint forward to attack, put it that way.

With about five minutes to go, the crowd started going ballistic. Something had happened. Watford were playing at Millwall and I assumed there had been a goal. I looked across at the manager. I couldn't hear him but I could see that he was mouthing 'Watford are losing'. Millwall had taken the lead in the 83rd minute. If it stayed that way, it meant we were up whether we got a point or not. I tried to ignore it. I told the players to concentrate. "We've got to get this done," I kept saying.

The crowd celebrations did us a favour. It brought the game to a premature end, effectively. The last five minutes turned into a bit of a practice match. It was one of those strange psychological things where Charlton didn't really want to do anything to spoil the party and we didn't want to do anything to jeopardise what we had.

I saw the fourth official come to the touchline to hold up the board to show how much added time there was. It said three minutes. That was a relief. Things started to happen in slow motion. I noticed every single detail. I saw expressions on faces in the crowd. I looked around at my teammates. I saw the ref nodding to the linesmen, intimating that he was about to blow the final whistle. I saw him signal to the Charlton captain to get their keeper in before the crowd invaded the pitch. I realised that there were only a few seconds left.

Then he blew. When he blew that whistle I just dropped to my knees. One, because I was so knackered and two, because I couldn't believe it was done. I couldn't believe this thing that had seemed like an impossible dream had actually been achieved. I had come so close to things so many times in my career but this was the thing I wanted most and we had done it.

The fans came rushing on. It was carnage. Happy carnage. Eventually, I made it back to the tunnel and gazed around at the joy on the faces of the other players. I saw the club doctor, Len Nokes. We call him Doctor Len but he's actually a professor and I've known him my whole career, since I was 16 and he was the doctor of Wales Under-21s.

He has given so much for the club and I knew how much he had always yearned for this moment. We hugged each other for a couple of minutes. We were both tearful. I wanted to soak it up but it was difficult. Everyone got to share it. The staff, the people in the media department, the groundsmen. This meant an awful lot to an awful lot of people.

I went back to the changing rooms. We wanted to go out and thank the fans. I saw Ellis in the tunnel and he came out on to the pitch with me while we did a kind of abbreviated lap of honour. I went up to the private box I have in the stadium, still in my kit, to see all the people who have been there for me, all my best mates.

My dad was there, of course. He's followed me everywhere. He's followed Cardiff, too. He was there when they were in the fourth division, watching them scrape along the bottom. It was great to see the happiness on his face. He told me he could die happy now, which I mentioned to the newspaper reporters later. It made all the headlines the next day.

Even if I hadn't been involved, even if I'd been playing for Liverpool or Newcastle or Man City, I would have been delighted for Cardiff. But to be a part of it, to be a player in the team that made history, to be a player in the side that got promoted to the Premier League, to be a player that brought so much joy to the people of my city, well, I was just incredibly grateful that I was involved in that occasion on that night. It will live with me forever.

I felt a deep sense of professional satisfaction, too. I felt I had given my all to the team. I had sacrificed individual ambitions and dedicated myself to the greater goal. I loved it. It gave me a kind of fulfilment I hadn't had before. I only scored four goals all season. But I had played well and enjoyed myself. I learned a lot from that and from the players around me.

That's part of the reason why I feel being promoted with Cardiff is my proudest moment in the game. I've never had a feeling like it. When you win something at Liverpool, it is great for you personally but you are always conscious that the club has won about 50 trophies. It is another trophy for the club, another trophy for the fans. Everyone's happy but, let's be honest, they have seen bigger days.

The Olympics was special, too, because it was unique but to be able to share that promotion with everyone was different because it tapped into my background and my history. Sometimes, it's hard to believe it's been more than 50 years since Cardiff were in the top flight. Where's this club been? To clear that final hurdle filled me with a huge sense of achievement.

I intend to stick around, too. I hope this is just the beginning for Cardiff. I hope that we can do something different with what we've achieved. I hope we can capitalise on the fact that our Welshness can give us an advantage. We are a city of 350,000 people but it isn't just the city. It's the valleys as well. You add that up and we are a club of a million people round this region who are all connected with the club and adore Cardiff.

A lot of those people probably followed other clubs like I followed Liverpool. It was a lot more fashionable for a kid to do that 20 or 30 years ago. We always had our eye on the stars. But now, that can change. Now we can build on our regional identity in the same way Athletic Bilbao have placed themselves at the centre of Basque culture and Barcelona have become a focus for Catalunya.

This is our identity. It's strong. It's separate. This is who we are. Playing for this club is first and foremost. So many boys who have come from this region have never played for Cardiff. Gareth Bale's never played for Cardiff. Ryan Giggs has never played for Cardiff. We have had players like Aaron Ramsey who have left too young. I have only played for the club towards the end of my career.

I am the only person from Cardiff who played for the team last season. We have to change that. We have to make the most of our area and our identity. We can produce the players but we have to be 'more than a club', as Barcelona say. We have to be about a region and an idea. You have to have the idea that playing for Cardiff is everything.

If there are lads running around like I was when I was a kid at ABC Park all those years ago, those kids will gravitate towards Cardiff now that we are in the Premier League. And even if the club lets a kid slip through the net, his parents will be on the phone telling you about him and saying they want him to be part of what we're building. The kid won't have to go to Norwich, to the other side of the country, to play football. The parents won't have to listen to their boy crying down the phone, standing in a phone box outside a chip shop, because he's homesick and far away.

We could control Merthyr, Rhondda, Caerphilly. We could have them in lockdown. All the kids from those areas playing for us. That's what makes us unique. The main core of the valleys is with us. We know how deprived those areas are. With the money we are able to receive now we are in the Premier League, we are hoping we can invest in those areas and invest in bringing those kids from those areas into ours and help with their schooling.

We have to get to the point quickly where players won't want to go anywhere else if they're from round here and we won't allow them to go. That is how we want to breed the football club. We want the top young players and preferably we want them to be Welsh. They don't go elsewhere and they are the future of the club and the backbone of the club.

I know that more and more clubs want to follow this route but we have got the kind of separateness that gives us an advantage. We have got the fan-base, too. When you go and play for Wales, most of the fans are Cardiff fans. Swansea have done brilliantly and I have always been vocal about how much respect I have for them but we are a bigger club by miles. Our attendances will shoot up in the Premier League and we have to make the most of it.

What we have achieved will hit home when we are building towards the first game of the 2013-14 season. The fixture list comes out, you look to see when the big clubs are coming to town. You go into the changing room and you see those shirts hanging on your pegs with the Premier League logo on them, the Nike balls instead of the Mitre ones we have in the Championship.

My older boy, Ellis, is 16 now and he has earned a scholarship with Cardiff. He is representing a Premier League club now. It will make a difference to his life, too. If we do it right, we have the manager to take us forward to the next level, a manager who believes in the vast potential of this club. There is no limit to where we can go.

We have the opportunity to create a club for the next 10 or 20 years. I am committed to staying because I want to be a part of it all. I want to see Cardiff become a power in the game. I don't know when my career is going to end. It could end me. But I am not looking to move on. Far from it.

I've never felt comfortable feeling comfortable before. It goes back to my time at Norwich when the club guaranteed me an apprenticeship a year ahead of time and I went off the rails a bit. Since then, I've been suspicious of planning ahead. I've always tried to live one season at a time. I never wanted that feeling of being comfortable again.

I've changed a little bit now. Steve Peters has had a huge effect on me. And my divorce made me realise I had to open up and relax a little. Sometimes, you can obsess and want something too much. Sometimes, you can lose sight of the fact that feeling content about something is actually what you should be striving for.

When I first started talking to Steve Peters in the aftermath of Speedo's death, I thought my life wasn't going to get better when I finished playing football. My life was going to be dark. I was going to be lost.

That was the thing that really petrified me: the idea that I wouldn't be able to stay in the game. If I had remained the way I was, I knew going into management would be out of my reach. Because of the intensity I worked at, I wouldn't be able to cope with players. I wouldn't be able to cope with unprofessionalism. My inflexibility, my lack of man-management skills would undermine my chances of succeeding as a boss.

If I hadn't started seeing Steve, if I hadn't begun to change, my people skills – or the lack of them – would have destroyed my chances of being a successful manager. I had always worked on the basis that if you have got something to say, say it, and deal with the consequences later. But you can't do that as a manager. And I knew that would be a stumbling block for me.

In the time since I have been talking to him, my people skills have improved beyond all recognition. I actually think before I speak now. Nothing's black and white for me any more. There is grey as well. I listen to people. I have actually become a proper human being.

I am not a saint. Watch me on a football pitch and there is still a percentage of me that exists in chimp mode. But it's a vastly smaller percentage than it used to be. I am more open to mistakes. I am more forgiving. And you know what, I am beginning to feel happy. My quality of life is much, much better.

Now I can be a better influence around people. Before, because I felt like shit, I wanted to make everyone else feel like shit, too. Now, if I am in a mood, I can get myself out of it. If I'm in a strop, I think of things that make me happy. Making someone else feel better about themselves makes me feel better, too. Like I said, I feel like I am becoming a functioning human being for the first time for a long time.

I am opening myself up again. That process of shutting myself down emotionally that I forced myself to endure after I moved away from home as a teenager – that's over now. I am starting to reverse it. I have become a lot closer to my parents again. I have allowed people back into my life. After Speedo died, I only saw emptiness ahead. Now I feel differently.

There's not a single day that goes by when I don't think about Speedo. Every time I play, I think about him. Why wouldn't I? He's still helping me, even though he's not here. His death forced me to take a look at myself. If I hadn't done that, I don't know what would have happened.

I've always listened to people talking about winning – win this, win that – but I've done more than I could have dreamed of in my career. I've already won. The two things I ask my kids after they have played a game are 'did you enjoy it' and 'did you do your best' but I wasn't asking myself the same questions.

I think differently now. Be thankful for what you've done. Keep trying hard. And don't let it ruin your life.

I did that for too long.

Index

Statistics

PROFESSIONAL CLUB CAREER 1996-2013

Norwich City	August 1996-August 2000
Coventry City	August 2000-June 2001
Newcastle United	June 2001-July 2005
Celtic (loan)	January 2005-May 2005
Blackburn Rovers	July 2005-June 2006
Liverpool	June 2006-July 2007
West Ham United	July 2007-January 2009
Manchester City	January 2009-August 2011
Cardiff City (loan)	August 2010-May 2011
Liverpool	August 2011-August 2012
Cardiff City	August 2012-

CLUB SEASON BY SEASON (Appearances/goals)

1996-97	Norwich City	3 (0)
1997-98	Norwich City	37 (13)

1998-99	Norwich City	45 (19)
1999-00	Norwich City	4 (2)
2000-01	Norwich City	1 (0)
2000-01	Coventry City	39 (8)
2001-02	Newcastle United	36 (14)
2002-03	Newcastle United	36 (9)
2003-04	Newcastle United	24 (9)
2004-05	Newcastle United	29 (10)
2004-05	Celtic	15 (9)
2005-06	Blackburn Rovers	32 (17)
2006-07	Liverpool	42 (9)
2007-08	West Ham United	9 (4)
2008-09	West Ham United	17 (5)
2008-09	Manchester City	11 (4)
2009-10	Manchester City	40 (11)
2010-11	Cardiff City	36 (11)
2011-12	Liverpool	37 (9)
2012-13	Cardiff City	33 (4)

WALES SEASON BY SEASON (Appearances/goals)

1997-98	3 (1)	2006-07	11 (4)
1998-99	4 (1)	2007-08	5 (2)
1999-00	2 (0)	2008-09	5 (1)
2000-01	3 (0)	2009-10	2 (1)
2001-02	4 (2)	2010-11	4 (1)
2002-03	4 (2)	2011-12	7 (1)
2003-04	5 (0)	2012-13	4 (0)
2004-05	8 (3)	Wales Under-21s: 8 (1)
2005-06	2 (0)	Wales Under-18s: 9 (6)

CRAIG BELLAMY

TEAM GB 2012 OLYMPICS (Appearances/goals)

20/07/12	GB & NI 0-2 Brazil (Olympics warm-up)
26/07/12	GB & NI 1-1 Senegal (1 goal)
29/07/12	GB & NI 3-1 UAE
01/08/12	GB & NI 1-0 Uruguay
04/08/12	GB & NI 1-1 South Korea, aet (4-5 pens)
TOTAL:	5 caps, 1 goal

INDIVIDUAL HONOURS

2001/02	PFA Young Player of the Year
2004/05	Scottish Cup winner
2005/06	Player of the Year (Blackburn Rovers)
2006	FA Community Shield
2006/07	Champions League runner-up
2007	Welsh Player of the Year
2011/12	League Cup
2011/12	FA Cup runner-up
2012/13	Championship winner

PERSONAL LANDMARKS

15/03/97	First-team debut: Crystal Palace 2-0 Norwich City
12/08/97:	LC debut: Norwich City 2-1 Barnet
01/11/97	First goal: Norwich City 2-2 Bury
03/01/98	FAC debut: Grimsby Town 3-0 Norwich City
25/03/98	Wales debut: Wales 0-0 Jamaica
04/06/98	First Wales goal: Malta 0-3 Wales
11/08/98	First LC goal: Swansea City 1-1 Norwich City

22/08/98	First hat-trick: Norwich City 4-2 QPR
19/08/00	PL debut: Coventry City 1-3 Middlesbrough
23/08/00	First PL goal: Southampton 1-2 Coventry City
06/01/01	First FAC goal: Swindon Town 0-2 Coventry
14/07/01	European debut: Lokeren 0-4 Newcastle United
21/07/01:	First Newcastle goal: Newcastle United 1-0 Lokeren
18/09/02:	CL debut: Dynamo Kiev 2-0 Newcastle United
20/02/05:	SPL debut: Celtic 0-2 Rangers
27/02/05:	First Celtic goal: Clyde 0-5 Celtic (Scottish Cup)
19/03/05:	First Celtic hat-trick: Dundee United 2-3 Celtic
28/05/05:	First cup final:
	Celtic 1-0 Dundee United (Scottish Cup final)
21/09/05:	First Blackburn Rovers goal:
	Blackburn Rovers 3-1 Huddersfield Town (2 goals)
09/08/06:	First Liverpool goal:
	Liverpool 2-1 Maccabi Haifa – on debut
28/08/07:	First West Ham United goal:
	Bristol Rovers 1-2 West Ham United (2 goals)
28/01/09:	First Manchester City goal:
	Manchester City 2-1 Newcastle United – on debut.
	Becomes only the fifth player in Premier League
	history to score for six different top-flight clubs
21/08/10:	First Cardiff City goal:
	Cardiff City 4-0 Doncaster Rovers
	– on debut, as captain
26/02/12:	Man of the Match:
	LC final, Liverpool 2-2 Cardiff City,
	aet (won 3-2 on pens)

(PL –Premier League; CL – Champions League; SPL – Scottish Premier League;
FAC – FA Cup; LC – League Cup)

Stats up to and including May, 2013

CRAIG BELLAMY
FOUNDATION

The Craig Bellamy Foundation (CBF) is a charity that offers underprivileged children in Sierra Leone the chance to reach their true potential through sport and education, enabling them to build a better life for themselves and their communities. It focuses on personal and community development, running a not-for-profit football academy and a national youth football league, developed with support from UNICEF.

The aim is to build a better future for Sierra Leone by offering children the opportunity to reach their full potential by playing the sport that they love. CBF harnesses this passion for football and uses it to promote healthy choices, education for all, peace building, gender equality and sustainable development.

For more information, log on to
www.craigbellamyfoundation.org